IF MAMA WERE HERE

By Donna Jean

ISBN 0-9703177-0-0.

First Printing

St. Jacques Publications
E-MAIL HDPomeroy@uplogon.com

Acknowledgments

First, I would like to thank my husband of thirty years for being my most treasured friend and greatest support. Also, I thank my four adult sons Wellyn, Colin, Ashley and Levi for listening to bits and pieces of my book over the years and for teaching me how to use the computer. Thanks for being patient when I couldn't figure things out on my own.

To the instructors I had when attending Bay College; I thank you. Gaining knowledge helped me to gain self-esteem and self-worth, which is what enabled me to write my book.

To Darby and the others at the Eighth Street Coffee House Writers' Guild. Your genuine feedback each week gave me the insight that I did indeed have something to offer.

Finally, I will never forget the help I received with this book. Thanks to Susan Hansen, Bonnie Jacques, Kathy White, Duane (Jacq) LaMarche, Judy Lauria, Gayle Nelson, Ruth Ann Ritter, Diane Pomeroy and my brothers and sisters for their insights. Your viewpoints and gentle criticisms are what brought my life story together.

To my dad
and
my five brothers
and
my five sisters

Chapter One

"**P**lease don't make me get on that bus!" I pleaded with my husband, Bryan.

"Don't back out now," he said, as he took my arms from around him, breaking my tight embrace. "If you don't get help, Sweetheart, I'm afraid the kids and I will lose you."

"But you know I've never been anywhere alone. What if the workshop doesn't help? What if I come back still depressed and with these same thoughts of wanting *out* of this big old world? Then what?"

"*It will help!*" Bryan said, lifting my chin and giving me a peck. "After all, Elisabeth Kubler-Ross is an expert on helping people deal with grief. I know it's hard for you right now, but please think positive about this trip. Heck, you'll be in the heart of the Catskills where Rip Van Winkle fell asleep for twenty years."

"I know, but I'd feel better if you and the kids were coming."

"Hey," he said. "Do you have *any* idea how much I want to go with you? You know I have to stay to be home with the kids. Heck, *you* wouldn't even be going if it weren't for Father Frank lending us the money to get you there."

"But I hate being away from the kids. What if something happens when I'm gone?"

"*Nothing will!*" Bryan assured, and called for our sons, who were exploring the Greyhound from the bus station window.

I stooped to my knees and gathered my four little boys in a big hug. I had planned to keep my tears in storage, as usual, but I sobbed as I kissed them good-bye.

"You're coming back, right, Mama?" my seven-year old asked, holding his *Return of the Jedi* figurine.

"Yes, Mama will be back soon," I managed as I questioned my ability to *get* to where I was going—*let alone* return home again.

"Come on," Bryan said, putting his arm around my shoulder and walking me to the door. "They're waiting on you."

After our final kiss and hug, I started walking out to the bus. Bryan stood with our boys in the doorway. "Don't go worrying," he hollered. "My mother will help while you're away. We plan to have fun!"

I kept my cocoa-brown, tear-filled eyes firmly on the bus. I feared even one last glance would keep me from getting on. Trembling, I walked to a back seat, purposefully not making eye contact with any passengers. I quietly sat next to the window. Once settled, I placed my Green Bay Packer blanket over my slender legs and propped my pillow behind my tense neck. It was then that I realized I was the only passenger on the bus leaving Michigan for New York. At first I thought that being alone was an opportunity to empty the reservoir of tears I held within me. But then I thought, as I had as a little girl, that I didn't deserve to cry. After all, what would the driver think if all of a sudden he heard me wailing? A few times over the last twenty-five years I had given in to the sorrowful emotions and it had only proven to set me further into the past. And besides, I reasoned, there's no in-between for me. It's either a few silent tears painfully making their escape, or I wail, bringing others to my rescue. Just last year I'd had a wailing episode. I thought I was alone in the church, but a cleaning woman heard me and rushed to my aid. "What on earth is wrong?" she asked, brushing my long, curly, light-brown hair from my tear soaked face.

Since that embarrassing outburst, I guarded my emotions closely, for I thought of them as a volcano waiting to erupt. It frightened me to think that even I probably wouldn't know when or where this outburst of emotions would occur or how many people would witness the event. I pushed the painful memories of the past into the cellar of my mind and tried to visualize securing them with a dead-bolt lock, as I had done at other times in my life when the haunting memories came lurking out. But as I gazed out the bus window into the darkness of the night, the memories came darting through my mind. Soon I was recalling the events that were responsible for my being in route to the Death, Life, and Transition workshop.

⌒

A young mother of five little girls from my community had died. Her death triggered memories of my own mother's death whenever I saw the little girls outside playing. Being alone was something my sisters and I had endured. And like us, on Sundays their father would drop them off at church. I felt like crying every time I saw them cuddled together in a pew. Their father had seemed bitter since the day his wife had died. One day I asked him if he'd soon be returning to church. I was surprised when he bluntly told me he'd never step foot in a church again, yet he did bring his children and I felt thankful for that.

Yvonne, his wife, had always reminded me of my own mother. She was a woman who was gentle and compassionate. Her family was her world. And although they had very little materially, her girls were always dressed neatly and their hair well groomed. Nowadays the little girls were usually in stained or dirty clothes with straggly, snarly hair. I wanted desperately to help the situation, so one day I stopped by their house to see if the girls would like me to trim and shampoo their hair. Their father politely thanked me but said they were managing just fine. So I asked if I could be of any other service—wash or iron, do dishes, scrub, or cook, but then very adamantly he said that everything was under control. He didn't even allow me beyond the doorway. What I could see of the inside of the house looked messed and in need of cleaning, but this came as no surprise. It was in exactly the condition I had expected. I wasn't foreign to such a situation. My own father had walked in this father's shoes. Who in her right mind would expect a parent to be able to keep a spotless house after he worked all day, prepared supper, washed clothes, tended to homework and did other chores. The only person who seemed to expect that was the little girls' father.

3

As I turned around to leave, my heart felt like pleading with him to at least let me pick up the two-year-old, wipe her snotty nose, get her into clean clothes, and rock her off to sleep. She looked pitiful clinging to his leg. The other girls were hungry for attention too. The four-year-old reached for me to pick her up, while the others all talked at once, each trying to tell me her own little story. But when I responded, the father shooed his children away. Another woman had told me that he was too proud to accept help. She had once tried to give him blankets, because one of the little girls had told her, following church one day, that she and her sisters were always cold at night. When she asked why they didn't put more blankets on their beds, the little girl told her they didn't have any more blankets; they were wearing their coats to bed at night to keep warm. When it was real cold they also covered with the rugs from the floor.

As I walked away, I was angry. The father had accepted a couple of my casseroles, so I had thought he'd also accept my help. My inner wish was to eventually become close to the little girls. But now I felt hopeless in that becoming a reality. I'd wanted to some day share with the girls how my own mother had died when I was little, too. I had faith that by sharing my own life of living without a mother, I could help them to not feel singled out as I had felt.

Knowing the girls were alone at times tore my heart to pieces. As the days passed, I couldn't stop thinking and worrying about them. Soon memories of my own past raced to take center stage in my mind. Try as I might to force the old hurt back, it began dominating my normal way of thinking until my concentration was dimmed and confused. I was already living in a state of depression and feeling physically, mentally, and emotionally drained. Negative thinking soon plagued me. Shortly thereafter, I felt saturated with fear. Even a phone call or a knock on the door was cause for panic. My family's daily good-byes became a time of immense grief. Each day as they left, I believed I'd never see them again. I convinced myself something surely would happen. Perhaps I would die and leave my children behind, as my mother had left my ten siblings and me.

⌒

Years earlier I'd seen a psychologist several times to try to overcome some of the fears I was living with, but he never asked me anything about my childhood. Time was spent working on exploring ways to change the negative behaviors. "I don't practice Freud's ways," he said, on my first visit. "Behavioral modification is my bag."

In an effort to help me overcome claustrophobia, the psychologist assigned me the task of getting into an elevator. I spent nearly two hours in a store, sampling perfume, trying on hats, and examining every dress on the rack while trying to build up enough courage to go into the elevator. I had promised my counselor that I'd at least step into it that day. Going up one floor would be my task for the following week. It had taken me several weeks to get this far. My previous sessions were spent watching a video about people going in and out of elevators. That in itself made my heart race and my stomach turn until I could hardly breathe.

I wanted desperately to enter the elevator, but each time as I went near it, panic overtook me and soon I was gasping for air. Disappointed in myself, I left, believing that I'd never return again. But each week I'd somehow get the courage to drive the thirty miles to town to the only store equipped with an elevator. Each week I'd leave, again disappointed in myself. Finally, fearing that someday I'd lose my breath completely, I quit trying to overcome my claustrophobia.

After that day my time was spent spewing words of self hate. My inability to conquer even the most menial of tasks was killing every trace of self-confidence. Even passing by a mirror became an outlet for hateful thought. I despised the thin reflection looking back at me. What little positive self-image I once had soon crumbled. Bringing one of my boys to the doctor, or handling some other similar emergency was the only way I'd venture out of my safe zone. Giving up completely was tempting, but a fragment of hope remained. I needed to get better for my children's sake at least. I longed to be there for them—for their school plays, picnics, concerts, open houses, basketball games—yes, every minute of their lives that I could share with them. I didn't want them looking out to an empty parent's chair, the way I'd had to. But as the days turned into weeks and the weeks into months, I felt paralyzed to do anything more about my fears.

Hitting rock bottom, I threw myself to my knees one afternoon and cried out to God for help. It was only a few days later when my husband bought me a book called *Working It Through* by Elisabeth Kubler-Ross. After reading it, I realized that I had not dealt with my mother's death. Only a few nights later I began opening up to Bryan about my childhood. As I shared with him, I didn't quite know what was happening to me. I heard myself talking in a childlike way and realized that I was displaying childish behaviors, but I couldn't control my actions. At times I felt like a spectator to this strange event. Internally I scolded myself for acting so childish. Yet, as I let my story unfold, the child within, who obviously was aching to be heard, continued to dominate my adult way of thinking. The next morning, at Bryan's request, I called our parish priest, who in return directed me to seek counseling. On that Monday, Father Frank made me a Friday appointment with a psychologist.

As the days went by, I feared Friday's arrival. "Would counseling be a flop as before?" I wondered. My heart raced in anticipation of the appointment as I tried to carry out my daily tasks. What would I say to the counselor? What would he think when I openly admitted that I thought I had to grieve for my mother who had been dead for years?

When Friday arrived, I mustered up the courage to go to my appointment, praying that no one would recognize me. My heart beat to the speed of the wipers as I drove through an unexpected storm. The thunder and lightening and the wind and rain scared me. I was about to turn around and go home, when suddenly I remembered something that a friend's mother had once told me. "Storms, even the storms of life, are followed by a rainbow." For a complete *second* I was at peace and excited to be going to counseling, looking forward to my own personal rainbow.

☞

At the front desk I checked in and took a seat. I lowered my head as I waited for my counselor to call my name. I grabbed a *Time* magazine from a nearby table and opened it. I held it at eye level in hopes of hiding my identity, but when my counselor loudly called me, the magazine flew from my hands. Embarrassed, I grabbed it from the floor, returned it to the table, then nervously followed him down the hall and into his smoke-filled room. He lit a cigarette and with his back to me pointed to the couch that I assumed I was to sit on. He sat on a swivel chair next to his desk and did paper work, while continuing to smoke. After crushing the butt in an ashtray, he swiveled around, lit another cigarette and then introduced himself. At his request, I spoke a little about myself while he continued to puff away, never once shaking the ash from his cigarette.

"What's on your mind?" he asked after I finished my spiel of how I was married and a mother of four small boys, reciting their names.

I wanted to say it was his long cigarette ash on my mind, but I knew it was probably another diversion to skirt around the truth, so I answered as honestly as possible. "I believe I'm grieving my mother," I very nervously responded.

"I'm sorry to hear that," he said, finally flicking the ash. "When did she die?"

"Twenty-five years ago," I hesitantly answered.

He began to chuckle. "And *you* think you're grieving her *now!*"

"Yes… I… do," my voice choked out.

"*Well, I don't,*" he said. "That's way in the past and *wouldn't* be affecting the present. Now why don't you start talking about what's really bothering you? Let's get right to the meat and potatoes of it all," he said, as he crushed his cigarette, then grabbed his nearly empty pack from his desk.

"Please… I'd rather… you not smoke," I said, very cautiously. "I have asthma."

"But I have a habit. Which is worse?" he sarcastically answered. With that remark I began to cry.

"I'm sorry," he said. "If smoking is that offensive to you, I certainly don't need one. Now let's get back to what you came here for today."

"I think I better leave," I said. Rising from the couch with my hand cupped over my mouth, I muttered, "I feel sick."

"It's your call," he said. "But are you sure?" I nodded, so he walked me to the door. "See you next week. And don't forget, make another appointment."

On the way out I walked right past the receptionist and ran out the glass doors to the car. Tears flooded my face. I had been so sure that I was on the right track after reading *Working It Through.*

7

Faces of concern glanced through the window, as they walked by the car. Panic was about to overtake me when suddenly an inspiration came to me. I grabbed a wad of Kleenex, blew my nose, then dried my eyes. Backing out of the parking lot, I said loudly and with a twinge of sarcasm, *"I'll write to Elisabeth Kubler-Ross and ask her what she thinks."*

On my drive home, I thought of all the things I would say in my letter. Then, I wrote it shortly after I got home. I told Elisabeth about my visit with the counselor and how terrible it had been. I told of my counselor's view on things and about my own thoughts of why I was so depressed and fearful. Only a few days had passed when Elisabeth's reply arrived. After reading it, I breathed a sigh of relief. Elisabeth had confirmed my suspicions and invited me to the workshop—the workshop in New York where I was now heading.

⌒

It was November and the first snow of the year was falling. For the Upper Peninsula, this was not unusual. I had once witnessed snow flurries on a Fourth of July night, so I wasn't surprised. Yet the snow concerned me. Would my family make it home safely?

At the end of Highway 35, the bus slid across the intersection onto Highway 41 and I nearly lost my breath. It wasn't my own safety I feared, but the safety of my husband and children. I quickly reminded myself that the thirty-minute trip home for them had passed and the children would be safely tucked into their beds. Still my throat swelled from forcing back the tears—the tears of present-day worry and fear and tears of past sorrows. City lights soon crept into the darkness of the window view. I took a deep breath. "Will peace ever come to my life?" I asked myself, as the bus traveled on.

The snow continued to thicken, and except for the absence of flickering colored lights, it began to look like Christmas everywhere.

"Are you warm enough back there?" the driver hollered. I answered yes twice before he could hear my reply.

"It's beginning to look like Christmas, don't you think?" he asked in what seemed to be an effort to make conversation. Again I answered yes, but with only the slightest movement of my head. I feared if I were to even say a single word, the tears would flow.

Since the Christmas of 1960, I had never thought of Christmas as a joyous time of year, so I ignored just how festive the outdoors might be looking. I lay my head against the window, dozed for a few minutes, and upon awakening, asked myself, "What was I dreaming?" Something unsettling preyed upon my mind. I closed my eyes again. Suddenly I awoke and realized that I had dreamt about my mother's good-bye to my siblings and me when she had left for *her* trip to Chicago. For the first time in days, a smile came upon my face. I thought about my own boys and how they had begged me to take them with to New York, much as my siblings and I had begged my own mother to take us with her to Chicago. I reclined the seat of the Greyhound and silently prayed that my boys wouldn't miss me as much as I had missed my mother during her absence.

⌒

Back home, Bryan lay awake in bed thinking about his wife going off alone to New York. It worried him terribly. Lately her almost exclusive confinement to the house had concerned him deeply. Night after night, upon his return from work, the same story greeted him. "I'm so tired, Bryan," she'd say. And each morning would bring the same routine. He'd have to convince her that ten hours of sleep was enough and listen to her complain of being too tired to get out of bed. Often, it was *Bryan* who took the first step out of bed for her. With his medium frame, he'd lift her into his muscular arms and gently set her feet upon the floor. He loved being with her, but he desperately wanted her to be free of the fear and worry that haunted their lives. It bothered him when she confessed that she was afraid to even go shopping. "What woman doesn't want to shop?" he asked himself, and the red flags of concern went up.

Bryan knew that some of Donna's negative behaviors had gotten better over the years, but others had gotten far worse. No matter how much pleading he did, year after year it was the same old story. Even since their earlier days in Germany, when Bryan had been drafted into the army, he had encouraged her to seek help for the things that were tormenting her. But she'd either say that she didn't know what was on her mind or that she "just knew" no one would be able to help her. More recently, Bryan had to ask a

9

friend of hers to come and be with her and the kids because all she did was lie on the living room floor—not eating, not speaking. "Damn!" Bryan said, when she refused to move from the floor on the third night. It was the worry Donna detected in his voice that temporarily brought her out of self-absorption and enabled her to sip from the glass of water he held to her mouth. She looked at his face—his wrinkled brow, his eyes without their usual gleam. She knew he hadn't been getting much sleep lately, either. On two different occasions, she had heard him crying during the night. It frightened her because she had never known her husband to cry, except years earlier on the day he had proposed to her. She didn't know what to do or say, so she chose not to talk to him about his crying, just as she hadn't talked to him about the evening she heard his angry words as he piled the wood into the basement. "What am I doing to my husband?" she asked herself. And the guilt continued to mount.

Bryan had always surmised that deep within the depression was a sad story waiting to be told. "What has happened to the girl I married?" he wondered as he lay staring at the clock. "What happened to the cheerleader, the prom queen, the out-going girl that once loved to be around people?" He brushed his brown hair from his forehead. He hit the mattress with his fist. "It's three o'clock. I have to work tomorrow!" Then he continued scolding himself. "If only I could have helped her, I wouldn't have had to send her off on that bus alone." But as the night slipped by, he admitted that he was glad she was finally gone to seek help. He knew that lately she had let herself go, and this behavior, of all her negative behaviors, scared him most. Typically, she took pride in her appearance, dressing her five-foot-five frame in clothes of style— not expensive clothes—but clothes of good taste. He admired her ability to French braid her own hair and her wisdom in choosing hairstyles that complimented her age. He loved it when she dressed feminine. He recalled one evening earlier in the year when he had convinced her to go out dancing.

"I'm not quite ready," she exclaimed, as he entered their bedroom. "I still have my face to do." Bryan watched as she lengthened her short eyelashes with mascara and then carried out the rest of the make-up procedure. "I have to hide my ugliness," she smirked, as she grabbed a piece of paper from a notepad to blot her plum colored lips. Bryan walked to the mirror. Gently he placed his callused hands upon her soft, blushed-fed face. "You're not hiding your ugliness; you're bringing out your beauty." She turned from the compliment, which had not surprised him. She had never been able to take a compliment, then or now.

⌒

Bryan tossed and turned as the memories of the previous weeks floated through his mind. He relived the conversations that had brought his wife to agree to attend the workshop—the workshop where she'd, hopefully, deal with the unfinished business leftover from childhood. He recalled how the first night of the conversations had started as a typical night. He tucked the boys into bed, folded the laundry, put the linens in the bathroom closet, then continued on to the master bedroom. He assumed she'd be sleeping as usual, but to his surprise he found her sitting at the foot of the bed when he opened the door. Instinctively, he sensed something wrong. It had been fifteen years since he'd seen her in pigtails. He raised his thick eyebrows and was about to ask, "Why pigtails?" when out of the blue she started telling him about her past. Her childlike manner took him by surprise. Not just in her body language, but in the manner of her speech. She was talking in a voice like that of a little girl, and this behavior put a scare into him, making him wonder what might be next. Was she having a breakdown? He questioned. If not, he guessed she was surely standing on the threshold of one.

⌒

"She couldn't let us go."
"Who couldn't let you go?" Bryan asked.
"Mama," I answered. "I asked if I could go with her to Chicago. But, "No," she said, "you're too little, Donna Jean. You're not even seven."
My sister Bernadette threw her little white prayer book onto Mama's bed. "I'm eight, can I go with you?"

11

My oldest sister Sarah thought she should be the one to go, because she was nine, but Mama still said, "No." And when my three little sisters started begging to go, Mama almost cried. Suddenly John, Luke, and Mark came running in the house. "Can we go with you too, Ma?" they hollered.

"Oh me, oh my," she said.

They wanted to go so that they could see our biggest brother Matthew. He was eighteen and living in Chicago with Auntie Celia.

"I'm sorry, but none of you can come with," Mama said. She knelt down and put her arms around my three little sisters and then looked at everybody and said, "There won't be any room."

See, at first, even Mama didn't know if she'd get to go to Chicago. Mama wanted to go real bad. She wanted to go to my Godmother's wedding. But when she asked Dad what he thought, Dad said, "I'd like to say go, but I don't think we have money to send you to Chicago."

"But," Mama said, and her bottom lip started to shake, "I've never… been able to see Matthew… since… he moved from home!" Mama put her hands over her eyes. My dad took her hands and kissed them and said, "Well, maybe we can flip a coin and if you win, you can go!" Then he got up from the chair and walked toward the refrigerator. "Maybe there's a coin in the yellow glass teapot."

"The yellow glass teapot that always gets the money?" I asked.

"The yellow glass teapot with the broken cover?" Bernadette said.

My sisters didn't break the cover to the yellow glass teapot. And I didn't break the cover. No, way! My brothers broke the cover of the yellow glass teapot. One day Luke and John were throwing their baseball in the kitchen. Mama asked them not to. Then Mama *told* them not to throw the ball, but John kept saying, "Just one more time. Come on, Ma, let us play!" And Luke said, "Just let us throw it once more, Ma, then we'll quit."

"For heavens sake Luke, you're fourteen, and John, you're twelve. By now you boys should know better! You'll end up breaking something!" she said.

All of a sudden CRASH, BOOM, BANG! Luke and John made the yellow glass teapot fall from off the refrigerator. I heard it hit the floor. Mama ran to the teapot. She knelt by it and picked up the cover. I heard her say, "No, no, not my yellow glass teapot. It's the only thing I have left from my wedding day!"

"It's only the cover, Ma," Luke said, "I'll glue it."

"You'll never be able to fix it!" she said. "It's got one big piece out of it now, and that piece is all broken up." Mama's shaky hands set the broken cover back on top the teapot and then she put the teapot back on top of the refrigerator. Next she took the broom from the corner of the room. I thought she was going to sweep up the yellow glass, but she took the broom and booted the boys out of the house with it.

"If I catch either of you in the house before it's time to eat, I'll have you both kneeling in corners!" The boys went running, and then Mama swept the glass off the kitchen floor.

The day after John and Luke broke the cover was the day that my dad made my sisters and me go outside to find a caterpillar. See, after Dad came in from doing barn chores, he said, "It's sure a nice day! You kids are going outside this morning!" Then he went to the wash basin. I watched my dad wash up, then put lots of soapy soap on his face. Next he took his shaver and cut off all his picky whiskers. Then he went into the kitchen. I followed him. Mama was putting dishes up into the cabinet and my dad went up behind her. He hugged her around her skinny belly. I saw him whisper something into her ear. Mama turned around and smiled at my dad. She shook her head into 'Little Yeses.' Then Dad turned around and said, "All right you girls...outside with your brothers!" Dad wouldn't even let Monica stay in the house. He made us take her outside with us.

"We don't want to pile wood with the boys" we cried.

"You girls don't have to pile wood," he said, handing Bernadette a Mason jar that had a cover with holes in it. "Go find a caterpillar and put it in this jar."

"What if we can't find a caterpillar?" I said.

"Just look and look, you'll find one," he said as he opened the door, then yelled to the boys. "Keep an eye on your sisters. Make sure they stay in the yard."

We looked and looked and looked for a caterpillar. Monica found the button off Mama's long gray coat and Sarah found Catherine's doll that Catherine thought had been stolen at school. Sarah saw its arm sticking out from under a pile of snow. We got tired of looking, so we watched Luke and John punch down our shrinking snowman. Then we started looking again for a caterpillar. We looked under stones, boards and tree branches and by the barn too, but we still couldn't find one. Finally, I spotted a night crawler creeping out of a big mud puddle.

"Let's put the night crawler inside the jar!" I said.

"A night crawler isn't a caterpillar," Bernadette said. "Caterpillars are fuzzy." But Bernadette took a stick and she lifted the night crawler up and into the jar anyway. Sarah screwed the cover on and Bernadette tucked the jar under her arm. Sarah lifted Monica and I grabbed Anna's hand and we ran to the house. Dad was looking out the window of the door, brushing his hair from his forehead, when he saw us coming and opened the door. He took the jar and looked inside. We didn't make a peep.

"Ah ha," Dad said, "you found a bald caterpillar!" Then he said, "Everyone is going outside this afternoon, too. Even your mother says that she can come with us!"

"Yippee!" we screamed.

So after lunch we went outside again. First Dad had us help him pile wood and then help him clean up the yard. Mama just played. I watched her make a snowball and then throw it right at Dad. It knocked his hat off.

"Hey!" Dad said, running over by the shed where there was still snow. "Two can play this game!" Mama dashed away, but he caught her, laid her on the ground and rubbed the snow onto her face. Then she rubbed snow onto his face. They laughed and laughed. We saw Dad kiss Mama right on her lips. Sarah started singing the K I S S I N G song, so all six of us sang together!

When Dad stood up, he rubbed his hands together and said, "It's Holy Saturday! What do you say we all go collect holy water, like the early Christians used to do."

"Where will we find holy water?" I asked.

"Well, get in the car," he said, "and I'll show you."

So we piled into the car and Dad took us to the Valentine Creek. On the way, he told us how, on Holy Saturday morning, the early Christians would go get water from a river and then bring it to the church to have it blessed. Dad had taken a jar to the Valentine and he let us take turns filling our hands with water and dumping the water into the jar. My brothers thought it was dumb. They wouldn't do it. When the jar was filled, we took the water to Father Dishaw and Dad asked him to bless it. When we got home, Mama sprinkled the house with the holy water.

"Is our house dry, like the clothes that need ironing?" I asked. Mama laughed. "No, I'm asking God's blessings upon our house so that we will love God with all our heart, mind and soul, and to keep us safe from harm. Then she made a sign-of-the-cross on each of our foreheads and asked God's blessings on us, too. And every Sunday after church she blessed us again, and our house, too, until all the holy water was gone.

☞

That was a long, long, long time ago, so I asked Dad if he'd take us to get more holy water. I wanted to bless Mama so she'd be safe if she got to go to Chicago.

"It's June," Dad said. "It's been too hot. The water in the Valentine is dried up." I followed Dad to the refrigerator. "Stand back," he said. He reached on top of the refrigerator and took down the yellow glass teapot.

"What you doing, Dad?" I asked.

"I'm looking for a coin to flip, to see if your mother gets to go to Chicago, or not," he said, winking at me. He lifted the broken cover off the teapot and turned the teapot upside down. An Indian-head nickel fell out. He took the nickel and flipped it over and over and over in his hands. Then he said to Mama, "If the Indian-head lands up, you'll get to go to Chicago, but if the buffalo lands up, you'll have to stay home."

Dad smiled, Mama cried, and I screamed, "Don't go Mama, don't go!" when I saw the Indian-head land on the floor.

Mama hurried to her bedroom and looked inside her dresser to see what she could take to wear. "I only have a couple pieces of clothes that are good enough," she said to Dad.

"You better bring cool clothes. It's hot in Chicago during June, a lot hotter than here," he said.

"But I don't have much of anything that fits now. I wear your big shirts around the house when I'm expecting, but I don't want to bring those to Chicago. Oh, well," Mama said, "what I have will have to do!"

"So how did your mother get to Chicago?" Bryan asked Donna that night when she opened up to him about her past. She was still sitting at the foot of their bed. She didn't seem to hear his question and continued talking in the same peculiar way.

Chapter Two

D ad climbed into the attic and got down a little brown suit case. He pushed on the round gold button of the suitcase and a gold buckle popped up. Looking at us he said, "The lock still works. It was a long time ago when I bought this. Your mother and I weren't even married!"

"I didn't know you and Mama weren't ever married," Catherine said. And I said I didn't know Dad had a little brown suitcase up in the attic!

"Here," he said, giving Mama the suitcase. "Use this for your trip. The last time I used it was on my way home from the CC Camps. Those were the good old days. Cold, but good. I sure had fun in the kitchen. And then at night, all I did was read."

See, my dad was a great cook for all the people in the CC Camps. Dad told us that he made the men really yummy things to eat and they all told him how good everything was. Even the captain did! He was my dad's boss. And before Dad left the CC Camps for good, the captain gave him a very, very important paper that says DISCHARGED with HIGHEST OF HONORS. We can't ever touch that paper—only my dad can and Mama.

Before Mama started to pack, she put Monica on my dad's lap so that he'd rock her. Then she put on records to play. Not our favorite songs, or hers, but the records that my dad liked best. Dad watched while Mama looked into the pockets of the suitcase. When

17

Little Rosa played, my dad sang with the song. And when it was over I heard him say, "I'm sure going to miss you when you're gone." "I know," she said, smiling at Dad. "I'll miss you, too. And by the way, when I get home Sunday night, I'll make your birthday cake."

"No, you don't have to make me a cake," Dad said.

"But you'll be FORTY! We have to celebrate that!" Mama giggled.

"You're only two years behind me," he said, making a ha-ha face. He got off the rocker and put Monica into her crib, and then went back outside to work.

Mama took the sugar cookies from the oven and then put in the pies. Then she put all the stuff that she needed for making bread onto the table.

"Why are you making so many things," Sarah asked.

"I don't want your dad to have too much to do when I'm in Chicago," she said.

My sisters and I knelt on kitchen chairs and watched while Mama made the bread dough. When she was done kneading it, she let me pour some flour onto her sticky bread dough hands. She rubbed her hands with the flour until pieces of dough fell off onto the table. We got to eat them. I watched Mama put the dough into the big green bowl. Then she made a sign-of-the-cross on top of it. After washing her hands, she looked around the kitchen for a place to put the bowl.

See, Mama always put the big green bowl on top of the little white table, but my dad had taken the little white table outside. He was using it to stand on because he's building us a bigger house.

"Maybe up here," she said, as she lifted the bowl to the top of the refrigerator. "The dough has to double in size, and it's going to take awhile, so I guess I'll have to put it up here where it won't be in the way." Mama reached up again and put a towel over the bowl. "Ouch," she said, grabbing her tummy. "I better sit down for awhile."

Anna and Sarah rubbed Mama's feet while she drank a glass of water and rubbed her tummy. When she got up, she greased all the tins. Then when the dough was ready to be made into buns and loaves of bread, she let us help shape it. Later, when we were washing our hands, Mama told us that she couldn't wait to get moved into the new part of the house. "It'll be great having a nice big kitchen. Three rooms are way too crowded."

Mama changed the record. She put on my favorite song, then said, "If my girls help me sing Mockingbird Hill, it'll surely take away the smell when I wash this pail of diapers."

So while Mama's hands lifted the diapers up and down and up and down in the soapy, bleachy water, we all sang:

When the sun in the morning comes over the hill
And kisses the roses on my window sill,
My heart fills with gladness when I hear the thrill
Of the birds in the tree tops on Mockingbird Hill
Tra La La Fiddleley Dee Dee it gives me a thrill
To wake up in the morning on Mockingbird Hill.

"There," Mama said, when she got the diapers hung on the line. "That's one more job done. Wednesday will be here soon." I held Mama's hand on the way to the house, but she asked me to let go. Her hand was all scratchy and I saw drops of blood coming out of it. I grabbed her other hand, but she asked me not to hold that one either.

"Do your hands hurt, Mama?"

"Oh just a little," she said. But she kept saying, "Ouch," when she scrubbed the bedroom floor. She kept taking her hands in and out of the pail of hot soapy water and swishing them back and forth, like Lily our cow swishes her tail to keep the flies off her back.

Mama's hands were always red and picky. Once when Father Dishaw came to eat supper at our house, I heard her talking to him. "I hope the Good Lord will let me in when I reach heaven's door. Maybe he'll think I've been too big of a sinner," she said.

"Why do you say that, Rose?" Father asked, lifting up his eyebrows.

"Because sometimes I really get mad at the kids, and I yell."

"Oh, Rose," Father said. "When you get to heaven's door, just show God those hard working hands. Just show Him your hands," he said as he picked little Monica from off the floor.

⁀

The next day Mama scrubbed the rest of the floors. She

told us that she wanted all her jobs finished before she left for Chicago. When she was done, her knees were all red. They were red like Luke, John, and John's friend Calvin's knees were red the day Mama made them kneel on the ground under the crabapple tree—right where she could see them. She punished them because they did something very bad. It was because Luke dared John and John's friend Calvin to sneak up on a skunk and pull its tail—and John and Calvin did it! Mama was very mad and she made the boys sleep in the barn that night. Calvin slept there too, because his Mama wouldn't let him in their house, either.

⌒

After Mama got the floors scrubbed, we helped her by putting the dirty clothes into piles.

"Where's Anna?" Mama called. "Where's my little four-year-old?" We looked around the house for her, because Anna always hides. Mama says that Anna's always up to mischief—and mischief, Mama says, means trouble! So we looked in the living room and the kitchen and the bedroom, but we couldn't find her. Then I saw the pile of dirty towels moving.

"Mama the towels are moving!" I screamed.

"No," Mama said, putting her finger over her mouth to shush me, "towels can't move!" Mama snuck down by the towels. "BOO!" she said.

Anna jumped up out of the towels giggling. "I 'cared' you, Mama!"

"You sure did scare me," Mama said, tickling Anna's tummy.

"Ha, ha, ha," Bernadette laughed, "I told Anna to hid there." Just then I saw Monica sitting on the towels.

"What you doing, Monica?" I asked. She pulled a towel over her head and then she started saying, "Tree, den, tree den."

"She's counting, Mama!" I shouted. "She wants you to find her, too!"

"Oh, dear," Mama said, putting her finger to her cheek. "Where, oh, where could little Monica be? Does anyone know where she's at?" I had to hold my hand over my mouth, because I almost laughed out loud as Mama walked loud on the floor, then stopped and looked behind the refrigerator, "Nope, Monica's not there." Mama walked some more, stopped again, and this time she looked behind the folding bed. "Nope, she's not there either. Where can my little girl be?"

Monica pulled the towel from her head. "BOO!"she hollered. Everyone laughed. Mama picked up Monica and gave her a hug and kiss, and then pinched her balloon cheeks. "You little stinker! You tricked Mama," she said.

After supper Mama ironed Catherine's doll's dress, and her own dress, skirt and blouse. She folded them and put them into the little brown suitcase.

"I don't want you to go away, Mama," Catherine cried.

"How you going to get to Chicago?" Bernadette asked.

"She's going to go on the train," I said. "Like Matthew did, right, Mama?"

"No, I'm going to get there with your Aunt Alice and Uncle Homer. We're going in their car."

"You mean Uncle Homely," I said. And everyone laughed, but that's what people call him—Uncle Homely. I think it's because his face is all cracked up. Sometimes he takes out his fake teeth and he makes really funny faces that are ugly faces, too. He always makes us laugh. He can put his hand behind the lamplight and make a horse gallop across the wall. He can even make the horse talk. I like Uncle Homely.

"Yes," Mama said, "I'm going to Chicago with my brother Homer. But enough talking about that." And Mama hollered, "Rosary time!" She hollered loud because once, when the boys didn't come for rosary time, they told Mama that they didn't hear her call. And for three days, John and Mark said that they didn't hear her call. So after that time, Mama always hollered loud to make sure everyone would hear. The boys don't like rosary time because they don't like kneeling on the hard floor, but I don't care. I get to be by Mama.

"Tonight we'll be doing the Sorrowful Mysteries of the Rosary," Mama said.

"Is the Sorrowful rosary about the bad men that put big long nails in Jesus' hands and big long nails into Jesus' feet to make Jesus die?" I asked.

"That's right! Donna Jean," Mama said, as she patted my back.

"Can we do the rosary where Jesus comes alive again?" I asked.

"No, let's do the rosary about when Jesus was born!"

21

Bernadette yelled out. But Mama still did the Sorrowful rosary and when we were done with it, she read to us from the Bible. She read the part where it says that we should go to our bedroom and close the door and pray.

Then John said, "If the Bible says that we're suppose to go to our room and pray, we shouldn't have to go to church on Sunday, right?"

"No," Mama said. "The Good Book also says that we should meet and worship in the house of the Lord in holy attire."

"What's holy attire?" Sarah asked.

"Clothes that you keep for special times," Mama answered, and she got off her bed. "Come here, everyone, to the kitchen. I'm going to show you something that my mother showed me. I can't remember many things about my mother, because I was so young when she died, but I remember her showing me and my sisters and brothers this."

When we got into the kitchen, Mama took a butter knife and some hard white baking beans. "Here, John," she said, "hold this knife by the handle." Mama put four of the beans on the knife and told John to walk kind of fast around the kitchen table with it. And so that's what John did, and all the beans stayed on the knife. Then she added four more beans. This time when John walked around the table, one-by-one the beans fell off and by the time he got back by Mama there weren't any beans left on the knife.

"You put too many on!" John complained.

"That's right," Mama said. "It got too hard for you to balance. We need balance in our lives."

"What the heck is balance?" John asked.

"Well," Mama said, "just because something is fun or even good doesn't mean that you can do just that all the time. Like praying, you need to pray in your bedroom behind closed doors sometimes, but you also need to pray with others at church. Both are important. Besides, you can't just pick out the things that you like about the Bible, and throw the rest away."

"So," John said, with a puzzled look on his face. "If I want to keep the beans on the knife, I have to go to church on Sunday!"

"That's right," Mama said, and she and my dad and my brothers laughed, but I don't know why.

My sisters and I wanted to play the bean game, too, so Dad

got out more butter knives and let us have bean races around the table. Mark and Luke watched. They laughed when the game was over, because Monica was slow like a caterpillar, but she won! Dad had only put one bean on her knife. I would have won, but John pushed me out of his way and then blamed me when the beans fell off his knife. John and I started fighting, so Mama made us quit.

"Next time we play the bean game," I said, "I'm going to win!"

⁀

Bryan chuckled to himself at the simplicity of the game and thought briefly of how their own boys would probably like to play it, but rather than verbalizing his thoughts, he let her continue with the stories from her past.

⁀

During the night I got up and went into Mama's bedroom and shook her arm. "The moon is scaring me, Mama," I said. Mama lifted the blankets and I crawled under. "Why do you have to go to Chicago?" I complained.

"Donna Jean," Mama whispered, "I'll be back before you know it. Now go back to sleep."

In the morning, when it was still dark, Mama came and kissed me good-bye.

"Donna Jean," she said, "where did you put my clothes? Mama's in a hurry this morning."

"I hid them behind the chair. Please, Mama, can't just I go with you?"

"No, Sweetheart," she said.

I watched as she carefully put her clothes back into the suitcase and then took her suitcase to the door. "Come here," she said, stretching out her arms. I ran to her and she hugged me really tight. "I'll be back soon, I promise."

While Mama kissed and hugged everybody good-bye, my dad told Mark that he was in charge of us until he got back from bringing Mama to Uncle Homely's.

When they left I snuck under Mama's bed to get her little girl storybooks—her little girl storybooks that she got from her mama when she was a little girl. I sat on the floor by Mama's bed to read them so that Mark wouldn't see me, because Mama doesn't let us read them without her. She's afraid they'll get ripped. Catherine and Anna came to listen, so I whispered the words from the pages. When I got done reading each page, I passed the book around so that they could see the pictures, too. Anna had to put the book right up to her face, like she always does, so that she could see the picture. She took so long that Catherine grabbed the book from her. Then Anna and Catherine started fighting for the book and a page got torn. Cinderella's head got ripped off, so I hurried the books back under the bed before Mark came to see what the fighting was about.

"Let's go! Let's get our jobs done," Mark said, clapping his hands together. So we made our beds and helped him clean the house really good. Monica wouldn't help us do anything. She just kept crying for Mama to come back home. When the house was all clean we wanted to make somersaults, but Mark wouldn't let us. He said that we'd wrinkle the rugs.

The next day Monica screamed all day because I accidentally burned her. The coffee poured out of the spout before I got to Dad's cup. It spilled over her bare legs. Dad jumped up and grabbed Monica from the chair and Mark jumped up and grabbed the coffeepot. "Oh, I wish Ma was home. Sunday will come none too soon," he said as he and Dad poured cold water over Monica's burnt legs.

On Friday Dad told us that the new part to our house was finished. "All I need now is a door for the new entrance. Luke, I thought that you and I could go to Escanaba to get one this afternoon."

"Can I go too?" Catherine asked.

"Me too," I said. But Dad would only let Luke go.

"Escanaba is fifty miles from Garden," Dad said to Mark, "so it'll take us about three hours, by the time we get there and back."

After Dad and Luke left, we noticed that Catherine was gone. Mark and John looked outside for her, and we looked all around in the new and old house for her. We didn't know it, but Catherine had left with my dad. When Dad got back home he told us what happened.

"Catherine popped up, out of the back seat when we were almost to Escanaba," he said. "I saw her in the rearview mirror. It was too late to turn around then, so I kept on going."

"Dad," Mark complained, "we thought Catherine was lost in Dupy's woods, (that's the woods next to our house) because we couldn't find her. John and I looked and looked and looked for her! The girls have been crying steady!"

Dad listened to Mark, then scratched his head with his matchbook and said, "There was no way to let you know that she was with us. She's fine and everything turned out okay, so let's not be mentioning any of this to your mother when she gets home from Chicago. It'll only upset her."

⌒

Sunday night finally came and we got to go with Dad to pick up Mama. She was waiting on Uncle Homely's front porch. As soon as Dad stopped the car, we jumped out to give her hugs and kisses. Mama hugged us, too. Then she looked at Dad and said, "I'm ready. Let's go!"

Monica sat on Mama's lap and Anna sat in the middle of the front seat, like they always do. I stood up on the back seat and leaned over, so I could hug up Mama.

"We had to wear wet socks to church today, Mama!" I said.

"Wet socks?" Mama asked. Her eyes got big and she looked over at my dad.

"Donna Jean," Dad said, "let your mother tell us about her trip."

So Mama told us about the things she got to see and do in Chicago and about how much she missed us when she was there.

"Well, I hope you at least had fun when you were with Matthew and your sisters," Dad said.

"Oh, I did have fun," she said, "but it doesn't mean that I could forget about all of you." Then she showed us pictures of the wedding. My cousin Marilyn had taken them with her instant Kodak camera so that Mama could bring the pictures home for us to see. Mama told us how she saw tall buildings that reminded her of the Tower of Babel. "It's as if the buildings were touching heaven," she said. Then she told us about all the yellow taxis and the stores with all the pretty clothes in the windows. Mama was smiling and sometimes laughing telling us about Chicago, but when my dad turned on the radio and Mama heard *I'm so Lonesome I Could Cry*, she started to cry. I saw tears rolling down her cheeks.

"What's the matter, Mama?" I asked.

"Oh I just miss everybody, especially Matthew," she said. Then she looked at Dad and said, "I wish Matthew still lived at home. It's like a part of me has been missing since the day he left for Chicago." Mama wiped her eyes with her sweater sleeve, "Yes, someday I'm going back there. We're all going to go!" she said as Dad drove into the driveway.

That night when I went to bed I asked my dad if I could use his little brown suitcase when we went to Chicago.

"Yes!" Dad said, "but get to sleep tonight!"

Chapter Three

"The boys!" I stammered, rising from the bed. "I have to check on them."

Bryan saw the fear and worry in my eyes, which added to his own fear and worry.

"They're sleeping. They're okay," he said, as he gently guided me back to the bed then asked if I'd like some water. "You sound hoarse," he said.

When he returned, I sipped from the glass.

"Am I boring you?" I asked, looking down into the glass.

"Never," he responded.

The compassion in his gray-blue eyes convinced me to continue, so I shared more of the memories that were now as clear in my mind as the day they had happened. I told about the day my sisters and I played hopscotch in the rain. And how, as we played, I could hear my dad and his friend Schuyler talking about who'd be the next president of the United States. So I stopped playing hopscotch and went over to talk with them.

⌒

"I know what a 'lection is," I told my dad and Schuyler. "Teacher told us all about it."

"An election," Dad corrected.

27

"Teacher had us pick the man that we want for president. We had to work on his canpane."

"Campaign!" Dad said. "By the way, didn't I hear your mother call? Your sisters have already gone to the house to help her. You run along now, too."

Schuyler laughed, "What man did you pick for president?"

"Kennedy," I said. And I told him and Dad how I was on Edwin's team and how at recess time we ran around outside the school shouting, "Kennedy's in the White House already elected, Nixon's in the garbage can waiting to be collected."

Schuyler laughed a great big laugh. I saw his tummy shake. He reached into his pocket. "Here, you can have this," he said, putting his hand out toward me. I unrolled his fingers. "A nickel! Thanks, Schyuler," I said, taking the nickel and running to the house to show everyone.

After everyone saw my nickel, I dropped it into my sock. When Schuyler and Dad came in, Catherine and I kept jumping off kitchen chairs trying to knock Schuyler's hat off, like we do to my dad and brothers. But Schuyler was so tall we couldn't even reach his neck.

After supper we went to Schuyler's house so my dad could help him move his piano. Anna saw a tree with purple flowers on it, so my sisters and I got out of the car and ran to pick some. Mama stayed in the car with Monica and watched us. When we reached up to pick the flowers, we saw buzzing bumblebees pecking the flowers. We screamed and went running back to the car. Mama was laughing when she opened the door for us. And Mama laughed again that night when we said our prayers. She laughed and laughed at how the bumblebees made us run.

The next morning, I could hear Mama's washing machine oinking. Mama says it makes that noise because it's had a real hard life.

"Don't quit on me now," Mama said to it, as she put the next load in. Then she walked over to our rollaway and asked me if she could borrow the nickel that Schuyler gave to me.

"I need it to mail a very important letter. I promise to give you another one as soon as Dad gets paid," she said.

I looked at Mama and then I looked at the nickel in my hand.

"Well," she asked, "can I borrow it, or not? The mailman

will be here soon."

"Okay," I said. But later when Mama carried her letter and my nickel to the mailbox, I started crying for my nickel. So Mama went back to the mailbox and got it for me.

"Are you mad at me?" I asked when she handed my nickel back.

"No," she said. "If the bill gets paid late, late will have to do."

⌒

Sarah and I were rolling old tires when the mailman came. When he drove away, I saw a big present tied on the mailbox, so I went to the kitchen window and hollered for Mama. She came running out of the house and crossed the road to get the present.

"Girls," she hollered. "The package is from Chicago. It's from Bernice and Joe, and we got a letter from Matthew!"

Mama sat on the front porch and we sat around her. She opened the package. Inside of it was a camera—a camera that Mama said could take even colored pictures. There was film to put into the camera, too. Mama found a letter inside the package and read it to us.

Dear Aunt Rose,
Thanks so much for coming all the way to Chicago for our wedding. My aunts all mean a lot to me, but you're more than just an aunt—you're a rose! We'll never forget how special your presence made our wedding day!
God Bless You,
Bernice and Joe

PS We hope you like the camera. Please send us some pictures as soon as possible.

Mama put the camera back into the box and set it on the porch. "Don't touch!" she said, and she started to open the letter from Matthew just as our car came speeding into the driveway.

"Honestly, John," Mama said to my dad when the car stopped. "Dust is everywhere! Why do you let that boy drive that jalopy so darn fast?"

29

"Wasn't going that fast, Ma!" Luke said, getting out of the car.

"Oh, yes, you were!" I said. "The chickens tried to fly away!"

"It's no big deal anyway!" he said.

"It certainly is!" Mama told him.

"Certainly isn't!" he said back to her.

"No more wise cracks! Maybe what you need, Luke, is to spend more time doing better things, like helping Donna Jean with her prayers. She's making her First Communion in the spring, and I need to be sure that she knows all the words to the prayers, so I'll have you help her with that."

"But…"

"But nothing!" Mama said. Luke stomped up the porch and into the house. Mama showed Dad and John and Mark the camera from Bernice and Joe. Then she read the letter from Matthew.

Dear Ma and Dad,

Hope things at home are okay. How was your trip home? The weather here is getting hotter. Dad, did you get the house finished yet? I should have told you when you were here, Ma, but I joined the army. I'll be home in a week. Don't go crying, Ma. I'll be okay.

God Bless,
Matthew

Still Mama cried. She handed the letter to my dad. Dad didn't cry. He just put his arm around Mama and said, "Rosie, this is a good thing what Matthew's done! He's going off to the Army—not to prison!"

"What's the Army?" I asked.

"That's when you're a soldier," Dad said.

"Like the tin soldier?" Catherine asked.

"Actually, Ma," Mark said, turning his head from Mama and looking out at the sky, "I've been thinking of doing about the same thing. I want to join the Marines."

"Don't tell me that; at least not today!" she said, putting her hand out in front of her, toward Mark. "One of my boys leaving here at a time is enough!"

"But Ma, it could help us all. I will be able to send money home. Dad thinks it's a good thing, so I'm quitting school and leaving as soon as possible."

"But you only have one year to go, then you'll graduate. Plus, you're only sixteen!"

"I know," he said, "but I need to do this, for all of us."

～

Five days went by and then Matthew came home. Then after Sarah crossed seven more days off the calendar, Mama told us that it was the day to bring Matthew and Mark to the train station.

Mama's eyes were filled with tears when we got in the car. We each climbed up on a brother's lap, except for Monica. We complained, because we didn't like sitting on a brother's lap. Sometimes they'd pinch our butt and it would make us scream and then we'd get in trouble.

At the train station Mama cried when she hugged Matthew and she cried when she hugged Mark, so I cried, too. My dad shook their hands. He didn't cry.

On the way home Dad sang the *Smoke Along the Track* song and puffed on his corncob pipe. We sang too, but sung, "Ice cream, you scream, we all scream for ice scream!" The closer we got to Rapid River, the louder we sang. When we passed the Dairy Queen though, Dad wouldn't stop.

Dad turned to Mama. "Well, where do you suppose the boys are now?" Mama didn't answer. She just started to cry again. So I asked her if she wanted to play *Button, Button who's got the Button*, because that's the game that makes her giggle. But Mama said, "Not today."

I watched as Mama hugged Monica and looked out the window. I listened as she hummed *Silver Threads and Golden Needles*. Dad kept hollering at us to sit down, but I stayed leaning over and hugging Mama and wiping away her tears. And for about one-zillion days I wiped away Mama's tears, because whenever I came running into the house from our sandbox to give her kisses, her cheeks were always wet.

～

"You don't look like you're feeling very good. Be sure to

31

get some rest today," Dad said to Mama before he left for work.

Mama was sick that day. She couldn't even help turn the jump rope, so that we could jump doubles. She'd get up and do a job, and then go right back to bed. She couldn't even holler for Luke, so she told me to. When Luke came, Mama asked him if I knew my First Communion prayers.

"I haven't had time to listen to them," he said.

"Oh, Luke, it's been days. You've had long enough. Go now, to the kitchen, and have her say her prayers to you."

"But, Ma, I'm tired. I just got done cutting wood."

"Right now!" she said. "And be sure she's not just mumbling words."

"Ya, ya, ya," Luke crabbed as he grabbed my hand and took me to the kitchen.

The fat hand of the clock went from the two to the three, and then Luke called out to Mama. "Ma, Maaaa, Donna Jean knows her prayers now. Want her to come and say them?"

"Please," she said, when we went in to her bedroom.

Just as I was about to say my prayers, Bernadette came running. "Mama, Monica's writing on the wall with color crayons!" Just then, Monica walked into the bedroom chewing on a purple crayon. Mama almost rolled off of the bed when she tried to get it from her. Monica zoomed out of the room.

"She could swallow it!" Mama hollered. So Luke ran and got the crayon.

"Okay," Mama said to me, when Luke got back into the room, "start your prayers."

"OUR FATHER WENT TO JAIL, STEALING PEANUTS BY THE PAIL," I said, looking at the floor.

"WHAT WAS THAT?" Mama asked as she twirled her eyes up toward Luke.

I knew Mama was mad, because when she's mad, her lips look stuck together like the lips on Catherine's Eskimo doll Moe. Moe always looks mad. I don't like to touch him because he has on a picky, furry coat and leggings and picky, furry boots, too. And his arms and legs don't move. He's stiff—like wood! His eyes don't move like other dolls' eyes—his eyes are glued shut. But Catherine still likes Moe.

Anyway, my dad came in from outside so Mama had me say the prayer to him. I saw my dad smile, but when Mama looked at him, Dad's face got mad. Then, even when Mama was looking, Dad kept smiling until he laughed out loud.

"Really, John," Mama said. "Did you hear that? Did you hear what your son has taught Donna Jean?" Dad smiled again.

"John!" Mama said.

"It's not all that bad, is it Rosie? I'm sure Luke was just having some fun."

"Well, Luke, is there anything else you taught your sister that your dad can laugh about?" Luke shook his head no, but Mama sat up on the end of the bed and put her hands on my shoulders.

"Did Luke teach you anything else, Donna Jean?"

"The Hail Mary," I whispered.

"Okay, let's hear it! Let's hear the Hail Mary."

"HAIL MARY FULL OF GRACE, WASHED HER HANDS AND FORGOT HER FACE," I said, looking at Mama. Mama looked very mad, but Dad smiled again. And when Luke laughed, I laughed, too.

"Did I hear what I think I heard?" Mama's face got bloody red. She lay back down. "Honestly, Luke, sometimes you can be such a pistol. If you seem to know so much about washing faces, I guess I'm going to let you wash your sisters' dirty faces and hands before bedtime."

So that night when we lined up for washing, Luke started washing Monica's face and hands, and he kept giggling and giggling. He giggled so much that he got dizzy and fell onto the floor. On the way down, his hand hit the wash basin and the water splashed all over. We all giggled. Dad tried to shush us, so that Mama wouldn't hear. When it was finally quiet, we heard giggles coming from Mama's bedroom. Then we heard her call for rosary time.

After the rosary Mama said, "Stay right where you're at." Mama slowly got off her bed and took the new camera from her dresser. "Take some pictures," she said handing the camera to my dad. Dad took the camera—the camera that Mama said she'd never take a picture with if Matthew and Mark left to be soldiers.

"Stay kneeling," Mama said, "and keep your hands folded."

"Nobody move," Dad said right before the flashlight on top

of the camera lit up. We couldn't see anything, but Mama said, "The light will go away." And it did.

Dad took nine pictures and then Mama told Dad that she wanted a couple pictures of him with us kids. So Dad got down on the floor and we sat around him. Dad gave Bernadette his pipe so she could pretend to smoke it. But when Mama saw the pipe in Bernadette's mouth, from the little window of the camera, she wouldn't take the picture.

"Get that pipe out of her mouth!" she said.

"For God sake, Rosie, it's empty!" Dad said, laughing.

So Mama took the picture and then took another one of us playing dog pile with Dad on the floor. "Hurry!" Sarah hollered, "I'm getting squished!" And so was I, because we were on the bottom of the pile, next to Dad.

"Come here," Dad said, and he lifted me to the top of the Victrola.

"Mama," Catherine said, putting up her arms, "lift me up, so I can get my picture taken up there, too."

Mama was about to lift Catherine to the Victrola when Dad hollered, "Don't you dare go lifting her, Rosie! You're too weak!" So Dad lifted Catherine to the top of the Victrola, by me.

"Mama," I said, "why can't you lift Catherine anymore?"

"Because my tummy will hurt. I can't lift much of anything," she said.

"Can't you even lift Wilhelmina?" I asked. "Can Wilhelmina get her picture taken with us?"

"I suppose," she said.

Wilhelmina's our pet bunny. She has the softest fur in the whole wide world. When Luke brought her home from his friend Lee's, we tried to think of a name for her. I said, "Let's call the bunny, Bunny," but nobody wanted Bunny. When Catherine said, "Let's call her Whitey," nobody wanted Whitey. Then Mama came and lifted up our bunny. "Wilhelmina!"

"Wilhelmina?" we asked.

"Yes!" she said, "let's call her Wilhelmina, because her fur is as soft as my Aunt Wilhelmina's hands. And your bunny won't be doing any more work than my Aunt Wilhelmina ever did. So I think Wilhelmina would be a good name."

So that's what we named her—Wilhelmina.

Dad lifted Wilhelmina up to me. Then Catherine wanted something to hold, too, so Mama got Moe for her.

"Rosie," Dad said, "stand there, by the girls." And when Mama put her arm around me, Dad took the last picture.

☞

Recalling the memories that Donna had shared with him, Bryan thanked God that she was on the bus. Lately it had been hard for him to cope with her depression and her lack of self-worth. "How could I ever go on without her?" he thought. Scenes from their earlier days flashed across his mind. New Year's Eve 1968 when they had went out on their first date. Bryan smiled when he thought of how her dad had told him that if he didn't have her home by ten, his sixty-five Ford would turn into a pumpkin. And he thought about the days when he was a basketball player and she a cheerleader. Suddenly, he recalled something she had shared with him from her past. He'd felt bad, back then, when she had told him about the incident, but he had never given it any more thought until now, and *now* it was taking on new significance. He began to rehash the old information.

"Yes," he thought, "now I remember. It was the night of our basketball game at Grand Marais, the same night we came home on the bus in that terrible blizzard. When we got to Garden Corners, I transferred onto my bus and she continued on the Garden bus."

Piece by piece, Bryan put the night together. When the bus finally arrived at two a.m. there was no one waiting to pick her up, she had told him. So she had to walk the mile and a half home on the country road in total darkness. Freezing rain had followed the terrible blizzard, so all the plows had been called off, except for the main road. When the bus driver stopped at the intersection, he had asked the chaperone if maybe they should put Donna up at a house in town for the night, but to that the chaperone had responded that it was her own responsibility to get home. "But she's still in her cheering skirt and doesn't even have a hat or gloves!" the frustrated driver replied.

"Her responsibility!" the chaperone said once again, so reluctantly he opened the bus door.

Bryan remembered how tired she had seemed at school the

following day and how she talked about the cold and how the black of night had frightened her as she walked knee-high in the crusty snow.

Donna had not even told him the main scare of the night. Of how frightened she was when she walked past a place called Ikey's orchard. Her brothers had often spoken of wolves that hid within the trees of the orchard. She had always been afraid of wolves, because she knew that they could kill people. So when she came close to that area she tried running. Her heart sounded louder than the pounding of the basketballs she had heard just hours before on the gymnasium floor. In her panic she fell, scraping her knees against the hardened snow. She picked herself up and tried running again, but lost her breath. So, again, she lay upon the snow. It was there that she hollered for the wolves to come and get her so that she'd never have to worry about wolves or anything else ever again.

Suddenly, in the silence of the night, she noticed that the freezing rain had stopped. She lifted her head and saw a star twinkling in the distance. Instantly, it gave her a sense of peace. She rose and began moving at a steady pace until she reached the driveway, then ran to the door.

☞

Catherine restlessly tried to sleep, awaiting Donna's return. She checked the time, then went to her dad's bedroom. "Dad," she said, "Donna Jean still isn't home from the game and it's three o'clock!"

"Catherine! We got two feet of snow, followed by freezing rain. The road is plugged solid. I'm sure the chaperone will *insist* on her staying at a house in town. Now quit worrying about your sister and get back to bed," he said.

Catherine lay in bed looking out into the darkness. She prayed but was still unable to sleep, so at the first turn of the doorknob, she ran to the door. Upon entering, Donna collapsed into Catherine's arms and began to cry. "I was so scared," she sighed. "I could hardly see where I was going. I thought I was going to die!"

In the dim light of the utility room, Catherine took off Donna's shoes and socks and washed the blood from the cuts on her frozen knees.

"My fingers sting so bad," she said, as the two of them climbed into bed, then cuddled together for warmth.

~

"Oh, dear," Bryan said, putting a hand to his heart. "She had to walk alone in the dark." An overwhelming sadness filled his spirit. Now more than ever, he felt relieved that she was on her way for help. He recalled how he had rocked her the night she had first lifted the lid of her very own Pandora's box. It gave him an inner peace. He had rocked her, as if she were his own child. His heart ached as she, in a trance-like state, relinquished bits of her past. He felt grateful that he had the sense and courage to recommend professional help. She had disagreed with his suggestion, but later confessed that many times after he had left for work and the children went off to school, she felt too depressed to do anything. She admitted that it would take her until late afternoon to finally get a grip on things, only to be jarred back into it by some small happening, like her second grader arriving home with a 'special surprise' that he had made for her in school. Received at face value by other mothers, the 'special surprise' to her often carried within it flashbacks of her past—of times gone wrong—of times she wished she could forget.

"She's in God's hands now," Bryan said, as he drifted off to sleep.

Chapter Four

At Union Station in Chicago I bought a muffin from a vending machine. I had promised Bryan that I would eat on my journey. I knew from reading articles on depression that not eating would only add to the depression that had been suffocating me for years. Since committing to the workshop, I somehow held positive expectations for it. My hope was to return home with a sense that I was controlling my depression, rather than it controlling me, so I forced the muffin down. Then, after freshening up a bit, I re-boarded the bus.

"Excuse me, please," I said when I arrived at my row in the back of the bus. A man, who looked to be in his mid-twenties, grabbed a guitar from his lap and stood. I squeezed past his tall, lanky frame and took my place next to the window. I kept my head forward but turned my curious eyes. I noticed a red bandanna tied around his shoulder length hair, his tie-dyed T-shirt, and his peace medallion hanging from his neck. "Sixties!" I inwardly hissed, and a shiver went up my spine.

"Hi, I'm Simon," he said putting out his hand.

I reluctantly took it. I noticed his deep blue eyes and marveled at his long, thick, black eyelashes. "If only I could have had eyelashes like his. Maybe then my life would be…"

"Ah, I said, I'm Simon," he repeated.

"I'm sorry," I said, shaking my head in disgust. "I'm, I'm Donna," I managed, and then let go of his hand.

Simon needed no time to get acquainted. He immediately began talking about his favorite rock singers—the Beatles, the Doors, Dylan, Velvet Underground. To me, it was as if 1960 were branded upon him. For a minute I thought of changing seats, but after a quick survey I realized there wasn't another seat available, so I resigned to the situation by telling myself his presence was meant to be.

"So what year were you born?" he boldly asked.

His question caught me by surprise and I almost responded with, "None of your business!" But I found myself saying, "1952."

"1960," for me," he said.

My face flushed. I didn't want to be reminded of 1960 and yet lately 1960 was in every step I took, and even in the air I breathed. Yes, everything about that year and the year that followed had been lurking around every door I opened and every corner I turned. So to avoid "Sixties" conservation, I looked to the fields where corn once stood and where cattle now gathered for warmth. I found myself counting silos as we journeyed down the highway. Dispite my mood, I inwardly chuckled, because the rolled bales of hay with the dusting of new snow upon them looked like giant Frosted Mini Wheats.

"Next stop, Gary, Indiana," the driver announced. I continued window gazing as we entered the city. Next to a house, little girls had made a snowman and were putting a big straw hat on top of its head. The scene made me gasp.

"Did you say something?" Simon asked. I shook my head no and then quickly deleted the window scene from my mind. It was all too familiar. It brought back memories of my sisters and me and how often we, too, had made a Mama snowman. Then I'd run to the house to get my mother and take her by the hand to the front yard to see the surprise we had made for her.

☞

After a short stop at Gary, we returned to the bus. I rearranged my pillow behind my neck, closed my eyes, and immediately went into a deep sleep.

An hour or so must have passed. I had slept through miles of two old men talking loudly and Simon's guitar strumming. Upon awakening, I lifted my head from Simon's shoulder. "You can leave it there, I don't mind," I heard him say. I hadn't even realized that I had finally drifted off, let alone falling asleep on some *stranger's* shoulder. I was embarrassed, too, by the drool I felt on my face. While wiping my chin I noticed a wet spot on his shirt but chose not to say anything. I repositioned my head to the window, closed my eyes, and went into a habitual introspection of "if only's."

⌒

"Hey, Kiddo. You awake? We're almost to Pittsburgh," Simon said, nudging my arm with his. Although I had not slept a wink since falling asleep on his shoulder, I nodded to make him think that I had, finding it easier than explaining hours of inner thought.

"Can I buy you dinner?" he asked when the bus pulled into a restaurant parking lot.

"No," I said abruptly, without even offering an explanation or a measure of appreciation for his generosity.

"Hey kiddo, it's just dinner—not a date."

Feeling a bit foolish for my ungrateful attitude, I recanted and accepted his offer.

"Groovy," he said.

Simon's bell-bottom jeans dragged over the wet, dirty ground, as we made our way inside the truck stop. The waitress crushed her cigarette. "Two?" she asked, grabbing the menus. "Right this way."

Simon pulled out a chair for me. "Looks like there're pretty good specials on the slate," he said. "Eat hardy. You could use it!"

Who is this protective stranger? I wondered. First he's meddling by asking my birth year, then allowing me to sleep upon his shoulder, waking me upon arrival in Pittsburgh, and now he's trying to make sure that I have a *good hearty meal!*

After the waitress took our orders, Simon continued with a series of questions. His probing exhausted me. I felt more physically drained than I had remembered feeling in months, or maybe my fatigue was due to my anticipation of the workshop.

"Only child, right?"

"No," I responded with a tone of amusement, "eleven—five boys, six girls!"

"Wow, I can't even imagine that. I'm an only child."

Had I felt more energized, I probably would have told him how sorry I felt for him without the blessing of siblings, but instead I found myself thinking, "Ah, one of those. Born with a silver spoon in his mouth!"

"So," he said, "I've been wanting to ask you for miles, 'Where did you board?'"

"Escanaba, Michigan."

"Southern U.P. huh?"

"You've been to the U.P.?"

"I travel quite a bit," he said.

"Where are you headed," I managed.

"East coast. Always wanted to see the Atlantic. What way are you headed?"

"Phoenicia."

"Upstate New York, right?"

"You have been around, haven't you?

"Woodstock, but years after the fact. It's located near Phoenicia. And let me guess, you're going to spend time in the Catskills on retreat."

At first I was going to say that I was going to visit a sister or brother, but because of my ingrained childhood values, I found myself telling him the truth.

"Actually, a workshop," I responded, somewhat embarrassed. I was going to stop with that, but by the time we re-boarded the bus, I had told him about some of the things I had hoped to deal with at the workshop. My openness had surprised me, but gave me a sense of confidence that if I could tell this *stranger* about the painful memories of my past, certainly I could also tell others who were in the same boat.

⌒

Simon, being a person who tended to analyze much of life, took to rehashing their restaurant conversation. He thought of how Donna could hardly speak at times about the painful memories of her past. He noticed that she had only taken two bites of her salad and had left most of the fries. Sadness overcame him. He began worrying about her as if she were his mother, sister, or dearest friend.

He tossed up a quick prayer for her. It was then that an inspiritation came. "I have to make sure she gets to her destination," he said to himself as he watched her maneuver her pillow every which way. He sensed her fidgeting was due to her uneasiness about the week ahead. "Everything all right?" he asked.

"It's my kids. I'm worried about them. I feel as though something is wrong at home."

"Don't be letting your mind play tricks on you. I'm sure things are okay. You said that your dad took care of the slew of you kids when your mother went to Chicago, and he managed. In fact, I bet things went rather smooth."

I was about to let my worry take me into a full fledged panic attack, but when Simon referred to my mother's absence as a time that went *'rather smooth,'* it snapped me back into focus. At first I felt that I should explain to him that when a mother leaves a home, even for a short time, there's confusion and things *don't* go so well. But I passed at the chance to interject figuring it would be too unbelievable to an only child to hear of such family chaos, and instead reached into my carry-on for my *Psychology Today*.

☞

"Don't you change buses here?" I asked Simon when he re-boarded in Philadelphia.

"No, I was going to get off here for a few days, but I think I better keep going east before some major blizzard hits the coast, you never know what will happen this time of the year."

Simon had planned to spend a few days sight-seeing in Philadelphia, but now he had committed himself to seeing this bewildered woman to her destination, so he had gone into the bus depot and bought a ticket to Phoenicia. He figured that once he had seen her there, he'd continue on to the coast.

"So, you say you have a few rug rats?"

"Four," I said. "All boys!" Then I told Simon their names, ages, and their interests. It felt refreshing to think in the present, talk in the present, live in the present, but before long, the conversation turned back to the past.

☞

Simon listened with enthusiasm. He found himself experiencing large family life vicariously through this stranger. Something he had long wished for—an extended family. He had not only been an only child, but had been adopted, due to his mother's death at his birth. And although he always had his basic material needs and many of his wants met, he had secretively longed for a larger family. His adoptive mother had died when he was only twelve, so it had been just him and his father. In part, that was why he didn't mind traveling solo—he was used to being alone.

It was raining hard when the bus turned onto the New Jersey Turnpike. Simon watched as Donna traded her *Psychology Today* for a book on *Body Reflexology*. She had shared with him that her mother-in-law had bought it for her trip. He watched as she skimmed the pages in search of a technique to help ease her neck pain. After a few minutes she closed the book and shoved it back into her bag. "I can't even concentrate!" she told Simon. "Memories of my past kept floating through my mind, like clouds on a windy day."

Earlier on the trip, Donna had shared with him how her family had lived in small quarters. Simon desperately wanted to ask her questions about it, like, "How did so many of you get along in just three rooms?" Fearing she'd be offended by such questioning, but feeling that she needed, and maybe even wanted to talk, he stuck to a safer inquisition and asked if they had ever moved into the new part of their house.

"Yes, we did," she said, excited as a child, and began to tell him all about it.

⌒

One morning when I woke up, I could hear funny noises and I saw a light coming in by our roll-a-way bed. When I opened my eyes wider, I could see John and Luke looking at us from a hole in the wall—a doorway that went into the new part of the house. I jumped off the roll-a-way and looked through the opening. I saw our old kitchen table in the new kitchen and Mama sitting on a turned over pail, putting food into the refrigerator. "Good morning, Donna Jean," she said when she saw me peeking in.

"Our new house!" I shouted as I went sliding onto the kitchen floor. I ran to wake my sisters.

"Hurry, everybody," I said, jumping on the bed. "Get up.

We're moving into our new house."

My sisters and I ran through the house, until Dad made us quit. So we skipped instead. While Mama sang, *Skip to my Lou,* she pointed to Luke where she wanted the clock hung and where John was to put the little white table. I watched as Dad cut a hole in the wall and then put a stovepipe into it. Mama told Dad that she'd make blackberry pies the next day if he could get the oven working. "You know me, Rosie, I'll do anything for a blackberry pie!" he said as he pounded the stovepipe into the wall.

We ran to get things to carry, too. It was fun moving all the stuff. Mama carried her yellow glass teapot and she let Anna and me each carry one of her glass roosters, but she put them up on the little shelves above the kitchen sink. Sarah and Bernadette helped Mama hang the red and white checkered curtains that she had made for the window. Luke carried the flour can and dumped the little bit of flour into the big new flour bin that was part of the new cupboards.

After everything was moved out of the old kitchen and into the new one, my dad and brothers moved Grandma's old couch and beds from the woodshed into the house. My grandma gave them to us when she moved from her big house into her little apartment. We watched our brothers put up their big bed and then our two big beds. Then I ran to the old part of the house and watched Luke take down the old crib. "It's the first time in umpteen years that only one crib is in our bedroom," Mama said to Dad when we got back into the kitchen.

While Sarah hung the calendar, the rest of us rolled on the floor. Mama walked over us once, but then said, "Get up now, no more rolling. Mama doesn't want to be tripping over you. I could fall and hurt the baby."

"What baby?" I asked. Mama said that she'd tell me about "What baby," some other day.

Before supper, Dad went down into the cellar, and when he came back up he had a jar of his dandelion wine. We set the table and when John and Luke came in from doing barn chores, we all said grace, then started to eat. "Now just a minute before you all dig in," Dad said. He poured just a little wine into Mama's cup and he poured his chock-full. "Here's to moving into the new house," he said, holding his cup up to Mama's. They hit cups and Mama smiled and said, "Thank you, Lord," and then they drank their wine.

"I want some wine, too," Catherine begged. But Dad wouldn't give her any.

"That's for when company comes," he said.

That night at bedtime we got to wash up at the new sink in the new bathroom. But we still had to use the outdoor toilet. Dad said that he wouldn't have time for bedtime stories. "I still have things to do, but you girls get to bed. I'll be there soon to tuck you in."

On my way to bed, I saw Dad taking Mama's washing machine from the corner of the old kitchen to put it into the new utility room. "That's one thing Dad has to do," I said to Bernadette.

Mama was putting rag curls in Monica's hair and when Dad came in to our bedroom she finished the last curl. Dad was carrying his hammer and Mama's picture of Jesus. "Where do you want this?" he asked Mama.

"Right there," she said pointing to the wall, "where the girls can see it when they first wake up." So Dad nailed the picture of Jesus to the wall, right where Mama told him. Then she looked at the picture and said, "There, now I can sleep in peace!"

⌒

This time it was Simon who fought back the tears. He was moved by her family's love for each other and was amazed for what little they seemed to have, he believed they made up for it with love. Curiosity plagued him again, and this time without thinking of how she'd react to his probing, he asked, "Did any of you ever get to celebrate a birthday?"

"Of course," I said, "but if you're asking if we ever got a gift or had a party on our birthday, the answer is no! But my mother always saw to it that we had a..."

Simon noticed the tears in her eyes as she held her hand over her mouth. "What is it that you're thinking?" he coaxed. But she motioned that she couldn't talk. Then after a few minutes she regained her composure.

"I'll try to tell you what I was thinking, because I believe unveiling these memories is in God's plan. I think He's preparing me ahead of time for the workshop."

"You're probably right," he said. "But this has been good for me, too. I've been longing for social contact and I'm getting it through you."

I smiled, "Sorry for such *intense* social contact!"

"It's just what the doctor ordered," he said.

I didn't understand his comment. I sensed that he had life by the tail. But I appreciated his genuine kindness in listening to me, so I answered his question.

"My mother always saw to it that we had a cake for our birthdays. Some years were harder than other years, so instead of a two-layer cake it might have ended up a single layer. But a birthday that stands out in my mind was the time she tried to make my brother Mark a cake. He was coming home on leave from the Marines. I can see her now, as if it were yesterday, standing in front of the big flour bin in the new kitchen. My sisters didn't want to help bake that day, because they were playing games, so Mama put her yellow chicken apron on me! It was the apron that her friend, Molly, had made for her with the red rickrack. I liked looking at and touching that apron. I think I felt like I was Mama's best friend, and not just her little girl, when I had that on. She had a butterfly apron, too, but I only saw it on Sundays when company came to the house—like our aunts and uncles.

⌒

Mama stood in front of the big flour bin. "Dear Lord," she said, making the sign-of-the-cross over it. "This flour bin holds fifty pounds of flour, all I'm asking for is two cups." Then she took a measure cup and went down into the flour bin. When she came back up, she dumped the flour from the cup into the big green bowl. "One more, Lord, just one more, so I can have enough for Mark's birthday cake." Mama took a spoon with her into the flour bin. I heard her scraping the bottom of the bin with it. "Is there enough flour?" I asked her.

Mama's voice sounded far away when she answered.

"I think so!"

When she came back up she dumped the flour into the bowl, and said, "It'll have to do!" I swatted the white flour from Mama's black bangs.

Mama was making a Miracle Whip cake for Mark because she always said that we were her 'miracles from heaven.'

"Mama," I asked, "can I put the cocoa into the bowl?"

"Go ahead, but be careful not to spill, we need the rest for breakfast!" So I was very careful and didn't spill any. Then she let me put the sugar and soda in too, and let me keep the empty soda box for our pretend store.

"There, all I need to do when I get home from the store is add water and salad dressing and Mark's cake will be ready for the oven." She reached into her skirt pocket for the money Dad had given her that morning. She counted the money. "Eighty-nine cents," she said. "It'll have to do."

Before Mama left for the store she had to do other jobs, so she let us play store with the money. But she told us not to lose it. We played with the empty grocery boxes, jars and cans that we had been saving. I bought the box of Breeze at the pretend store, because of the towel that came in the box.

☞

"I remember Breeze detergent," Simon exclaimed. "My mother always bought it too, because of the bath or dish towel or washcloth in the box."

"We mostly had washcloths, at our house," I said, and then carried on with my story.

☞

Mama waited until everybody got a turn buying something from our store, then she counted the money again. "It's all here," she said. "A jar of salad dressing is thirty-nine cents," and she took a quarter and a dime and four pennies from the table and put them in her hand. "A pound of oleo is seventeen cents, a box of matches is six, soda eleven, plus tax will be three cents, I'll have enough!" she said. "With maybe a few pennies to spare!"

"Are you going to get more flour, too, Mama?" I asked, when she was washing up.

"No, not today. The flour will have to wait," she said, as she spread cold cream onto her face. Afterwards, she put dots of lipstick onto her cheeks then put the lipstick back into her purse. With her fingers, she spread the dots out. I wanted to put some dots of lipstick on my face, too, but Mama said, "Not now. I have to get going to the store." Mama reached for her purse that was on her bed and it was gone. Monica had it on the other side of the bed. Mama's red lipstick was smeared all over and around her lips. "Oh, dear," Mama said, "I should have known better than to leave my purse in the reach of a two-year-old!"

"Monica's getting a spanking," Bernadette sang.

I thought that Monica would be in big trouble, too, and so did my other sisters, but Mama just took Monica by the hand and helped her out from behind the bed. I started complaining about Monica not getting in trouble and so did my sisters. Mama sat on the edge of the bed. "Listen!" she said. "You girls know better, but Monica's only two. We have to teach her right from wrong. You only get in trouble if you know better."

Mama went into the kitchen and got her gray coat and black scarf from the coat hook. Her eyes looked sad, like Jesus' eyes in the picture on the wall when she put her coat on. "Line up," she told us. "I'm leaving for the store. I need my kisses!"

My sisters and I begged to go with, but "No!" she said, "Today I'm going alone. I need to hurry. It looks like it might rain, and it's really cold outside, so I want to hurry back. I'm not feeling very good."

"I'm in charge when you're gone, right Mama?' Sarah hollered. "Because I'm the oldest!"

"It's my turn!" Bernadette yelled.

"No, Sarah's the oldest," Mama said. "Sarah will watch you girls, but only when John goes out to milk the cows. I should be home before that."

We don't like it when John's in charge. One time he chased us with a snake. Mama came home early from the doctor and she caught him chasing us with the dead snake that we thought was alive! She got mad at John. "Get over here—now!" she screamed. John kept taking baby-steps to her. "Don't be strolling this way like a little old spider! Move it!" When John got by Mama, she spanked his behind three times. When John laughed, Mama's face got bloody red and drips of water fell down her forehead.

Since that day, Mama always hurries back whenever she leaves John in charge.

⌒

"That's not fair," Bernadette hollered, "Sarah always gets to be in charge when John goes out to the barn."

"Sarah's the oldest and in charge and that's final!" Mama said.

Bernadette got mad and wouldn't give Mama a hug and kiss goodbye. Mama waited and waited and waited. She kept telling Bernadette that she had to get going because it could start to rain, but Bernadette still wouldn't kiss her good-bye. So Mama opened the door. "I wish I could be taking your kiss with me, too, Bernadette," she said.

See, Mama doesn't like going anywhere if we won't give her hugs and kisses. Except once. She got really mad at us and told us that she couldn't stand all the bickering. "Luke, you're in charge! I'm leaving!" she said. We watched Mama walk down the road and over the hill. Monica kept crying and hollering for Mama to come back. I think Mama heard her screaming and crying because the window was open, but she wouldn't come back. Monica screamed and cried until she fell asleep on the floor next to my cat, Puff.

We watched and waited for her to come back home. We thought that she went to her friend Josephine's house because Josephine's house is on the other side of the hill.

"Donna Jean," Anna said, "Mama might never come back."

"She has to come back!" I said. "She's our mother!"

After a long, long, long time, we saw Mama coming. Catherine wondered what she was carrying, so we ran to meet her. Mama had a lard pail filled with strawberries. Anna and Catherine and I jumped up to try to grab some, but she lifted the pail. "They're for supper," she said. That's when I noticed that Mama's arms were all red, so I asked her why they were. "Oh, dear, I must have gotten sunburned," she said.

That night Mama's arms really hurt her, so I got a washcloth and wet it with cold water and put it on her arms. "The fever will go away soon," I told her.

When Mama walked to the store for the salad dressing, I knew she wouldn't get burned because it was cold. She had to put on her long gray coat—her long gray coat with the patch on the bottom of it. Mama looked at the patch. "What a shame!" she said.

See, one night my Uncle Elmer drank too much of my dad's dandelion wine, and his fat cigar burnt a hole into Mama's coat. Mama screamed when she saw the cigar against her coat. She ran fast outside to the pump and pumped water over it, but the hole stayed in her coat. She marched back into the house. She held her coat up for Uncle Elmer to see. "Look what you've done! I waited a long, long time for this here coat, you know!" Uncle Elmer giggled, and giggled, and giggled. Mama called for Luke and John. "Go throw him out in the haymow so he can sleep it off," she said.

The next morning Mama wouldn't make breakfast for Uncle Elmer. So he asked Catherine and me if we'd go for a walk with him. When we got to the edge of the woods, we helped him pick some of the picky pink roses. He carried the flowers to the house. Mama was ironing clothes when he handed them to her and sang, "I'm sending you a big bouquet of roses, one for every time I broke your heart." Mama turned her face. "Take em! Come on," he said, "I'm sorry!" So Mama took the flowers. She started smiling at Uncle Elmer. "Get out of here, you fool!" she said.

"Not until you say you forgive me," he told her.

"Okay! Okay!" she said, with a smile. "I'll forgive you, because you're my brother, and because that's what the 'Good Book' says that I ought to do."

Before Uncle Elmer went back to Escanaba, he played games with us so Mama could sew a patch on her coat. We played Simon Says. And when it was my turn to be Simon I said, "Simon says to walk like a duck." And Uncle Elmer said, "Oh, you mean walk like your mother!"

We laughed, but I was glad that Mama didn't hear. Mama hates when Uncle Elmer tells her that she walks like a duck!

Chapter Five

Two hours from Phoenicia the bus driver apologized when he stopped to rest. He asked us to remain on the bus, but most of the passengers got off, for at least a few minutes, including Simon and me. The air was cold and windy. I wrapped my black silk scarf, with its scrolled roses, around my head. Simon flipped up his collar, then turned his back to the wind to light his cigarette. I was glad he didn't offer me one. Even the smell of smoke flared up my asthma.

"So back to what you were saying on the bus. Did you get to go to the store with your mother?"

"A part of the way," I said. Then I continued telling him about the day my mother went to the store for the Miracle Whip.

⌒

Mama hurried down the driveway. When she got to the road, I snuck out of the house to catch up with her. She saw me coming and hollered for me to get back, but I kept sneaking through the trees and into the ditch until I caught up with her.

"Will you bring us back some pop, Mama?" I asked. "Because Cal's store has pop in a big, red, steel box. It's steamy cold inside of it and it has lots of bottles of pop. Like purple, orange, red, white and brown pop. I want a purple one."

"Pop," Mama said, "is just for when you're sick, or if something bad happens to you."

"Is purple pop grape pop, Mama?"

"Yes," Mama said, laughing. "Purple is grape, brown is root beer, white is cream soda and…"

"But, orange is orange!" I said. "And pop isn't just for when you're sick, because Timmy brought some to school."

Mama started smiling. "Your teeth are chattering. You're cold. Run along back home. You've already walked with me far enough. Your sisters and John will be worried about you."

"Mama, in just five days we start school again, right?"

"That's right."

"I'll get to see my friends again, like Janet, Krystal and Celeste. They're my best friends, but I like everybody. Except sometimes I don't like Mrs. Webster."

"I thought you liked your teacher."

"I like her, but she scares me when she gets really, really mad. Last year in second grade she hit her ruler on her desk so hard that it made me jump. Once when Peter peed his pants, she made him stay in the cubbyhole, and Peter cried. I still like my Mrs. Boudreau best."

"You didn't like Mrs. Boudreau the night of your kindergarten play."

"That's because she made me be Little Miss Muffet for the play."

"Didn't you want to be Little Miss Muffet?"

"No, I wanted to be Cinderella, or somebody else."

"So that's why you crossed your arms, rolled your eyes and didn't run when the spider came to frighten you away?"

"See, Mama, Mrs. Boudreau asked us who wanted to be Mary, from Mary had a Little Lamb. I raised my hand, but Janet got to be Mary. Then Teacher asked who wanted to be Little Bo Peep, so I raised my hand high and swished it back and forth, but Candy got to be Little Bo Peep. Krystal got to be Snow White and Celeste got to be Rapunzel because of her lovely, long hair. 'I have lovely, long hair, too,' I told Teacher. Teacher looked around the room, "Now for Cinderella," she said. I jumped out of my seat. I stood up on my tiptoes and waved my hand really, really high. I begged Teacher to let me be Cinderella, but she picked Debbie. Then everyone had a part, except for me. "Donna Jean," Teacher said.

"I've saved the best character for you! I want you to be Little Miss Muffet!" Then she said that we'd do my storybook character last, so that all the moms and dads would go home laughing! I tried to tell her that I didn't want to be Little Miss Muffet who sat on a tuffet eating her turds away, but the bell rang and we had to go home.

"Oh, no wonder!" Mama said laughing. "Little Miss Muffet wasn't eating her turds away, you silly goose! She was eating curds and whey! That's cheese, Donna Jean! Now you get back to the house before John worries about you. You don't even have your coat on!"

A big horsefly followed me into the house. John said that the flies were coming in to get warm. He caught the horsefly with just one hand. Then he took its wings off and the horsefly crawled over his arms. John thought the crawling horsefly was funny. He rolled on the floor laughing. Then he picked the horsefly up and chased us around the house with it, to scare us. When I screamed he said, "What? You still a big chicken of horseflies!" I told John that if Mama was home she'd spank him, but John said he didn't give a hoot what Mama thought.

After John left to go milk the cows, we pushed kitchen chairs to the window so that we could watch for Mama. We shared them because we all wanted to see her coming. Mama showed us on the clock that it would take one turn of the small fat hand for her to get to the store and back, unless someone came by to give her a ride. "Today," Mama said, "if someone stops to pick me up, I hope it's not Frank. I'd rather walk then ride with him!"

See, one other day when Mama walked to the store Frank and Stella stopped and picked her up. It was really hot outside. The only bugs that John could find were grasshoppers and Dad said that was a sure sign of it being hot. Anyway, Frank and Stella were going to the store too, so they stopped and gave Mama a ride. I thought Mama would be happy when I saw them dropping her off. She likes getting rides because she has corns on her toes and they make her feet hurt. But she was mad when she came into the house carrying the yeast for the bread. Her face was all snarled-up.

"I held my tongue in that truck," she said. "People like Frank don't belong on God's good earth!"

Mama's face got bloody red and the veins on her forehead

started popping out of her skin, like angleworms on cement after it rains.

"What happened?" John asked.

"On the way back home I had to sit in the middle and watch the two of them eat ice cream. Stella asked Frank to buy me a cone too, and I know he heard, but he didn't listen. Oh, if I had Frank's money," she said, "I'd buy everyone in the whole world ice cream, if they wanted some."

☞

"Everybody ready? Let's go!" the driver hollered.

"Sorry I'm such a scatterbrain," Donna said as she took her seat on the bus. "I was starting to tell you about the day my mother walked to the store for the salad dressing. We sang songs for awhile then Catherine and I touched tongues. It tasted terrible!"

"You touched tongues?" Simon asked, with a look of displeasure. "I don't think I'm going to try that one, unless it's with a chick!"

"Yes," I said, chuckling, "tongues!" And continued on.

☞

I looked out the window. I spotted my marbles on the sidewalk where Catherine and I had left them. "Whoops," I said. "Catherine! you and I better go and pick up the marbles! Mama said they have to be put away before she gets back!"

We started fighting, because she wouldn't help me pick them up.

"You better run and get them before Mama gets home," Bernadette said, shaking her finger at us.

"Mama's already home," Anna shouted, standing tip toed on the chair. "She's coming up the driveway!"

I hurried to get the marbles before Mama could see them. But just as I opened the door I saw her slip on my jumbo marble and fall onto the cement. I heard the salad dressing jar crash. Sarah and Bernadette were by the door and they saw Mama fall, too. So my sisters and I hurried down the steps to help her. Mama tried hard to help us lift her up, but her legs kept wobbling, like new baby cow legs, and she fell down again next to the ripped grocery bag. I pushed Mama's black bangs out of her brown eyes. That's when I noticed the tears.

"Wait," Mama told us when we tried to lift her again. "Give me a minute, so I can get my breath."

John saw us from the barn and ran to help. She was moaning and groaning like Lily, our Guernsey cow, when John got her to her bed. And she kept moaning, like the day when Lily pooped out a baby cow! Catherine called Lily's baby, Daisy, because it was her turn to get to name it. The next time it'll be my turn to name the baby cow. I'm going to call my cow Fancy.

⌒

"Are you getting ready to puke again, Mama?" I asked.

She shook her head no, but moaned again. I thought that she was moaning because she had fallen and it had made her knees bleed. Or that maybe it was because she was sad that she had used up all the money to buy the salad dressing, and now it was all broken.

"John," Mama said, "go throw that broken jar in the garbage, check the oleo for glass and put the matches up high. There are suckers in the bag, one for each of you. They're wrapped, but check them for glass too."

We ran outside with John to get our suckers. "Mama," Bernadette said, when we got back in, "after supper will Mark be coming home from the Marines?"

"No," she said. "Tomorrow night. After your Dad gets home from work, he and your brothers will go pick up Mark at the train station."

"Yippee!" I screamed.

I couldn't wait for Mark to get home. I missed him and Matthew, lots. Whenever we got a letter I was happy, like Mama. Mama would read the letters to us. Sometimes she'd cry. Like the day she got the pillow—the pillow that came as a present from Matthew. Mama tried to read the writing on the pillow, but she kept stopping and stopping, because she kept crying and crying. Finally, without stopping even once, she read:

> *To Mother*
> *To the one who bears the sweetest name*
> *And adds a lesson to the same*
> *Who shares my joys and times when sad,*
> *To the greatest friend I ever had.*
> *Long life to her for there's no other*
> *Could take the place of my dear Mother.*

Mama cried so hard after reading the words on the pillow that she puked. See, whenever Mama cries hard, she pukes. But sometimes she pukes because she's sick. Like all summer long. Thirteen times my sisters and I took turns running for the scrub bucket to put by the side of Mama's bed. One time Bernadette and I were fighting about whose turn it was to get the bucket and Mama puked spaghetti onto the floor. Bernadette and I felt bad, so we told Mama we'd clean it up. But Mama wouldn't let us. "No one is ever going to clean up my puke except me!" Mama slid slowly off the bed, wobbled to her knees, then wiped up her puke with the rag and bucket of water that we got for her.

⌒

"Are you going to throw-up again today, Mama?" I asked as I looked at the cuts on her knees.

"I hope not," she said. Then she asked Catherine, Anna, Monica and me if we would rub her feet and legs because they were swollen. So we rubbed and rubbed, even over all the long, fat wormy veins on her legs and the big corns on her toes. That's when I noticed Mama's tummy.

"Mama!" I said. "Your tummy is swollen, too! Do you want us to rub it?"

I lifted Dad's shirt that Mama had on. I giggled, because Mama's tummy looked like a giant hill of bread dough.

"Did you put bread dough on top of your tummy?" I asked. It looked like bread dough and it felt like bread dough when I rubbed my hands over it. Anna pretended to drive a car up the big hill of Mama's tummy.

"Holler for John," Mama said.

When he came she asked him to get her the old cowbell

from off the refrigerator. "I'll ring it if I need anything." Then she told us to be quiet so she and Monica could take a nap.

We played school. I put on Mama's pretty yellow dress, the one that Aunt Lu Lu gave her. Then I snuck into her purse for her lipstick. But Mama with her catlike eyes saw me, and she wouldn't let *even me* the Teacher put any of it on. She made me put it back and then told me to take off her church dress. I only got to use her green housedress and dabs of her cold cream.

When Mama rang the cowbell, John came running. "Help me out to the toilet," she said. So he did, then waited to help her back to the house. Then he left for the barn to do his chores. Right after he left, Mama had to go pee again. This time, Sarah and Bernadette helped her to the toilet, but we all went with.

"Mama, why do you have to pee again!" I asked, giggling.

"The baby is pushing on my bladder," she said.

I didn't like being in the outdoor toilet. I was afraid that I would fall into the dark, stinky hole where Luke and John told us bugs and snakes lived.

"Hurry up and go, so we can hurry back," Mama said.

We were freezing as we walked back to the house. Mama wobbled with her arms around Bernadette and Sarah's shoulders and almost fell two times. "Stop, I'm too weak to go any further," she said. Slowly she scooted to the ground. "Go get John at the barn," she told Sarah. But just then, Russell came running. Russell walks by our house almost every day on his way to the store to get his bottle of beer. Once when he stopped at our house, he played marbles with Catherine and me. Russell is old like my dad, but he can only count to ten like my little sister Anna. One time I asked my dad why Russell could only count to ten.

"Russell doesn't have all his marbles," Dad said. So I told Dad that I could give him some of my marbles, but my dad just laughed, and I don't know why.

Anyway, Russell saw Mama sitting on the ground and he came running. "What's da madder with da Mama?" he asked.

"The Mama hurts and can't walk," Mama said.

"Den Russell carry you."

"No, no, that's okay," Mama told him. But Russell picked her up anyway and carried her into the house and put her on a kitchen chair.

"Da Mama, okay now?" he asked.

"Yes," Mama said, "The Mama's okay. Thank you, Russell."

Russell went to the door, waved his hand up really high and said, "Russell better get ta store before rain pours down." And he left. Sarah and Bernadette helped Mama back to her bed. Monica climbed up onto the bed. She kept crawling over Mama's tummy. So I said, "Hey, everybody, let's play house. I'll be the mother!"

"I'm the dad!" Catherine hollered. Then in a dad's voice Catherine asked me if I wanted her to go to the store to buy a baby and some dollies. I started laughing. "You don't get babies at a store! You have to go to the hospital to buy them, right Mama?" I asked as I grabbed Monica off of her. When I did, Dad's shirt got lifted up and I could see her big tummy again. "Why is your tummy so fat, Mama?" I asked.

"Because there's a baby growing inside of it," she said.

"A baby!" I said, giggling.

"It's true!" she told my sisters and me. "Babies grow from a seed that dads put inside of mamas!"

I thought that sounded pretty yucky, so I didn't ask Mama anymore questions about babies or seeds, because I know what happened. Mama and Dad were kissing and she let Dad spit an apple seed into her mouth. Then she swallowed it. When it got all the way down inside of her tummy it started turning into a baby! I know this because once I asked Luke how the baby cow got inside of the big cow's tummy. Luke said, "The cow must have swallowed an apple seed!"

"Come here," Mama said, and she took my hand and put it on her tummy. "Feel that? That's the baby moving inside of me."

One-by-one she took my sisters' hands, too, so they could feel the baby. Monica kept trying to get Mama's tummy to herself, so Catherine pulled her off, and Monica started crying. Bernadette came into the bedroom and yelled at Catherine, and Sarah came in and yelled at Bernadette. Then Sarah pulled Bernadette's hair, so Bernadette pulled Sarah's hair. Catherine kept carrying Monica and Monica kept screaming. Anna pulled my cat's tail, so Puff scratched her. I was going to go and get two wash cloths and a big towel so that I could make myself titties and a big tummy, like Mama's, but John came in and yelled at us.

"Ma isn't going to get any rest if all of you keep being loud and fighting." He booted us out of Mama's bedroom and into the living room.

"Want to play a game that I learned at choir practice called Rock, Paper, Scissors?" Bernadette asked Catherine and me.

"Sure," we said.

"Okay," she said, "but watch what I do with my hands. First you have to take one of your hands and when I count to three, you have to be either a rock or paper or scissors. If you want to be a rock, you have to scrunch up your fingers into your hand. If you want to be paper, just hold all your fingers out, or if you want to be scissors, just put two fingers out like scissors—okay?"

So every time when Bernadette counted to three, we had to either be a rock, paper or scissors. Bernadette and I did it right, but not Catherine. She kept being a rock, a rock, a rock, a rock, a rock. She wouldn't be anything else, ever. She was being a big brat, so I quit playing and went to see if Mama was sleeping. Very quietly I opened her bedroom door, but John still heard.

"Can't you keep away from that bedroom door you little snot? Let Ma sleep!"

Chapter Six

"Look! It's snowing," Simon said, as if it were the first snow fall he had ever witnessed.

I watched as the huge flakes fell. Soon a cloud of darkness blanketed the bus. It reminded me of a particular cloudy, windy day when I was a child, so I told Simon about it.

I could hear the wind blowing, so I got out of bed and went to the window. I pulled back the curtain and watched as the leaves blew to the ground. I ran to the kitchen. "Mama, Mama," I shouted, "it's snowing leaves." But Mama wasn't in the kitchen making breakfast.

"Your mother's still in bed," my dad said. "Let her rest."

I waited and waited to see her, but she didn't get up for breakfast. When she finally got up, she sat on the couch and, one-by-one, she had us girls sit between her legs so that she could comb our hair into ringlets. She found gum in Bernadette's hair, so she had me to go to the kitchen to see if there was any peanut butter left. When I came back with the empty pail, Mama took her finger around the inside of it, then rubbed the peanut butter into the gum. Bit-by-bit, the gum came out.

"There!" she said to Bernadette, "go wash your hair and rinse it really good. I'm going back to bed."

When Dad and the boys went outside to pile wood, my sisters and I hurried to get our jobs done. We made our beds and did the dishes. Then Catherine sprinkled the white shirts so Bernadette could iron them. Sarah scrubbed the kitchen sink and the wash basin and I took care of Anna and Monica. When our jobs were done, we hurried back to Mama.

"Mama," Catherine asked, "at lunchtime, can we bring our sandwiches into your bedroom so we can have a picnic?"

"I think that's a wonderful idea," she said. "Then I can eat with my little girls."

So when it was time, we carried the scrambled-egg sandwiches and jars of water into Mama's room for a bedroom picnic. We each took a spot on the floor, but Mama stayed on her bed. While we were eating, Sarah said, "I can see people swimming in the water."

"I can see boys playing baseball," Bernadette shouted. Then Catherine stood up, spread out her arms and waved them up and down. "Butterflies are on picnics, right Mama?" Catherine, the butterfly, flopped her wings up and down and up and down and went all around the room until she flew off Mama's bed, and onto the floor.

"I'm the picnic grasshopper," Sarah shouted, and she jumped, jumped, jumped.

"Taterpillars are on picnics, right, Mama?" Anna asked. And Anna the caterpillar crawled up onto Mama's bed. Bernadette pretended to be an ant. She put her hands up over her head and stuck out her pointer fingers to make the ant's antennas. Monica cried because she didn't know what to be, so Catherine told her to be a cricket. "Just make a clicking sound with your tongue," Catherine told her. Then she showed her how to do it. Mama shushed us so everyone could hear Monica the Cricket. Monica made us laugh.

Then it was my turn to be something at the bedroom picnic.

"Ouch!" Bernadette yelled.

"Don't!" Catherine screamed.

"That hurts!" Anna cried.

"Donna Jean, what on earth are you doing?" Mama asked.

"I'm not Donna Jean. I'm Charlotte the spider. And I'm

biting everyone."

"Ouch," Mama said as she rubbed her arm. "I guess it's time to be done with the picnic. Now go get your dishes done, then hurry back so that I can read to you."

⌒

Bernadette carried the big white *Bible* to Mama's bed and handed it to her.

"Aren't you done reading that book yet?" I asked.

"Never," Mama said. "I will never finish this book. This book is different from all the other books in the whole world. This book is God's Book!"

"Then why do you have it?" Catherine asked.

"All families should have a *Bible*," Mama said, "because it teaches right from wrong. It's God's laws for us. If we follow His laws, we'll be happy." Then she read the names of some of the books from the *Bible,* but it still looked like just one book to me. Mama read to us from the Book of Jude. She told us that Jude is the saint of hopeless cases. So I asked her what a hopeless case was?

"Oh, like me I guess, because I'm too tired to stand up by myself. I can't even do the washing or ironing or baking—nothing!"

"But we can do them, Mama." Bernadette said. "I'll make some biscuits! I know how."

"I'll put the dirty clothes into piles," Catherine told her.

"And I'll wash them," Sarah shouted. And they ran out of the bedroom. Tears rolled down her face. "What's the matter, Mama?" I asked.

"You little girls shouldn't have to do those big jobs," she said. "And it's Mark's birthday today! He's coming home tonight and I can't even get up to make him a cake."

"Then I'll make him one!"

"No, we don't have anything to make it with," she said.

"We can make him a mud cake, like we do when we're playing house outside on the flat stones! Can we use your angel pan?"

"I suppose," she said as she laughed and wiped the tears from her eyes. "But let me know when you get the mud made. I want to help."

"Yippee," I screamed, and I ran to tell my sisters and to get the angel pan from Mama's spot for it in the kitchen. Then my sisters and I ran outside to make the cake. I took an empty jar and pumped water into it. Catherine took an empty lard pail to mix the dirt and water in. When the cake batter was ready we went and got Mama. It was hard getting Mama and her big, fat tummy outside, so John helped us. But he said he wasn't going to help make "a stupid mud cake." He got mad at Mama and told her she should be in bed. Mama got mad back and said she was helping even if it killed her.

Mama sat on the hard, cold ground under the crabapple tree. She told us that she had something special to put inside of the cake. I wondered what it could be. I looked into her hands. She didn't have the food coloring for the Christmas cookies and she didn't have the Christmas cookie sprinkles. So I wondered what the "something special" could be.

Mama had us bring the muddy batter and the angel cake pan to her. She took the mud and patted the pan half full. Then she reached into her shirt pocket and took out a dollar.

"Mama," I said, "I thought we didn't have any more money!"

"This is the dollar I had put away for Christmas," she said. "Right now Mark's birthday is more important." She folded the dollar and put it on top of the mud and then filled the pan with the muddy batter while we watched. Then she turned the cake over, onto her prettiest plate—the plate with the pink roses. Very carefully she lifted the pan. The cake kind-of fell apart, but we patted it back together until it looked like a cake from the oven. "There," she said. "It's the best we can do." On the way to the house, Sarah got to carry the cake.

Mama lay back down and when she fell asleep, we went into the kitchen and got around the little white table to look at the cake. Catherine found two used candles up in the cupboard and she stuck them into the center. We could hardly wait for Mark to get home from California to see it. For a minute, I thought I could smell chocolate. I was just about to take a lick of the cake with my finger, when Sarah slapped my hand and giggled, "Donna Jean, remember, it's mud!"

☞

Dad and my brothers changed from their work clothes into

their good clothes. Then after supper they left to go and pick up Mark. We waited and waited. Finally Mama said they'd be home soon. Sarah and I started watching for car lights. Three cars went by before lights turned into the driveway.

"Mark's coming!" we screamed and ran to the door. When I pulled it open, there was Mark.

"Ah ha, my little sisters!" he said.

Mark is very strong, so he lifted Anna with one arm and Monica with the other. I hugged his legs and tried to pull him to the little white table to see his cake, but he wouldn't come.

"Not right away," he said, "First I want to go see Ma."

We all went with him into her bedroom. Even my dad! Mark hugged and kissed Mama. Her eyes filled with tears, but she smiled. I pulled on Mark's arm again to have him come to the kitchen, but he kept talking and talking. I heard him ask Mama if she could iron a shirt for him in the morning. Mama told him that she didn't do that kind of stuff anymore. "Not until the baby comes," she said. "I spend most of my days in bed now."

"Hey, Ma, don't give it another thought," he said. "Uncle Sam taught me how to iron, so I guess I can iron at home, too."

"I didn't know we had an Uncle Sam!" I said. Mark, Dad, Luke and John, and even Mama laughed, and I don't know why.

"Uncle Sam," Mark said. "He's the President of the United States! The President is the boss of us soldiers, so we call him Uncle Sam!"

"Then is the President's wife your Aunt?" I asked. They laughed again, and I don't know why.

After a long, long time in Mama's bedroom, Mark helped her to the kitchen. When she sat down, he put a chair in front of her and put her feet up on it.

Luke lit the two candles on the cake. "Happy birthday brother—you just turned two!" he said.

"He's seventeen!" Sarah hollered. Everybody laughed and then we sang happy birthday. Mark made a wish and then blew out the candles. And when he lifted the knife to cut the cake, we screamed, "It's MUD, it's MUD, Mark!" Then we told him exactly how we made it. Mark laughed and looked at Mama. I saw him wink at her and then he said, "I never would have known!" I jumped up and down, and said, "Cut the cake, Mark! Cut the cake!" When he did, the dollar came out and Mark laughed again. He took the dollar and shook off the crumbs and handed it to Mama.

"Here," he said, "you can have it back. Then he reached into his front pants pocket and got out a bunch more money and gave that money to Mama, too!

"Oh, no! Oh, no you don't!" she said, trying to give him back the money. But Mark said, "Oh, yes! Oh, yes I do! There's one hundred and four dollars and fifty-two cents that I've been saving for you. You can do whatever you need to with it."

Mama covered her face with her hands. "Oh, Mark!" she said as tears popped out of her eyes. "My sons are something else. Matthew has already sent money for the mortgage."

"Hey, Ma," John hollered, "if it's going to make you cry, you can give me the money. I sure the heck won't cry!" But Mama took the money and gave it to Dad and he put the money into the yellow glass teapot. "Thank you so much, Mark," she said. "I know the Good Lord will bless you for this."

Later, Mark helped Mama back to bed. He lay by Mama and told us Marine stories. Afterwards, he reached into his duffel bag and got a blackjack candy and a lollipop out of it for each of us. Then he held out a pack of gum. "Who wants a piece of Spearmint gum?" he asked. Everyone started fighting to be the first to get a stick, but Sarah beat us. When she pulled on the gum, it stung her. Mark laughed, but Sarah cried. "Come on Sarah, don't cry, it was only a joke," Mark said as he showed us how it was *trick* gum.

After we got our pajamas on, we ran back into Mama's bedroom. Mama's forehead was sweaty, so I wiped it with her hanky. She has two hankies—one with the purple flower in the corner of it and one with her name on it. Mama said that it's not really her name. The R.J. is her initials and initials are like your name. "Someday when I'm big," I said, "I want a hanky with my initials. My hanky will have a D. J. in the corner of it."

We listened while Mark told us more stories about being a soldier. When I heard Dad firing the stove, I knew that, pretty soon, he would holler, "Oh, my little girls, bed time!"

Mama stayed in her bed, but we knelt by it for the rosary. I got to kneel by Mark. When we were done saying it, we all got to pray for something. When Mama's turn came she prayed that I wouldn't have any more bad dreams. So I started telling Mark about my dream, of how the wicked witch of the west came and stole all our marbles, but Dad shushed me and said, "Not now. It's your turn to pray."

"God bless Mama and Dad and God bless my brothers and my sisters and the baby boy inside of Mama's tummy."

After prayers Mark tucked us into bed, and said, "We won't know if the baby's going to be a boy or a girl until after it's born, Donna Jean." But all of us started telling Mark that Mama said she *just knows* it's a boy—and that the boy is going to be called Jude. Then we told him how Mama let us feel the baby kicking, and how she said, "Only a boy could kick like this!"

Chapter Seven

At four o'clock in the afternoon, the bus pulled into Vango's restaurant outside Phoenicia. As I gathered my belongings, sadness overcame me. In the two days of bus living, I had enjoyed communicating with Simon and appreciated him listening to me. I wondered how I'd ever repay him for his kindness, knowing that I'd never see him again. When leaving the bus, I thought of saying something like, "I'm glad our paths crossed." But hating permanent good-byes and, once again trying to avoid an explosion of tears, I shook his hand quickly. "See you later," I said. As I moved down the isle, I could hear him saying goodbye. Tears streamed down my face as I transferred to the shuttle that was waiting to take others and me to the resort.

Gazing from the window, as the bus slowly traveled down the narrow, winding road, my eyes became fixed on rays of sun beaming down through the clouds. I thought the scene heavenly. It reminded me that I was in God's hands. Still I found it hard to relax. Even the beauty of the surrounding mountains with their tranquility could not ease my nervousness. I was silently wishing I could vanish into the mountains, when I realized that it was the *Catskills* where Rip Van Winkel had gone to escape his wife's nagging and had fallen asleep for twenty years. Oh, if I could be so lucky, I thought. At that moment, I felt sure I understood Rip more than any other person ever had. I, too, wanted to escape knowing that I'd soon be facing the stale old grief of years gone by. "Time Heals All Wounds," was as far from accuracy to me as "Time Will Make You Younger." Time had only kept my wounds in storage. That is, until that fateful day when I decided to explore reasons for my depression and had lifted the lid of my very own *Pandora's Box*. In it I found feelings of abandonment, loss, and separation that I now was forced to deal with.

As the Shanti Nilaya resort, nestled in the valley, came into view, I lowered my head to pray. I noticed my blouse moving with every beat of my heart as the shuttle came to a stop. Trembling uncontrollably, I gathered my belongings, then worked my way to the lounge where I registered and proceeded on to my room. Fumbling for the key, I was surprised when my roommate opened the door.

"Thank you," I told her, as I entered.

"Hi," she said. "I'm Flossy. I arrived this morning from Maine. I came a little early. I needed to take some time to sort out my thoughts before I shared them with the world. I haven't been able to function too well since my little boy's accident. I'm hoping this workshop will help me… to know… he's okay."

I nervously took her hand. I noticed the pain glaring out through her tear-filled eyes. "I hope you gain that insight, too," I said. I introduced myself, then began unpacking while she talked. I only half-heartedly listened to the pain-stricken women as I placed my clothes in the dresser. Then, in an effort to escape it all, I began comparing myself to her. I compared our height, weight, bust, teeth, and fingernails—my stubbles to her long luxurious, creamed colored ones. I compared our hair—the texture, the thickness, the color, the length. Her sad gray eyes to my once brown eyes that had turned hazel over the years. But soon my thoughts were back in focus. I wondered if her acute pain was greater than my stale, old grief. And I wondered if she had any of the fears and worries that I had.

⌒

Later that evening I invited Flossy to walk the grounds with me. Now more relaxed, I listened to her every word as we circled the grounds, then visited the sanctuary before retiring for the night. It comforted me that I was on the giving end instead of groping for a reassuring word from somebody, from anybody who would tell me that the dark clouds of life would soon make way to sunny skies.

Throughout the night I was restless. I was too hot, then too cold. I threw my blankets off, then back on. I flung my over-stuffed pillow at the door, then covered over the head. Frustrated, I got up and threw on my robe and walked to the sanctuary again. I took a mat at the doorway and lay upon it on the hardwood floor. I looked out through the glass-topped roof and marveled at the magnificence of the stars as I pondered what would take place during the weeklong workshop. Suddenly I became frightened. I realized that although I had shared memories with Bryan and Simon, I had always stayed within the comfort zone, always staying away from the more unpleasant memories. So again I pleaded to God for the courage to help me let go of the painful memories of the past and the memories I wished had been, but had not.

Returning to my room, I looked at my watch. "Two hours until morning!" I said to myself, as I climbed back into bed.

I felt sluggish at the breakfast table and didn't join in on much of the conversation. Afterwards, when we walked to the conference room, the crisp morning air revived me. As we entered, Elisabeth Kubler-Ross greeted us. She was casually dressed in jeans and a sweatshirt. Her short, slightly graying blonde hair seemed fitting for her height. She had no make-up or jewelry on. Her simplicity, along with the genuineness I felt as she shook my hand, helped me relax.

When everyone was seated, she welcomed the ninety-seven participants and introduced the eight counselors that would be assisting her during the week. "The six days of this workshop will be very intense," she said, and continued to explain the peculiar setting at the front of the room, a mattress on the floor. "When a person feels ready to share, they can come forward to the mattress. A rubber hose and expired New York phone books have been placed on the mattress to assist you in venting your anger." She knelt upon the mattress and demonstrated to the group by hitting one of the old directories with the rubber hose, while hollering out words of anger. Then after giving a few rules of the workshop, like how we were never to touch the person while they were venting feelings of anger, it began.

By early afternoon, several of the participants had shared their grief. A woman in her mid-forties told how she had contacted AIDS through her job as a nurse. She shared how her grief wasn't only due to the fact that she was dying, but from the rejection she was receiving from her family. Tears flowed as she told of their fear of coming into contact with her. "They leave my meals outside my bedroom door! I miss their touch so much, especially their hugs and kisses. It's been months," she cried.

From my seat, I couldn't help but cry too. I felt sorry for the woman. When she left the mattress, Elisabeth called out to me. I heard my named being called, yet looked at my nametag.

"Why are you crying?" she asked when she had finally got my attention. As was proper procedure, I stood to answer.
My legs felt like dry twigs ready to snap. I thought I was going to collapse.

"I just think it's so sad when people don't want to be with you," I finally responded, with a very shaky voice.

Elisabeth motioned me to the front. As I sat upon the mattress, tears began streaming down my face. Elisabeth knelt beside me.

"Donna, who is it that doesn't want to be with you?" I lowered my head and gave no answer. Elisabeth continued to speak, directing her statement to the group. "See, when we think that we're crying for another, often times we're really crying for ourselves—a deep hurt within us has been triggered." I wiped my face with my hands. "You can cry here," she said. "Don't hide your tears. Don't put anymore band-aids on your wounds. This is the place where you can expose them so they can finally heal."

I began to twirl my hair around my finger and quite childishly, I said, "But my aunt said that if I cry, I would make my dad sad."

"Is it your mother then that you're grieving?" I nodded my head and faintly replied, "Yes."

"We would all like to hear about your mother? What was she like? What did you and she do together?"

I knelt up, slouched my body back upon my feet and without much hesitation I started telling the group about my life with my mother. Elisabeth took her chair.

⌒

"Mama was always sick. At meal times my sisters and I took turns bringing food to her bedroom. One day Mama said she didn't want any more eggs, because they were making her sick. Another day she said she didn't want any more milk, because milk was making her sick. And on Halloween she wouldn't even eat the Almond Joy that John gave her, or any of my Sugar Babies. So the next morning my dad asked, "What can I make for you that won't make you sick?"

"Bread," she said. " I miss my homemade bread." So my dad made bread for her. At lunchtime when it was done, I got to carry a slice with butter on it to Mama. She ate it and didn't even puke! So Dad let me stay and talk with her. I sat on the bed and brushed her hair. Mama liked it whenever my sisters and I did things with her hair. She didn't even care if we made little braids all over it. One time Sarah made spit curls in Mama's hair and once Bernadette made little ponytails. I tried to make a French braid, but my sisters laughed at it. Mama had me get her powder thing with the mirror on it. While I held Mama's hand mirror behind her, she looked into her little one to the back of her hair. "Oh, it's beautiful!" she said. "The braid is just fine!"

Bernadette and Sarah giggled. Mama heard them and said, "It's certainly better then the Beehive your Aunt LuLu made for me one time."

"A Beehive?" Catherine asked.

"Yes," Mama said. "A Beehive. A hairdo way too fancy for me." Mama tried to show us a Beehive on Catherine's hair, but her arms couldn't stay up long enough and Catherine's hair fell down. "Someday, when I'm feeling better, I'll put a Beehive on all of your heads!" she said.

"I don't like bees! I don't want a Beehive!" Anna screamed, as she swished her hands around her head, as if a bee was there.

"Then Mama won't do a Beehive on your head," she said.

Anna was afraid of bees. Once she had a bad dream that bees were chasing her. She called out for Mama during the night and Mama came running. Sometimes I yell for Mama, too. Once a bear was chasing me and twice a wolf. And once I yelled, "Don't fall, Mama. Don't fall!" I yelled that, because in my dream I saw Mama hanging from a star. Mama came running. I hugged her really tight. "I thought you were going to fall from a star," I said.

Mama brushed the hair from my face. "Everything's okay! I'm here!" she said. And she stayed by me until I wasn't scared anymore.

The next morning Mama told my sisters and me about the dream that she keeps having over and over and over again.

"I'm always on a picnic. Lots of people are there. When everybody sits down to eat, I notice lions and bears and other animals have come to eat with us."

"Is the picnic at Indian Lake, where we go?" Catherine asked.

"No, it's not there, but where it's at, it's really pretty. I can see waterfalls coming down the mountains and beautiful butterflies that rest on my arms."

"Do you see me there? Do the butterflies land on me?" I asked.

"Am I there?" Anna asked.

"No, but you're all here with me right now, and that's all that matters," Mama said, giving us hugs and kisses.

☞

"Donna Jean," Dad called. "Get in here and play with your little sisters. I'm trying to get ready for the holiday."

Mama had eaten her second slice of bread, so I took the empty plate from the bed and ran to the kitchen with it. I played with my little sisters and watched as my dad and Luke made supper. When it was ready, John helped Mama to the table.

"Are you sure you're up to this?" Dad asked.

"It's Thanksgiving Day, John," she said.

On that day, we get to have turkey, mashed potatoes, cranberries, green Jell-O, and pumpkin pie with whipped cream on top. Everybody took everything, except Mama. She only took an itty-bit of mashed potatoes, like Monica. And she ate them really, really slow, like Monica. Then when everyone was done eating, we turned our plates upside down. Luke got up and went to the cupboard to dish up the pumpkin pie. "Hey Ma," he said, as he cut the pie, "I think my pies turned out like yours! I made the crust by myself—like you taught me. Want a piece?"

Mama looked at Luke and smiled. She started to say yes, but Dad whispered, "You better not, Rosie, pumpkin pie is really spicy." Mama patted Dad's hand. "That sounds excellent Luke. I think I'll have a sliver!"

"Dut da da!" Luke said as he placed a piece on Mama's plate. He waited for her to taste it. Mama's tongue washed over her lips. "Luke, it's delicious!" she said. "Will you make the pies for Christmas, too?"

"Okay," he said, "baking is fun!"

⌒

When school closed for Christmas vacation, Mama told us *Bible* stories everyday after lunch. One day, Anna and Monica were really, really tired and they fell asleep right under Mama's wings. (Her wings are really her arms, but she calls them wings.) After Mama told us about *Daniel in the Lion's Den,* and *Jonah in the Belly of a Whale*, Dad came in the bedroom and told us that he was taking his little kittens (that's my sisters and me) and Mama for a ride to Fayette. "As long as the kids are out of school, we won't have to hurry back. Maybe we can stop and visit Roland and Thatis on the way back, if you're up to it," he said.

"Yippee!" we screamed, as we jumped up and down.

We like it when Dad takes us for rides. Especially when he take us down the hilly road. "Hold on for your life," he says, then he goes really fast over the hills.

"Faster, faster!" we holler. "Go until our tummies tickle!"

It's always so much fun, until Mama hollers, "Slow down, John!" Then Dad has to quit going fast like a humming bird and goes slow like a crow.

Anyway, after Dad warmed up the car we got in and then Dad helped Mama out to it. After he lit his pipe, away we went. We only got as far as the old white school when Mama told Dad that she needed him to stop the car. "I'm having trouble breathing. I need some air," she said. Dad opened Mama's door and helped her out and held her up when she bent over to breathe. When she got back in the car, she had the shivers. Cold air came into the car, too, so Anna and I blew the cold smoke out of our mouths to

73

pretend we were smoking Dad's pipe.

When Dad drove away from the old white school I was glad because, Luke once told me that a ghost lives in the old white school. I didn't want that ghost to get Mama. But after just a little ways, we had to stop again. This time we stopped by Humbert's house. After Dad helped Mama out of the car and back in, he turned the car around. We started to pout, because we still wanted to go to Fayette, but Dad said, "There'll be none of that pouting today! Be good for your mother." So we sat quiet. Dad wouldn't even let us sing. I thought we'd still get to stop at Roland and Thatis, but we didn't. I heard Dad tell Mama that she better not go to Midnight Mass. I thought Mama was going to cry. "I just have to go to church," she said. "It's Christmas!" My dad told her that he'd talk to Father Dishaw after church to see if he could stop by our house on Christmas day with communion for her.

Mama once told us that communion is Jesus' body. When we laughed, she said, "It's true!" She opened the *Bible* and read to us about Jesus' body from the Book of Mark.

> **While they were at supper, Jesus took bread, said a blessing, gave the bread to his disciples and said, "Take this, all of you, this is my body."**

"Maybe he was just joking," Sarah said.

"No," Mama said. "The *Bible* doesn't joke."

"Father Dishaw blesses the bread, too, but how does he turn the bread into Jesus?" Bernadette asked.

"I'm not sure either!" Mama said. "It's a mystery of our faith. But when we get to heaven we'll find out how it turned from bread and wine into Jesus' body and blood."

"Why can't I go get Jesus in my mouth at church?" I asked.

"Because you have to make your First Holy Communion, then you'll be able to. That'll be in May. Around Catherine's birthday," Mama said.

☞

Luke didn't come with us to Midnight Mass. He stayed home to take care of Mama, because my dad didn't want to leave her home alone. On the way to church we sang Christmas songs. First we tried to sing *Silent Night*, but John kept singing *Deck the Halls*. So we started singing *Deck the Halls*, too. When John started to sing *Up on the Housetop*, Dad made us all be quiet.

Just as we got in church, I told Dad that I wanted to go sit in the front PU, but he grabbed my hair. "I want to go sit by the Jesus, Mary and Joseph window, not by Moses, again!" I told him. But he wouldn't let me, so I had to crawl over John, because he wouldn't let me sit by the edge.

I don't know why they called the seats PU's. It doesn't even stink in church, except when Father Dishaw used the incense. Mama told me the incense was like sending our prayers up to God in heaven, but I never once saw any prayers rising up, like the incense. The incense always stinks up the church and makes Mama and me cough, and Anna sneeze. One time Anna sneezed and sneezed and sneezed, and she got us wet. Mama took Anna's hand and put it over Anna's mouth and whispered, "Anna Rose, please cover your mouth."

When everyone was singing *Joy To The World*, Oliver, the man in front of us, farted. It stunk really, really bad! I pulled on Dad's coat sleeve. "Is that why the seats are called PU's?" I asked.

"Shhhhhh," Dad said. So I squeezed the holes of my nose. Dad made me put my hand down, so I had to smell the stink.

Sarah carried Monica to the car when church was over. Monica had fallen to sleep right after she put Dad's quarter and penny into the collection basket. Dad always let Monica and Anna take turns putting the money into the basket. I wanted a turn, too, but Dad said that I already had had my turn, but I didn't remember getting one.

When we got into the car, my brother John started laughing and said, "I couldn't hear the whistle of the train in the pew in front of us, but I sure could smell the smoke!" I giggled, because I knew John was talking about Oliver. John kept talking like a man, while we waited for Dad to talk to Father Dishaw. "Oliver, Oliver, Oliver!" he'd say. "In church? Oh Oliver, God is surely going to send you to hell for that one!"

"Watch your tongue young man," Dad said, when he got into the car. "Or you might end up in the same place you say Oliver's going."

On Christmas day Dad carried the big chair out of the living room and into the kitchen for Mama. After she sat down, Luke put the stool by her and put her feet unto it. Mama was sad because she didn't get to go to Mass. "Are you going to be too sick to go to my First Holy Communion too?" I asked.

"That's a few months away," she said. "But I'll be there, even if I'm *dead*!"

"Where?" Dad asked.

"To Donna Jean's First Communion. I just told her that I'll be at her First Communion, even if I'm dead."

"That's a long way off. You'll be better by then," he said, as he peeled the potatoes for the Christmas supper.

We all played with our present from Santa, except John. John said that he couldn't play with his baseball glove without a ball, so he kept going around the house with his hand in his armpit, flopping his bent arm up and down until farting sounds came out. Then he'd say, "Hey, Ma and Dad, Oliver's here!"

I watched Mama in the big chair. She kept falling asleep. But every time the clock that Matthew sent us from Germany coo-cooed, she'd wake up again. "It's going to be suppertime soon," she said. "I wonder if Father Dishaw has forgotten about me."

All of a sudden we heard bells and a "Ho, ho, ho," and in walked Santa! He had a white pillowcase on his back with presents sticking out of it. Santa put the pillowcase of presents down. I saw Santa's eyes. They weren't blue, like when Santa came to school to give us a stocking with candy, an orange and a popcorn ball in it. His eyes were brown. Monica and Anna were scared of Santa, so they ran and hid under the little white table, but the Santa found them and gave them each a present. They jumped up and down. They were happy because they each got a doll. I touched the dolls' eyelashes. They tickled my fingers. Their eyes looked like glass, so I felt them, too. They felt just like marbles.

Next, Catherine got a spinning top from Santa. It was all different colors. She had it turning really fast. Luke was helping her. Bernadette and Sarah each got a sweater. Bernadette was hugging her blue one and Sarah was showing Mama her green one. Luke got a deck of cards and some comic books. John got a baseball, so he started throwing the baseball into his new glove. Mama got a soft, yellow blanket and Dad got long johns—two pairs! Then Santa said, "And where's this little girl by the name of Donna Jean? Does she live here, or is she from another family?"

"Santa! Santa!" I shouted as I jumped up and down. "I'm right here!"

Santa laughed a big laugh. "Are you the little Jacques' girl that likes marbles so much?"

"YES!" I said, very excited. My eyes got big as cow eyes when Santa handed me a great big present. It was the biggest and prettiest present I'd ever seen. It was wrapped with snowmen paper and on the top of it sat a big, red bow. I carefully peeled the snowmen paper off. "Chinese Checkers! Oh thank you Santa! Thank you Santa!" I ran and gave Santa's leg a big hug. That's when I noticed that Santa didn't have his red fuzzy pants on. He had on black, slippery pants. And Santa didn't have on big, black boots. He had on black, peaky-toed shoes that had lots of little holes in them with laces through the holes, like my grandma's church shoes.

Just when I was about to ask Santa why he only had on his red hat and red coat and why he didn't come down our chimney, he said "Ho, ho, ho," once again, and he left.

I hid my Chinese Checkers behind Mama's chair and hurried to her bedroom window to watch Santa leave. I stood on Mama's bed and ducked behind the shade. I scraped a hole in the Jack Frost so I could peek to see Santa on his sleigh with his reindeer. But when I looked, I saw Santa take off his red hat and coat. I saw him take off his white whiskers and reach into his shiny black car—not his sleigh! He took a hat out of the car and put it on. It was a black hat that looked just like Father Dishaw' black priest hat—Father Dishaw's black priest hat with the three sides and the fuzzy ball thing on top.

Santa turned around. "Father Dishaw? Father Dishaw!" I said.

I watched Father Dishaw in the wind and the blowing snow as he tried to put on his long coat-thing that he took from his car—his long, black coat-thing with zillions of buttons that go all the way down the front of it that he wears at church. It looked like a dress blowing in the wind. The wind blew so hard that he could hardly get his arms into the holes. And then when he tried to put his black cape on, the wind blew it away. Father ran and caught it. When he finally got it on, he closed the car door, then knelt down in front of his car. He made the sign of the cross and said his prayers right on the snow. Then he stood up and slowly walked to the house.

Quickly I got out from behind the shade and jumped off Mama's bed. I saw Mama getting under the blankets. She asked me if I wanted to lie down by her. "Not now," I said, and I went running to the back door. When I got there my dad was opening it for Father. My dad didn't say anything to Father Dishaw and Father Dishaw didn't say anything to him. He just stood there while Dad went to tell Mama that the priest was at our house. See, when Father comes to our house to bring Mama communion, we're not supposed to talk to him until he's done giving Mama communion. And Father can't talk to us either, until he's done giving her communion.

Father walked into the kitchen. He took off his black cape and set it on the back of Mama's big chair. Around his neck I saw the chain holding the little round, golden pix-thing, with the cross on top.

One time at Catechism class, Father Dishaw came to show us the little golden pix. He lifted the cover of it. It looked like when Great Uncle Willy lifted the cover of his shiny gold pocket-watch. But the pix didn't have anything in it. Father Dishaw told us that it's always empty except when he puts communion in it, to bring to a sick person.

⌒

I looked at the pix-thing again. "Jesus' body is in there," I said to myself. Then I whispered to Father. "I know you're the Santa!" But Father wouldn't talk to me. He just rolled his big brown eyes and looked up at the ceiling and put his tongue at the corner of his mouth. Then he looked back down at me and smiled. But he still wouldn't say if he was that Santa, or if he wasn't that Santa.

When he went in to see Mama, I listened by the door to see if he was going to tell Mama that he was the Santa, but instead, I heard him ask her if she had any sins she wanted to tell him. I thought Mama was going to say, "No, Of course not! I don't have any sins!" But Mama said, "Yes, I do."

"Donna Jean," Dad whispered loudly. "Get away from that bedroom door—now!"

I waited in the kitchen for Mama's door to open. When it did, I ran to Father. "I know you're that Santa that came here," I said.

"How do you know that?"

"I watched you from the window!"

Father Dishaw put his finger over his mouth, "Shhhh," he said, bending down by me, "This will be our little secret, okay? Don't tell your little sisters." So I said I wouldn't tell.

When we were walking into the living room, Catherine asked Father why he always wears a dress and Father said, "Because I'm a girl!" Everybody laughed.

"You're a boy!" I said.

"Oh, really," he laughed, "then how come I wear this dress?" My sisters and I looked at each other and put up our shoulders.

"We don't know!" we said.

Father sat down in a chair and lifted his black dress and showed us his black high-heeled shoes. "Don't girls wear high-heels?"

"Grandmas and Mamas do," Anna said.

"And don't they wear stockings?" Father giggled while he lifted up the bottom of his pants to show us his stockings.

"Girls wear *long* stockings!" Bernadette giggled.

"Well," he said, "My name is Connie. Boys aren't named Connie, are they?"

Sarah's eyeballs got big. "No," she said, "Only girls are named Connie!"

Father and my dad laughed, as Father bounced us one-by-one on his knees to give us pony rides, because Dad said he was too tired to give rides. After we all had a turn, Father said, "Enough fun for one day. I've got to get going." My sisters ran to get their present, but I ran to the door.

"Father Dishaw," I said, holding open the door so I could see him. "What's your real name?"

"Conrad," he said. "It's Conrad!"

"Donna Jean," Dad hollered, "Must you always be up to mischief? Close the door!"

"What a priest!" a women in the front row of the workshop exclaimed.

"You mean a saint!" another voice remarked.

I raised my head and looked at Elisabeth and the other counselors. "Are you sure I'm not boring you to smithereens?" I asked.

"No," Brandi replied. I looked. It was the counselor with the flaming red hair. If only I'd had pretty hair like hers…maybe then my life would be…

"Stay with it," she said. I closed my eyes, retraced my thoughts, then continued on.

Chapter Eight

"Are you sure it won't be too much trouble if I go stay with Geraldine and Roy?" I heard Mama asking Dad.

"I told you, we can handle it," he said. "You're feeling halfway decent and the weather is good, so I'm taking you there today. Maybe then you'll be able to get the rest you need."

"But, what about the kids? Will you be able to get them off to school? And who'll watch Anna and Monica? How do you expect to make the meals, do the wash and ironing, and the scrubbing? If I stay, at least I'll be here to watch the little ones."

"Don't go worrying about anything. I'll keep Luke out of school for awhile. The kids and I can handle it. Remember, too, my mother will be here in about a week. And don't forget, Rosie, the ladies from church have been bringing up supper. The only thing I'm worried about is whether or not the old Chevy is going to make the thirty miles to Manistique and back home again. The tires aren't very good and the motor's been missing. But we'll give it a try," he said.

Later that day, Dad packed some of Mama's clothes in the little brown suitcase. Anna and I ran to our bedroom and jumped on our beds while we waited to take Mama to Auntie's house. Suddenly I had a great idea. I jumped down and ran to my dresser drawer to get out my crayons. "Anna," I said, "I'm going to make

Mama some pretty flowers. And I'll write GET WELL by the flowers, like on the card I made at school for Paula when she was sick."

I looked and looked all around the house for paper, but I couldn't find any, so on the wall, behind the dresser, I drew a purple daisy, a yellow lady slipper and a pink rose. Then I wrote GET WELL MAMA. When I was finished, I ran and asked Mama if she could come to see the surprise I had made for her.

"I'll try," she said, taking my arm.

"Don't go over doing it," Dad crabbed, as we passed through the kitchen.

"Where is it?" Mama asked, after she looked all around the bedroom. I took her hand to the dresser that I had wheeled away from the wall. "SURPRISE!" I said when she looked behind it.

"Donna Jean!" Mama said. "You know better then to write on the wall! This makes me so sick! It's our new wall, honey!"

"What's the matter?" Dad hollered on his way into the bedroom.

"Donna Jean colored on the new wall! And it sure makes me sick!" Mama put her head down and her hand over her eyes.

"She knows better than that! She's getting a spanking!" Dad said.

"No," Mama told him, "let her go. She meant well. It's a get well card."

Mama started to shake all over, so Dad made her sit on the bed. I ran and got the dishrag so I could wash the flowers off of the wall. But when I washed them, the flowers got all scribbled and wouldn't come off.

"Forget it," Mama said.

Mama stayed lying on our bed until it was time to bring her to live with Aunt Geraldine and Uncle Roy. Slowly we started walking with her to the car. I couldn't even see her face; it was so black outside. But I wasn't afraid because Mama let us grab onto her coat, because my sisters and I are chickens of the dark. At least that's what our brothers say.

It was the very first day of nineteen hundred and sixty when we slid our feet on the icy snow toward the running noise of the car. "Stop for a minute," Mama said. "What a beautiful night! Look at those stars! Now that's heaven."

"What's heaven?" Catherine asked.

"Heaven," Mama said, "is on the other side of the stars. It's where God and the angels live. It's where we go when we die. My mama lives there."

"How did your mama get up there in that heaven?" Anna asked.

"Well," Mama said, "when I was seven years old my mama died. And when a person dies they go to heaven to live with God and the angels."

"Look!" Bernadette yelled. "That star is twinkling, like *Twinkle Twinkle Little Star!*"

Mama laughed. "When a star twinkles, I think it's my mother winking at me from heaven," she said. Then she slowly lowered herself down to us. I could smell her Ponds cream. "Mama is going to tell my little girls something very, very important," she said, as she opened her arms and we cuddled in around her big tummy. I want you to always remember what I'm going to say—so listen.

"Look at that sky!" she said again. So we did. I could see zillions of stars. "Always remember girls, that as long as you can see the stars of heaven, you'll never need the diamonds of earth." Then she said that she wanted us to say what she had just said. So again she said, "As long as you can see the stars of heaven," and we repeated, "As long as you can see the stars of heaven,"

—"you'll never need the diamonds of earth."

—"you'll never need the diamonds of earth."

"Okay," Mama said, "one more time, all together." Again we all said what Mama said: "As long as you can see the stars of heaven, you'll never need the diamonds of earth."

"What are diamonds of earth?" I asked. But before Mama could answer, Dad tooted the car horn. When he did, it scared screams out of us. Mama got mad and hollered, "Are you trying to make me have the baby right here? For goodness sake, John, at least give us some light!"

When the two big lights came out of the night, Dad came out of the car and hollered for us to get in before we froze to death. Dad helped Mama into the car and after he got back in, he lit his pipe. "You're too weak to be standing out there in the cold," he said as we sputtered out of the driveway. Then off we went to Auntie's house singing the grandma's song *Over the River and Through the Woods.* Even my dad sang.

83

⌒

Four days after we brought Mama to live with Auntie, we got to go see her. At Auntie's house I asked Mama if she'd play Chinese checkers with me, but she said she was too tired. All she could do was look at the marbles that belonged to my game. Anna and Monica brought their baby dolls with them. They were walking them up Mama's tummy, but Dad made them stop. "You could hurt the baby that's inside your mother," he told them.

"When will summertime come again, Mama?" Bernadette asked. "I can't wait to play games outside again."

I like to play games outside, too. It's a lot more fun than games in the house, because there's a lot more room. We can play marbles and hopscotch and jump rope. (It's fun, especially at school.) Krystal, Janet, Celeste and I jump the O'Leary's on the cement.

"Mama," Sarah asked, "when summer comes, can we put the new metal tub under the crab apple tree like we did last summer, so we can take a bath again?"

See, last summer Mama had Dad haul pails of hot water and pails of cold water to put into the tub. Then she hung sheets on the branches of the crabapple tree, so the boys and Dad wouldn't be able to see us. After Mama sprinkled Breeze into the water, she swished it around to make bubbles. Then we got to hop naked into the tub. Mama knelt by the tub and soaped our hair with Prell, until it stood up high. She laughed and said, "Look at all my little princesses—each of them has a crown!" And then she laughed again. Mama laughed so hard that she tumbled onto her back to the ground.

"Gosh, oh gee," she said, looking up to the sky. "I forgot how beautiful the outdoors is!" She watched as the robins flew into their nest and as a butterfly sat on an Indian Paintbrush.

"Wild roses must be near by," she said as she took another big breath.

We watched as Mama's black hair blew across her face and her green housedress lifted high with the wind. We hollered to her. "We can see your bloomers, Mama!" We giggled, too, but she still didn't hear us. Mama had fallen fast asleep—like *Little Boy Blue* in the haystack. Then Sarah whispered a song for us to sing. So we sang: "I see London, I see France, I see Mama's underpants!" Mama woke back up when she heard us singing and then poured water over our princesses' crowns and washed them all away.

⤳

"Another outdoors bath under the crabapple tree!" Mama said, smiling. "I'm afraid we won't be able to do that Sarah. Dad bought that tub to water the cows with. Now it's in the pasture, but maybe someday soon we'll have an indoor tub. Then you'll be able to take a hot bath whenever you want to."

"Mama, can we go up Aunt Geraldine's stairs to see what's up there?" I asked.

"No," Mama said, "Auntie doesn't want you up there." But when Auntie was in the kitchen, Catherine and I tried sneaking up anyway. Auntie caught us and made us come back down. Mama was *very* mad when she heard Auntie telling us to stay off the stairs.

"You girls know better!" she said, when Auntie sat us together on the big red chair. "You have to mind your elders!" (Mama says elders mean big people.)

When Auntie went for milk, (not from a cow, but from a store) Mama had everybody come and sit around her. Then she told us that Aunt Geraldine and Uncle Roy asked her to stay and live with them for awhile after the baby is born. "It's so I can get rested up before I go back home to take care of everyone again. I'm thinking I just might do that," she said.

My aunt and uncle don't have any babies at their house, but they want a baby really, really bad. So I asked Mama if she was going to give them our baby. Mama laughed. "We've got lots of babies, Donna Jean, but I'd never give any one of my precious babies away. You're all too special! If I stay, it's just so I can get rested up. And then your aunt and uncle can have a baby around their house for a couple of weeks. But if I could have a baby for anyone in this world, it would be for them," she said.

Dad helped Mama sit up. One by one she had us sit on the floor, between her legs, so she could brush our hair. I could feel her hands and legs shaking when she brushed my hair around her finger until it fell into a long curl. When she finished, I brushed her hair.

"We better get going," Dad said. "I don't want to leave too late, in case the car breaks down. We'll be back on Saturday, unless we hear the baby's been born."

I counted on my fingers to Saturday. "That will be January ninth," I said to Bernadette.

"Mama," Catherine asked, "is the doctor going to cut your tummy open with a butcher knife and pull the baby out of your guts?"

"Don't be such a lamebrain," Luke said. "They don't do it that way."

Mama kissed everyone. I was last. "Mama," I whispered, "last night I had a dream that you pooped the baby out. It was a boy and he kept crying and crying for you to rock him! I tried to wake you up, to tell you that the baby was a boy, but you wouldn't wake up! I shook your arm, but you still kept sleeping. Mama, are you going to poop that baby out? Is that how it's going to get out of your tummy?"

"Donna Jean," Mama laughed, "You have way too many dreams and you ask way too many questions! Get out to the car. Your dad's waiting for you."

⤌

"Up and at em!" Dad hollered, when he opened our bedroom door the next morning. "The rooster forgot to wake me up, so if you don't want to miss your school bus, you better hurry!"

We all hurried like ants getting ready for winter. We had to eat our pancake, rolled up with sugar in the middle of it, when we got on the bus. At school, my friend Krystal and I raced to our classroom.

"I beat!" I hollered.

"I did!" she said.

We looked into our room. Teacher wasn't there. We have to behave even if she isn't in the room. We're not even allowed to play piano unless we get Teacher's permission, but Krystal and I decided to play it anyway. First she played, while I watched to make sure Mrs. Webster wasn't coming. Then when it was my turn to play, Krystal had to watch for Mrs. Webster. "I'm going to play *Three Blind Mice*," I told Krystal, as she walked to the door to spy for Teacher.

See, my Aunt Geraldine taught us how to play *Three Blind Mice* and *Doctor, Doctor Can You Tell*. My dad tells everybody that Aunt Geraldine plays piano with her ear, but Dad's telling lies because Auntie plays with her fingers. I've never ever seen her play piano with her ear. I hope my dad doesn't go to H E double L for telling those lies about my auntie.

"The coast is clear," Krystal hollered. So I started to play. I like to play piano. My dad once told me that someday when he gets an extra dollar, he's going to let me take a piano lesson from Mrs. Lyons, at the school. Dad says that I have piano fingers because my fingers are long.

Anyway, I started to play on the white, soft, slippery keys. "Three blind mice, three blind mice, see how they run...."

"What are you doing playing the piano? You're in big trouble, little girl! How many times must you be told to mind your P's and Q's? You know the rules!" Teacher said as she marched to the blackboard to get the hanging paddle. "Come over here now!" she shouted as she sat down on one of the little chairs.

I knew Teacher was really mad because when she gets really mad her lips squeeze together and look like a bellybutton. The paddle in Teacher's hand scared me as I slowly walked to the front of the room. I kept begging and promising Teacher that I'd never touch the piano again.

"You better believe you won't!" she said, and threw me over her lap. "One, two, three, four, five, six, and seven! A seven year old should know better," she shouted. Her words were really loud and they went far, far into my ears.

"Mama!" I hollered, with each hit.

"This hurts me more than it hurts you," she said. "But it's my job to teach you to obey the rules! Now get to your seat and don't expect to leave it for the rest of the day!"

On my way to my desk, I saw Krystal. She was walking back into the room, holding and talking to her new baby doll.

When the morning bell rang, Teacher called our names, and when she did, we had to holler, *clear and loud*, "Here!" But when it was Edwin's turn, he hollered "Absent!" Teacher got mad, again. She made Edwin go to the chalkboard and stand on his tiptoes with his nose in the circle of chalk that she drew on the board. When she called Frederick's name, Frederick hollered, "Here!"

"Come to the front!" she shouted. She checked his head for lice, like she did almost every morning. When she found some again, she pulled the piano away from the wall and shoved Frederick's desk behind it. "If you come to school with head lice that's where you're staying!" she said, pointing to behind the piano. "Don't all of you be looking up here, get out your spelling books, NOW!"

When spelling was over, we took turns going into our reading groups. I got to read *See Spot Run* all by myself. Then after lunch Teacher said that if we were good for the rest of the day, she'd let us do *Show and Tell* instead of arithmetic. And we were good, so one by one, we got to get up and show what we got from Santa, except for Frederick. He could only come out from behind the piano if he had to go to the bathroom.

Timmy got to do *Show and Tell* first. He showed us his new train and told us about his other train at home. "But I wanted another one, so I asked Santa for another one, and I got it," he said. Timmy started to tell us about the other things he got, too, but Mrs. Webster smiled and said, "Honey, I don't think we have time to tell about more than one, or it'll take us too long." Timmy sat back down.

Next, she called Janet to the front of the room. "My, don't 'we' look pretty today," Teacher said. Janet swished her new dress with the cancan underneath it, as she showed us her new Raggedy Ann. Her dress was really pretty. Mrs. Webster said she liked Janet's doll. "Thank You, Sweetie," she said. "You must have been a very good girl." Then one by one, Teacher called everyone except for Donna Tifen and me. When she finally called my name, I jumped out of my seat. "Just wait a minute, little girl. First, I want you to know that I shouldn't even let you out of your seat for misbehaving this morning, so consider yourself lucky!"

I couldn't wait to show everyone my Chinese checkers. When I did, Teacher asked, "Didn't you get a doll? I thought Santa would bring you a doll."

"My little sisters got dolls," I said. "And their dolls are really pretty. Their eyes feel like marbles!"

"Maybe she was bad!" Alvin hollered.

I tried to tell Alvin that I wasn't bad, but everyone started laughing and asking me if that was all I got from Santa. I was going to tell them about my thick coloring book and my box of sixty-four crayons, but Mrs. Webster stood up and said, "All right, that's enough!" Teacher came up to me and put her arm around my shoulders. "I'll write to Santa myself for you next year and I'm sure he'll bring you a doll."

"Thanks, Teacher!" I said as she walked me back to my seat. Then she went over to Donna Tifen's desk and asked her if she'd like to show the class her teddy bear. Donna Tifen is big like my brother Mark, but she can't read yet. Not one word! Even my sister Catherine can read, but not Donna Tifen. At first Donna smiled and shook her head yes, but when Teacher took her teddy bear, Donna started crying and throwing one of her fits. Teacher had me reach into Donna's desk for her smelling stuff that stops her fits. When I was giving the tiny little jar of oily stuff to Teacher, I saw Donna Tifen's eyes roll back into her head, until I could only see the whites of them. "Donna," Teacher said, as she softly slapped Donna's face, "You can keep your teddy bear."

Teacher held the little jar under Donna's nose until she woke back up. I thought that Donna might swallow her tongue. Richard once told me that somebody once told him that Donna almost swallowed her tongue one time. Her mother, or maybe it was her aunt, had to hold her tongue with a clothespin so it wouldn't fall down into her throat.

I didn't like it when Donna Tifen threw a fit. One time she said weird things like she was going to bite our heads off, and at recess time she chased us all around. I ran and ran away from Donna, until those pains came into my throat, and I had to huff and puff like the *Big Bad Wolf.* I hid from Donna Tifen under the tree by the merry-go-round, but she found me under there. I covered my head with my hands so she couldn't bite it off.

"Want to play wiff me?" she asked as she lifted the branch.

"Okay," I said, because I was afraid to tell her, "No." Donna wanted me to take her hand, so I did. Mama says that Jesus smiles when we're nice to people that don't have friends. So I took Donna's big hand to the seesaw. When I sat on my side of it, Donna hardly went up, but every time she sat down on her side, I flew high into the air, then land back on the seesaw. I screamed each time, because my tummy tickled and because I thought I was going to fall off.

On the bus ride home that day, I told Bernadette about Teacher spanking me and how I was going to tell Mama on her. Bernadette and I counted how many more days until we'd get to see Mama again. We tried to tell Sarah how many more days, but Sarah had her knitting needles and yarn and got mad when we talked to her. "Can't you see? I'm trying to make Mama potholders with my Christmas yarn!" The yarn was pretty yellow.

The bus was really, really noisy. My brothers and lots of big kids were talking loud, but Catherine fell asleep anyway. Almost everyday after school my sister sleeps on the bus and we have to wake her up when we get home. Except once Luke had to carry her to the house, because she wouldn't wake up.

It had been nearly an hour since I had nervously walked to the front of the room and sat on the mattress. As I shared memories of my past, I felt numb. At times the whole episode seemed to be a dream that I couldn't awaken from. But then one of the counselors would say something to me and it would bring me back to reality. Then I'd continue to share my experiences.

Chapter Nine

O n Saturday morning, Dad got us up early because he and my brothers were going to work.

"I've already stoked the fire, girls, so don't go near the stove when I'm gone, and don't go back to bed. I want you *up* in case of fire."

"Today's the day we get to go see Mama again, right, Dad?" I asked.

"That's right, we'll go once the boys and I get home from work."

Dad looked out the window. "It's pretty dark out there," he said. "It may be wintertime, but it looks like we're in for one heck of a summertime storm."

Dad reached high over the refrigerator and took the little metal box from the cupboard. "If lightning strikes the house, make sure you girls get out and take this little metal box with. It has important papers in it that say we own this place." Dad told Sarah and Bernadette they were both in charge of all of us. He looked at the boys, "Let's go!" he said.

We watched through the foggy window as they drove away. Then we hurried and got dressed in case the house caught on fire. Afterwards, I made the cocoa for breakfast, Bernadette made the oatmeal and Sarah made the toast. We ate and then did the dishes. Later we played *Follow the Leader* and *LeapFrog*. When we were playing *Jack Jumped Over the Candlestick,* a big sound of thunder came. We screamed and hugged each other. "We don't have to be afraid," Sarah said. "Remember what Mama said about thunder? She said that it's just the apostles rolling big beer barrels up in heaven. They're getting ready for a party!" But when the next thunder came, even Sarah screamed loud, so we all ran to the door. When we saw lightning light up the sky, we ran out of the house. Sarah carried Monica, Bernadette carried Anna, Catherine carried Moe, and I carried the little metal box. It thundered and lightning again as we ran in the rain. "Where should we go?" Sarah hollered. We looked around.

"Under Mama's crabapple tree," Bernadette shouted.

"No," Sarah said, "lightning hit a cow that was under a tree. Dad said *never ever* stand under a tree in a storm."

"The outdoor toilet," I hollered. "Lightning doesn't catch toilets on fire? Does it?" My big sisters put up their shoulders. We ran to the toilet. We waited and waited in the stinky toilet watching the lightning and blocking our ears when the thunder came. And we prayed to Jesus so that the lightning wouldn't catch our house on fire.

"The rain's turning into baby stones," Anna said, as she peeked out between the boards. We could hear it knocking on the roof. "That's hail!" Bernadette said. Then the hail turned back to rain. It blew in through the open spaces and got us wet and stung Anna in the eyes.

"What if the rain covers the whole world, like it did for Noah and the Ark boat that Mama told us about," Catherine said, shivering.

"No, remember, Catherine? Mama said that God promised he'd never flood the earth with water again," Bernadette said. "That's why there are rainbows!"

The rain stopped. We started running to the house because Monica's nose was freezing and so were our hands and ears. Catherine slipped and fell with Moe onto the wet, icy snow. I fell, too, and the cover of the little metal box flew open and Dad's important papers blew out. Sarah and I chased them around the yard. Mama and Dad's wedding picture got wet and so did the envelope with Luke's yellow curls in it.

When we got into the house, we saw Dad and the boys coming

home. We went lickety-split and pushed the important papers back into the metal box.

"Girls!" Luke hollered, as he came into the house. "Girls, look out the window. There's a rainbow."

We ran and looked. We saw two rainbows together in the sky. I counted the colors in the rainbow. Luke called and called for everyone to hurry to come and see it, but while we were waiting for Anna, the snow started falling and the rainbows disappeared.

⌒

"Holy wah!" Dad said when he looked outside. "Guess we made it in from the woods just in time. Look at that snow coming down! I sure hope it clears up before we leave to go see your mother. Uncle Herb is supposed to bring Grandma here today, but he's not going to come if there's a blizzard. "Well," Dad said, chuckling, "here he comes now."

I ran to the door and waited for Grandma. Once they were in the house, Uncle Herb drank a cup of coffee, then said that he had to get right back to Escanaba because of the storm.

Sarah took Grandma to our bedroom, because Grandma had to sleep in our bed with Sarah. Dad told Monica and me that we could sleep with him until Mama came back home. Grandma put her suitcase in the bedroom and then sat down in Mama's chair that was still in the kitchen. Anna climbed up on the arm of the chair and started rubbing Grandma's face. "Grandma," she said, "why do you have fur on your face?"

Grandma laughed, "That's not fur, Anna Rose, that's hair! That's what happens when you get old like me." Then Grandma sang:

The old gray mare, she ain't what she used to be
Ain't what she used to be, ain't what she used to be
The old gray mare she ain't what she used to be
Many long years ago!

Catherine and I laughed at Grandma as she bounced her knee and clapped her hands to the song. Then Catherine ran and jumped on her.

"Don't be jumping up on your grandma," Dad said. "You girls should be outside making a snowman. The snow is heavy—perfect for a snowman." So we got dressed and went outside to make one. We rolled three snowballs.

"This is Papa snowball," Sarah said.

"I made Mama snowball," Bernadette shouted, and Catherine said that she made Baby snowball. We lifted the snowballs on top of each other. "It's a Mama Snowman!" I said when Sarah put Mama's old straw hat on it. Bernadette put buttons for the eyes and mouth and Anna put a carrot for its nose. I ran and knocked on the window. "Everybody, come see Mama Snowman!" I hollered through the glass. Grandma smiled and waved and said something, but we couldn't hear her. Dad said it was nice and then he said that we had to get back in the house. "We're eating supper and then leaving to go see your mother."

"Yippee!" we screamed, and ran to the house.

After the boys finished their barn chores and Sarah and Bernadette finished the supper dishes, Dad fired the stove so it would be warm in the house for Grandma. "We're going to take the back way to Manistique," he told Grandma. "It's shorter and will save on gas."

On the way, we sang *Oh Black Joe* and *Did you Ever See A Lassie*, and lots of other songs, too. And just when we were singing *Pop Goes The Weasel*; the car made a big bang sound and it started going from side to side. I grabbed onto Bernadette's leg and screamed until Dad got the car stopped.

"I think we just had a blow-out," Dad said. "It was all I could do to keep the car from going over the cliff!"

"We must be by Poodle Petes," I thought. That's where the road doesn't have any sides, and it looks like our car will fall off the edge.

Dad, Luke, and John got out of the car, but they got right back in. The jack broke, so they couldn't lift up the car to put the other tire on.

"It's not much of a tire," Dad said. "It's got a big bunion on it, but if someone comes with a jack, I think it'll get us to Manistique and back."

"What's a bunion?" Sarah asked.

"It's a big bump on the tire," he said.

The trees, the road, the car, and even *us* all turned to pitch black as we waited and waited for a car to come with a jack. I heard Dad whisper to Luke. "There aren't any houses for miles and very few cars ever travel this Little Harbor Road. I should have taken the highway. We'll freeze to death if someone doesn't come soon."

"Car lights are coming!" Catherine shouted.

Dad got out of the car. I could see snow blowing all around him. He waved his arm up really high when the lights came closer, but the car went right by. Dad got back in the car and rubbed his hands together.

"Ahaaaaaaaa!" Bernadette screeched. I looked at her.

"I think Bernadette's tongue is stuck on the metal thing around the window."

"Wait!" John hollered. "Don't move. I'll come back there and help you get it off!"

But Bernadette didn't wait. She jerked her tongue from the window and then started screaming and talking funny. We thought she said that it hurt.

"We can't understand you," John said. "Quit crying!" But Bernadette cried even louder. Then Anna started crying, because she had to go pee.

"Hold on, Anna. I'm going to get the tire fixed soon," Dad said to her.

I had to go *pee,* and *poop, too.* My tummy kept twisting around and around on the inside, like the inside of Mama's washing machine. Then Monica started crying, because she was cold. So I gave her my hat to put on—my hat with the knitted curls hanging down the back. The one Wendy's mother knitted for me, with mittens to match. (Wendy and I play together when my dad goes to her dad's house.) Luke told me that I should let Monica wear my mittens too, so I put them on her. Catherine was lying up by the back window and crying, because she was cold, too.

"Get down from the window," Luke said. "If you stay up there, you'll be cold for sure." Catherine crawled down from the back window and I put my hands up through my coat sleeve. I could feel the crayon on my fingernails.

I had polished my fingernails to make them pretty for Mama. After I was done polishing them, I put the red crayon on top of my dresser and then sat on the floor to put on my shoes. "I gonna give

Mama tolor train tisses," I heard Monica say. I looked up and saw that Monica had crawled up onto the top of the dresser and was trying to color her lips. "Monica," I shouted running to take her down. I stretched out my arms and she jumped into them. "Did you say you're going to give Mama color crayon kisses?"

"Yup," she said, putting her cold lips onto my warm ones.

⌒

"Car lights are coming," Sarah shouted. This time the car lights stopped in front of our car.

"It's my buddy Monty!" Luke said.

Dad and our brothers got out and talked to him. Then Monty came to our car and told us to get into his warm car. After we were in his car, he turned it around so his car lights would light up the dark. Then he got out to help Dad change the tire. We saw Monty put the jack onto our car and watched when the car lifted up and then fell back down. Monty jacked up the car again and then it stayed up, so Dad put the tire on.

"Get back into the car girls," Luke hollered to us through the window. Everyone piled in. Dad lit up his pipe and then we were on our way again. When we turned onto the highway at the store that's made of stones, I asked how much longer it would be until we'd get to see Mama.

"Soon," Dad said.

"How many minutes is soon?" Catherine asked.

"Ten, fifteen maybe, then we'll be inside where you can all get warm. And don't forget when we get inside your Aunt and Uncle's house, it's shoes off! And absolutely, positively no jumping on your mother!"

I knew Mama would be lying on the couch in the room with the piano. That's the room where she always is—on the big red couch that has lion's hands and feet.

"Go faster, Dad," we hollered.

Freezing air was blowing the cardboard off the holes on the floor of the car. Dad had put it there so we couldn't get our feet caught in the holes when the car was moving.

When we turned to go downtown I clapped, because I could see the giant Paul Bunyan man and the giant sign he holds that says, "I HELPED BUILD MANISTIQUE 100 YEARS AGO." My tummy tickled, because whenever we see Paul Bunyan, I know that pretty soon we get to see Mama, too.

Dad parked the car in front of the tall yellow house. "We're finally here!" I said.

"I get to ring the door bell!" Catherine hollered.

"No way,'" I said pushing my way out of the car. "You did last time. It's my turn!" Dad put his finger over his mouth. "Shhhhh, be good now," he said. "I don't think any of you want to sit in the car on a night like tonight, do you?"

Dad carried Monica to the door and he let *her* ring the bell. Luke carried Anna. We waited and waited on the steps under the light over the door. Bernadette grabbed snow and put it on her tongue.

"Bernadette, there's dirt in that snow!" I said.

See, Dad gets mad whenever we eat snow, because he thinks there're little bugs in the snow. And he hates when we break icicles off the house and suck on them, because he thinks there're bugs in the icicles, too. We have looked and looked for bugs, but we still haven't found any. One time an icicle on the roof of the house was so long that Monica reached it and broke it off. But it was too heavy for her to carry, so she gave it to me. I started sucking on it and went running to the house to show Mama. When I got to the porch I tripped and fell, and the icicle cut my mouth and made it bloody. Mama heard me crying and came to get me. "Oh, my gosh!" she said. "You've cut the roof of your mouth!" Mama took me into the house and rocked me until my boo-boo was better.

Mama is always nice. Once when I cut my knees on the fence and twice when I got scratches from the blackberry patch, Mama made my boo-boos all better. Mama very softly washed my boo-boo. Then she put the medicine from the little blue bottle on my boo-boos—the Mercurochrome. (We don't like the red medicine— the Iodine, because it stings). Then she kissed my boo-boos and they got all better! And one time I went running through the big mud puddle after it rained and I stepped on a piece of glass. It got stuck in the bottom of my foot. Mama very carefully took the glass out of my foot. She kept asking me questions like, "What grade are you in at school, Donna Jean?"

"Mama," I said, "you know I'm in second grade!"

"Who's your teacher?"

"Mama, you know my teacher is Mrs. Webster!"

"Ha, ha!" Mama said. "The glass is out!" And she showed it to me.

We won't let Dad even take out slivers! But we let him pull out our baby teeth. Once Dad said that he was going to pull my tooth out with his pliers, so I screamed. But he was just joking. Instead, he grabbed my tooth with his fingers and said, "Abracadabra!" and the tooth came out, and it didn't even bleed! I put my tooth under my pillow so the tooth fairy would come and give me money, like she gave to Sarah and Bernadette. They each got three pennies, so I thought I'd get three pennies from her, too. But in the morning when I lifted up my pillow, nothing was there. I started crying. Mama put her arm around me and said, "The tooth fairy must be awfully busy these days. Try again on *Friday* night. Then she'll have more time."

Sure enough! On Saturday morning when I lifted my pillow, money was under it. "A Nickel!" I screamed. Quickly I ran to ask Dad if he'd take me to the store so that I could buy a popsicle.

"But, then your sisters will want one, too!" he said. He put his hand over his chin and moved it back and forth, as he looked up to the ceiling. Then he looked back down and pointed his finger at me and said, "Oh that's right, I almost forgot, the popsicle truck tipped over!"

☞

A woman sitting a few rows back at the workshop began to chuckle. I sat up, blew my nose, wiped my eyes, tossed my hair to the back of my neck and then looked in her direction. Very adult-like I said, "That was the ninth time that year that the popsicle truck had tipped over! I guess it was my dad's way of keeping me satisfied, and us kids from fighting."

"You betcha," an elderly man replied.

"Elisabeth!" one of the counselors said trying to get her attention. When she looked he pointed to his watch.

"Oh my," she said, "it's that time already!" she stood up. "You're excused until tomorrow morning."

Chapter Ten

Before daylight came to the Catskills, I walked with others to the conference building. I gripped my scarf tightly as the brisk wind blew. Losing my scarf would mean losing what little I had left of my mother, although lately I was feeling a close connection to her. Especially since leaving for New York. I felt as though she were my personal angel, guiding me. I took the ends of the silk scarf and brushed it over my cold, chapped face.

"Hey," Kevin said, elbowing me. "You were sure in deep thought. I've been asking if you think it's going to snow today?"

"I hope so," I said, a bit embarrassed that he had startled me. But to pretend he hadn't, I added to the conversation. "I love it when it snows—especially blizzards. There's a certain serenity about it, as long as I'm safe inside."

"My thoughts exactly," he said, smiling.

I listened, as he and the others continued to chat along the way. In some respect Kevin, a Californian, reminded me of Bryan. I had spoken with him a few times and, like Bryan, he always seemed poised and confident. In just the few days that I had been in his company, I could tell he was a joyful personality, with not a care in the world. He was always joking around and making someone laugh, despite the cloud of grief that encompassed the workshop. I assumed he came to the workshop as one of the several Hospice

Volunteers to gain knowledge on how best to help those in their final stages of life, and to help their families that would be left behind.

"Hello, Penelope!" he said, to a woman who was passing by. "So, do you think you'll take the stand today?"

"Are you asking if I plan to share my life with the group?" she remarked.

"Yes," he said. "There's not too many of us left that haven't."

As they continued to chat, I eyed Kevin more closely. I watched his saddle-brown hair blow in the wind. I guessed him to be around thirty and figured him to be quite a popular person by the charm he exhibited. I envied his calm, yet bubbly personality. And, as the old saying goes, "If looks could kill," I wondered how it was that my heart was still beating. Then, right then and there, I slowed my walk to have words with God. I asked Him why I couldn't experience a life less problematic, like Kevin's.

Kevin held the door of the conference building. "Slacked your pace, did you?" he chuckled.

"I must have," I admitted as I entered the building, then thanked him for waiting. I took my usual seat and watched as Kevin visited along the way to get the songbooks that he so graciously volunteered to pass out each morning. I watched as he joyfully sang *Edelweiss*. I envied the serenity he had. It made me think how serenity of heart and mind had only visited me on occasion, never staying long enough to even take root.

After songs, the day continued with the usual moment of silence. Then Elisabeth passed out paper and crayons and asked everyone to draw a picture. "Don't think about what you're going to draw," she said. "Just draw. Let your subconscious do the work for you."

When everyone was finished, she collected the drawings, studied them for a few minutes then asked Kevin if he could join her at the front of the room. Kevin reluctantly stepped forward. Elisabeth held his drawing up for all to see.

"Why do you suppose you have colored the bottom half of your paper solid black, while the top half is colored in red jagged streaks? What's been happening in your life?" she asked.

Kevin shrugged his shoulders.

"The color black usually signifies grief and red most often

alerts us to the emotion of anger." she said.

Kevin nodded. "It's about my fiancée. I've been very angry with her. I've been angry with myself, too. I should've known that something, obviously, was wrong. It's been over two years since she left me and I can't get her out of my mind."

"Once you have faced the pain," Elisabeth said, "then you'll be able to let go. What happened?" she asked.

"I don't even want to go there," he said. "I've closed the book on that chapter of my life."

"You struck me as being quite happy," said James, one of the counselors.

"It's a façade," Kevin said, throwing his hands up over his face and dropping to the mattress. "She committed suicide!" he shouted. "My fiancee killed herself and I'm probably to blame."

"So you found it easier to 'act happy' than to deal with what made her so unhappy," James said. "More than likely it was her inability to cope with whatever it was that was bothering her. And unfortunately, suicide is a permanent solution to a temporary problem."

Kevin grabbed the rubber hose and started beating on the phone books. The more he hit them the more apparent his rage became. He called for his fiancee by name and begged her to let him know what he had done wrong. He pleaded with her to tell him, then and there, why she had not confided in him about the plan to end her life.

"Do you see what's happening here?" Elisabeth asked after Kevin lay exhausted. "Kevin isn't only grieving his fiancee, but also for a future that never came to be. There is such extreme guilt when a person loses a loved one through suicide. They have to work extra hard to realize that it wasn't their fault. The deceased was destined to leave this world someday, like everyone else who dies. Unfortunately, suicide has such a stigma to it. I prefer to think of it this way. Some people die a natural death, and some die from cancer, or Aids, car accidents, fires, and some of suicide, to mention just a few. If we change 'committed suicide' to 'died of suicide' it takes on a different light. In some countries suicide is honorable. Kevin," she said, taking his hand, "I encourage you to think this way regarding your fiancee's death. If you think of it in this respect, the healing will begin."

Kevin stood and embraced Elisabeth. As he walked to his seat, Elisabeth motioned me to the front and then she rummaged through the pile of papers. "Your picture," she said, holding it up. Do you have an insight into it? I think it's pretty self-explanatory."

Without even thinking about it when I drew it, I had drawn a road on the paper. Ironically, my previous memories were about being in route with my family to go visit with my mother.

"It's a road leading to nowhere," I exclaimed.

"That's probably how you feel," she said, and then she encouraged me to pick up on the memories of the previous day.

⌒

"When we finally made it to Uncle Roy and Aunt Geraldine's house, we hurried to the door. We were so excited. We couldn't wait to see Mama. We stood on the steps under the porch light.

" I'm cold," Catherine cried.

"Ring the bell again," Dad said. So she rang it, but still no one came to the door.

"Bernadette," I shouted, "your coat has blood on it!"

Bernadette was shivering. She stuck her tongue out into the wind. "It burns," she cried.

"Maybe the bell is broken," Dad said, so he knocked hard on the door. Finally we heard someone coming. I could only see the top of Auntie's head as she slowly opened the door. At first I thought she was playing peek-a-boo with us, but when she came out from behind it, I saw tears popping out of her eyes. "Oh," she cried, as she covered her face with her hands. "It's terrible, John!"

"What's so terrible?" Dad asked.

"*I'm so sorry!*" she said. "I tried to call your neighbor, but she told me you had already left."

"What on earth's the matter? Where's Rosie?" Dad said, as he pushed his way into the house.

"She's left us!"

"WHAT?" Dad said, as if he didn't hear what Auntie had said.

"Rosie, she's gone! She has passed away!"

"NO! NO!" Dad shouted. "*That can't be true!*" And he ran to the couch where Mama was to be. None of us stopped to take off our shoes.

"I wonder where Mama went," I said to Catherine when we got into the living room.

"I don't know," she said and ran to the piano. Monica ran too, and crawled up on the piano bench. I walked over to Uncle Roy. He was kneeling and praying by the big red chair. When he looked at me, he started to cry. Then he stretched out his arms for me to come and get a hug, so I went over by him. He was hugging me when I saw Mama's black scarf and her fake teeth powder on the lamp table, so I took Uncle Roy's arms off my neck and went over to it. Anna came with me. We sprinkled Mama's fake teeth powder over our arms. I thought Uncle Roy was going to yell at us when he saw us with her stuff, like he always yells, but he didn't say anything! He didn't even come to chase us, or try to steal kisses. Nope, Uncle Roy just kept crying.

"Maybe Mama got mad at Uncle Roy and Aunt Geraldine, like she got mad at us sometimes," I said to Anna. "Maybe that's why she left."

"Maybe Mama went to Josephine's again," Anna said.

"That's what I think," I said. "Like the day Mama left because we kept bickering. Remember what Mama said, Anna? She said, 'I'm leaving, and I'm not coming back!' But she did! So, she'll come back, again," I told Anna.

When Auntie's phone rang, I ran to the kitchen. I heard Auntie talking to somebody. When she hung it up she said to Dad, "Rosie's still at the hospital."

Sarah heard Auntie talking about Mama and she started screaming, so Dad lifted her up. Luke heard too, and went running out the back door yelling, "No, not Ma!" Soon, lots of people were coming in the front door, and they were crying, too. I didn't know why the people were crying. "I don't think they got the chicken pox," I told Anna.

See, one time, Sarah got the chicken pox. At first she thought that a mosquito had bitten her. But the bump got bigger and bigger, and then she got another bump. Mama thought that a spider must have bitten Sarah. But when more and more bumps came, Mama said, "Sarah, I think you've got the chicken pox!" We laughed at Sarah's chicken pox, but Sarah cried, so I called her a big baby. Sarah scratched her chicken pox everyday because they kept bugging her and making her cry. Bernadette and I yelled at Sarah to stop crying, but she kept crying, because she didn't want those chickens pox on her. Mama said, "It's not nice to tell someone not to cry, if they need to cry." So we didn't tell Sarah not to cry anymore.

Next Monica got the chicken pox, then Catherine, then Bernadette, then Anna, then me! When I cried, because I couldn't go to school, Sarah didn't laugh. And she didn't laugh when I scratched the big chicken pox that was on my nose and made it bleed. Nope, Sarah didn't say anything. So I didn't say anything either when I saw the people crying at Auntie's house. I just sat in the corner of the living room and blocked my ears and watched them.

⌒

Anna followed the black cat up the stairs and I followed Anna. I was glad Mama was at the hospital, because if she saw us going up the stairs, she'd be really mad. I counted the thirteen steps to the top. I wondered why Mama didn't tell anyone that she went to the hospital.

Upstairs Anna and I went into a little room that had a Raggedy Ann doll, without eyes, lying on top of an ironing board. Anna took the Raggedy Ann doll and hugged it, then threw it on the floor.

"Anna!" I said, "you have to put things back, or we'll be in big trouble!"

We went potty in Auntie's indoor bathroom. But when I pushed down the handle of the toilet, no water came to push the pee and poop into the floor, like at Grandma Jacques' house. And when we tried to wash our hands, the sink wouldn't pour out water either. We didn't know what to do. Mama says we should always wash our hands. Grandma Jacques calls our hands patties. Dad said patties are Irish hands.

Anna found a round dish with a cover on it. She pulled the cover off. Inside was smelly powder. "Can I have that?" I asked. She wouldn't give it to me, so I tried to get the powder from her. She finally let go and I fell on the floor, and the powder fell on top of me.

"Now see what you made me do?" I said, coughing powder out of my mouth.

Anna climbed onto the counter. She opened the big cupboard doors. I counted four big towels and seven washcloths. And on the top shelf I saw a big jar with little pink curlers in it and a small jar with bobby pins. "Wow!" I said, pointing to the jars, "Mama would like those!"

Anna jumped down from the counter, so I climbed up. I stood on the counter. I opened the cupboard doors and held unto the door handles. "I can swing on these," I said to Anna, and I swung out to show her. When I turned around, Anna was in the bathtub and was trying to turn the water on. "I want to take a bath," she said. I jumped down from the counter and hurried to the tub to be sure no hot water came out, because Grandma Jacques once told us about a little boy who climbed into a bathtub and turned on the hot water and it burned him. He had to go to the hospital. "He was nearly dead," Grandma said.

"What's dead mean, Grandma?" Catherine asked that day. Grandma told us that it's when a person can't see or hear or touch or taste or smell anything anymore.

⌒

Anna turned the bathtub handles, but no water came out. "Come on," I said to her, "let's go see what's in the other rooms."

We opened a bedroom door and turned on the light. Boxes were all over the floor and the window shades were down. On the bed I saw a lady's black dress and a lady's black hat. The black hat had like a black spider web coming down from the top of it. On the floor were black peaky-toed hi-heel shoes—like the red hi-heels Auntie wears when she comes to our house wearing her red coat and big red hat.

We could hear the people down stairs crying and wondered why they were, and we wondered if Mama had came back yet, so we listened to hear if she was talking.

"I'm going to put this black dress on," I told Anna. I put on the black hat, too, and the high-heeled shoes. Anna started to laugh and said, "Donna Jean, you're very, very tall now."

I looked in the mirror that was on the back of the door. We

giggled because the spider web thing on the hat kept sticking in my mouth when I talked.

Anna and I climbed onto the bed, and as we jumped we did the *ItseyBitsey Spider*. Once we thought we could hear someone coming, so we hid in the closet until no more sounds came. I whispered to Anna, "We better go back downstairs." So I took off the black things and put them back on the bed. I closed the bedroom door, then noticed another door, so I opened it and we went inside. Everything was very, very pretty. I thought we were in *Alice in Wonderland*. Each wall of the bedroom was a different color. One wall was yellow, one pink, one blue, and one green. Anna and I ran to the pink wall, because there was a pretty white crib and dresser by it. I stood up on the edge of the crib. I saw a picture lying on a pretty pink blanket that was inside of the crib. I looked at the picture. The picture was of a little baby. The little baby had on a white dress and a white bonnet. The baby was sleeping in a box and flowers were all around the box. Someone spelled out words on the bottom of the picture that said, "Our Little Princess, Anne Marie." Diapers, baby bottles, baby powder and baby oil were on a table next to the crib. It was a table to dress a baby on, like one I saw at my cousin Bobbie Lou's house. Anna and I rubbed some of the baby oil onto our tummies. It smelled pretty. "We better not be upstairs," I said.

Anna wouldn't come with me, so I went back downstairs alone. I counted the thirteen steps and took ten giant steps through the crying people into the kitchen. Monica was in the kitchen eating a candy blackjack.

"Where'd you get that, Monica?" I asked.

"Aunt Nearldine," she said.

"It's Aunt *Geraldine!*" I said.

I tried to find some blackjacks, too, but I couldn't. I saw a pan of cookies sitting on the stove. The cookies weren't cooked, but I ate one anyway. Then I skipped to the dining room. I could see Bernadette and Catherine in the living room. They were sitting at the piano playing *Doctor, Doctor Can You Tell*. Monica ran by them and was trying to get up on the piano bench again, but Catherine kept pushing her down. Monica's mouth was dripping blackjack unto the bench.

I opened the two glass doors of Auntie's bedroom. I could

smell her perfume. I went to the little dresser with the mirror and sat on the little stool. I counted all the different colors of fingernail polish and lipstick and smelled her seven perfumes that were on the little dresser. Then I put some of the fire-red lipstick on and put dabs of it on my cheeks, like Mama. With the brown pencil, I made eyebrows like Auntie's. I opened the top little drawer of the dresser. Auntie's necklace and earrings, the ones with the big white beads were there, so I put them on. The earrings pinched my ears. Next I saw Auntie's big red hat, so I put it on, too. I looked at myself in the mirror and watched myself spray perfume over me. "Oh me, oh my," I said to myself, "I really must be going."

"Yes you better!" Bernadette shouted. "What do you think you're doing? You know we're not allowed in here!" Take off Auntie's things! And get out, now!"

"Can't I even leave the lipstick on?"

"No!" she said, "and you better hurry and get it off before she sees you."

After I took everything off, I skipped out to the living room, then through the dining room, and back to the bedroom. Bernadette was still in Auntie's bedroom. I saw her spraying perfume onto her arm. "You can't be in here, either!" I yelled.

"I know!" she whispered. "Get out!"

Lots of people kept coming to Auntie's house. Monica was sleeping on Josephine's lap, in the living room. I wondered why Josephine was at our Auntie's house, because Mama once told us that the only way Josephine would ever leave Garden, was if someone died. "Maybe someone died," I thought. Luke was crying on the couch, so I sat by him. I rubbed his head. I noticed Mama's purse again. I went and opened it and looked inside. I took out her watch and looked at it. "Mama will get very, very mad if I put this on," I said to myself. So I put her watch back into her purse.

"Daaad," Catherine cried, "I want to go home."

"I know you do," he said. "I better get the kids home," he told the people. Then he asked John to go out and start the car, so it would be warm for us. But when John came back in the house, he said that the car wouldn't start. So Uncle Roy's neighbor said that he'd go jump-start it. And jumping on it worked, because when John came back in again, he said, "Jumping it did the trick."

Aunt Geraldine handed my dad a quilt. "Here," she said,

"put it on the kids, for the ride home."

I ran to the car to get away from the ladies who wanted to give me hugs and kisses. "I only like Mama's hugs and kisses," I said, and ran out the door. It wasn't snowing anymore. I looked up at the sky. I could see a shining star. John was sitting in the car. "Look, John, at the pretty star?" I said, pointing to it. It just winked at me!" That's when I noticed that John had Dad's corncob pipe, and he was smoking it. I told him that he'd be in big trouble if Dad found out. He got mad and said, "Mind your own business, you little asshole."

"Oh, oh," I said. "I'm telling Mama that you swore."

John stuck his arm out the car window and then hit Dad's pipe against the door. "There, it's empty! You satisfied?"

He got out of the car and slammed the door really hard. I watched as he ran to the fat, tall tree. He punched the tree really hard, then screamed. I wondered why he kept punching and punching and punching the big tree. Then he shook his hand, like he does when he's trying to warm up his fingers.

"Why did you punch the tree?" I asked.

"Just shut-up and mind your own business," he hollered.

"What's the matter John?"

"You just don't get it! Do you? Get in the car," he said. John was kicking the car when I rolled over the front seat into the back.

"That's not nice," I hollered through the glass. "You're being mean to the car! God doesn't like it when we're mean."

"Oh really, Dick Tracy! Maybe I just don't care what God thinks. You can tell him to go to hell!"

"Oh, oh," I thought. "If Mama were here, she'd soap John's mouth!"

"Enough," Dad said, as he opened the car door.

Everyone got in. Bernadette sat by a door in the back and so did I. Catherine, Anna, and Sarah sat in the middle of us and Monica was on Sarah's lap. Dad reminded us not to put our feet on the cardboard that was over the holes in the floor, when he reached in to cover us with the quilt.

On the way home Dad asked us if we were warm enough. We said we were, but I could hear the cardboard lifting up and down and feel the wind down by my feet. Suddenly, I remembered that I hadn't showed Mama my color crayon nails and that Monica hadn't given her color crayon kisses. "Dad, Dad," I said, "We have to go back to Auntie's house. I didn't show Mama my polished fingernails?" Dad didn't hear me so I talked louder. "Pretty please, Dad? Monica forgot to give Mama color crayon kisses, too!" But my dad wouldn't answer me. I don't think he heard, because Luke and Sarah were crying so loud. So I asked him again, and when I did, John turned around and yelled at me.

"Can't you just shut your trap?" he shouted.

"Just forget it Donna Jean!" Bernadette said. "And Catherine, quit sucking your thumb!" But Catherine sucked it anyway.

When we turned by the Paul Bunyan man, I heard a noise go clankety clank. I told Dad about the noise, but Dad didn't hear me again. Then John said, "Donna Jean, don't worry about it. It's probably just a little stone that got caught in the hubcap when we changed the flat tire."

I put my head back against the door and listened to the little stone. It rolled over and over in the hubcap. "It's all alone!" I said to myself. "I bet it's scared."

When we got home, I asked Dad if I could get the rolling stone out of the hubcap.

"In the morning," he said. "We have company."

"Company!" I said. "It's too dark!"

Dad carried Monica and John carried Anna to the house and put them into bed. They got to sleep with their clothes on. Uncle Herb and Aunt Gereatha were at our house. "They must have come to see Grandma," I thought. See, Grandma Jacques isn't just my dad's mother, she's Aunt Gereatha's, Uncle Freddy's, Uncle Ernie's, Uncle Leo's and lots of other people's mother, too.

Grandma cried when she gave my dad a hug. And when Aunt Gereatha hugged my dad, Grandma Jacques looked at her and said, "Oh, Rosie, there you are! I knew it couldn't be true!"

"Mother, it's me, your daughter, Gereatha!" Aunt Gereatha said. Grandma's eyes closed and she fell to the floor. Uncle Herb ran to her. "She fainted!" he said. He picked her up and carried her to the couch. Aunt Gereatha put a wet washcloth on Grandma's forehead and then Grandma's eyes opened and she started to talk again. Uncle Herb took Catherine, Bernadette and me into our bedroom. He told us stories and he gave us horseyback rides on

109

top of his shoulders. When we were tired, he tucked us into bed and said prayers with us. I prayed for Mama to come home with our new baby.

Uncle Herb kissed us goodnight, and said he'd see us in the morning.

"Uncle Herb," I asked, "when do we get to see Mama again?" Uncle Herb put his head down and then took his big white hanky out of his pocket. He wiped his eyes and nose and said something, but I couldn't hear him.

"When?" I asked again.

"In a couple days," he said. He looked down to the floor, shook his head back and forth, and then left the bedroom.

"See, Sarah," I said, when she came into the bedroom. "You don't have to cry. Uncle Herb said that Mama's coming home in just two more days!" But when I said that, Sarah cried even harder!

Chapter Eleven

S arah was crying when I woke up the next morning. It was still dark outside, but people were at our house already. I could hear them talking. I jumped out of bed and peeked into the kitchen. I saw Uncle Herb, Aunt Gereatha and some of our neighbors, like Roland and Thatis, Josephine and Steve, and Molly and Paul. I heard Uncle Herb talking low to Josephine. I heard him say, "Grandma went kind-of berserk last night. She thought Gereatha was Rosie!"

Then I heard someone knock. When Dad opened the door—there was Mrs. Webster. "Oh no!" I said to myself. I ran and jumped on the bed. "Wake up, Bernadette! Wake up, Catherine! Mrs. Webster's at our house!"

"Who?" Bernadette asked, wiping the morning glories out of her eyes. (Dad calls that icky stuff in the corners of our eyes, cat shit. Mama gets mad at him for saying that. She says the icky stuff is morning glories because it's the glory of God to give us another morning to wake up to. But I don't think my dad cares about the 'glory of God,' because he *still* calls it cat shit!)

"My school teacher! She's here—at our house!"

Bernadette didn't believe me, so she ran to the bedroom doorway to see. She pushed her long hair from her face. "Yikes, it's true!" she said, and jumped back on the bed.

111

"Maybe she's here to tell Dad that I played the piano without permission."

"No," Bernadette said, "it's because of Mama."

"Oh," I said.

We were afraid to go in the kitchen, so my sisters and I played Statue of Liberty on the bed. Bernadette, Catherine, Anna and I jumped and jumped and jumped, with our hand up high in the air, until Catherine and I bumped heads. "Ouch!" we screamed.

Uncle Herb came running into the bedroom. "What the heck is all the racket about in here?" he asked. We told him and he said, "I'll make you girls *a deal.*"

"I don't want to play cards," I said. And Catherine said that she didn't even know how to deal yet.

"No, no! Not cards!" he said. "The *deal* I'm going to make with you is, if you girls are good, I'll give you all horsy back rides again today, like I did last night." So we played *Rock, Paper, Scissors.* I liked playing *Rock, Paper, Scissors*, because it's the game Mama likes playing. "It's a quiet game and I don't have to get out of bed to play," Mama says. Mama always wins. One time I got mad when she won, because she laughed when I lost. Mama put her hand under my chin, "Donna Jean, it's just a game. You're going to win, too, sometime. Do you want Mama to quit?" Sarah and Bernadette got mad at me for getting mad at Mama, so I told Mama that I wanted her to play. And sure enough, just like Mama said, I won the next game!

⌒

"Who wants a horseyback ride?" Uncle Herb asked. Catherine, Anna, and I screamed, "I do, I do." So one by one he galloped us on his back into the kitchen. When it was my turn, I wondered why people were coming in and out of our house.

"Their breakfast is ready," Aunt Gereatha said. So Uncle Herb put me down on a chair.

"I don't like *oatmeal!*" I told her.

"You better eat up," she said. When she and Grandma weren't looking, I put spoons of sugar on my oatmeal and so did Monica, Anna, and Catherine. Bernadette tattletaled on us, but no one heard her, so I put more sugar on my oatmeal, then so did my sisters. Then we raced to see who could eat their oatmeal the fastest. Catherine won! Monica didn't eat any. She just squeezed the oatmeal through her fingers then rubbed it into her hair.

"Monica's being bad!" I hollered.

"Oh, heavens!" Aunt Gereatha said, grabbing the bowl from her. She lifted Monica from the highchair. "This high-chair is going to be the new baby's highchair when Mama gets home from the hospital," I said. Aunt Gereatha didn't say anything. I thought she was going to say, "That's right. Monica will have to use a big girl's chair!" But nope, Aunt Gereatha just kept washing the tray.

I went by Grandma and asked her if Mama had gotten the baby out of her tummy yet and if she was still at the hospital. I don't think Grandma heard me, because she didn't answer. So I asked her really, really loud. "Grandma, did Mama get the baby out of her tummy yet? Is that why everyone's at our house?"

"Run along and play. Grandma's got things to do," she said. Suddenly I remembered why all the people were at our house, so I told Catherine. "They're going to help Mama with our new baby, like Aunt Celia helped Mama when she brought Monica home from the hospital."

See, even before my mama went to the hospital, some high-school girls came to do her housework. I liked it when they came. Like Diane and Jerlyn, Jeannie and Mary Ann, Mary Jane and other girls, too. Sometimes they'd stop ironing, or scrubbing, or doing dishes and they'd talk to us. Mama liked the big girls being at our house, too. I heard her telling the high-school girls that she wouldn't know what she'd do without them. I was in Mama's bedroom the night she asked Dad if Diane could be the baby's godmother and if Luke could be the godfather. I thought Mary Jane would be the godmother, because she brought a big wreath for us. Candies were tied all over the wreath. When I saw her come into our house with it, my eyes got big like they do when Dad brings home ice cream. After Mary Jane left, Mama told us that we had to wait until Christmas to start eating the candies. But by the time Christmas day came, there was only one candy cane left on the wreath.

☞

Anyway, more people kept coming to our house and getting

in the way of the marble game that Catherine and I were playing. By suppertime there were tons of people at our house. Uncle Ernie and Aunt Viola came with goulash. Uncle Homer and Aunt Alice and my cousin Della came with scalloped potatoes and Uncle Elmer and Aunt Betty brought beans. Mimein, a lady from our church, came too. She's the lady with the mustache. (My dad said one day after church, that when Mimein blows her nose it sounds like the foghorn of a ship!) She brought bread that she made—lots of loaves, like Mama used to make and she brought jars of jelly, too. She opened a jar of strawberry jelly and a jar of beet jelly and put them on the table. After she cut the bread into slices she said, "Well, don't just be looking, dig in!" Mimein poured coffee for the grown-ups and put jelly on Monica and Anna's bread.

I pulled on Mimein dress. "Your bread is yummy!" I said. "My Mama can make bread, too!"

"Oh dear! You poor little girl," she said, and she rubbed the top of my head.

☞

All day long people kept coming to our house. My dad made Catherine and me stop playing marbles, because he was afraid someone would slip on one. So instead of having fun, we had to get hugs and kisses. People tried to kiss Sarah, too, but she hid behind the kitchen stove. Sarah really, really, really hates hugs and kisses. But when Aunt Joanne and Uncle George came from far, far away, they found where Sarah was hiding and gave her kisses anyway. I was glad they came, because they bought a new dress for each of my sisters and me. Each dress was a different color with a can-can to match. Mine was yellow! They also bought new shirts and pants for Luke and John. Then when Uncle Freddy and Aunt Joyce came, they came with a new suit for Dad.

Aunt Celia cried and cried really, really hard when she got to our house. She's Mama's sister. I was glad she was at our house, because she has a very, very long braid. I ran to the couch where she was sitting, so I could play with her braid, like I always do. "Maybe later," she said, and she put her braid around to the front of her. She started to cry again and put me on her lap and kept hugging and hugging me.

"Why are you crying, Aunt Celia?" I asked.

"For your mother," she said.

"Mama's coming home from the hospital pretty soon with our new baby," I said.

I think Aunt Celia was *very, very* happy to hear that Mama was coming home, because she lifted me up and gave me a long, long kiss on the cheek.

At suppertime, another knock came. I ran and opened the door—there was Mrs. Boudreau—my kindergarten teacher. Mrs. Boudreau brought some food for us, too. She talked with Dad and then she lifted Monica into her arms. She looked at Monica. "What a pretty baby, just like a doll!" she said. I saw a tear roll down Mrs. Boudreau's cheek. "I really must be going." She put Monica down then took my dad's hand. "I'm so sorry, Mr. Jacques. If there's anything I can do, please let me know," she said, then hurried out the door.

I think teacher was sorry because she scratched my dad's hand with her long, red fingernail when she handed him the cake she made for us.

That night Molly and Josephine did our dishes while Grandma and Aunt Celia washed us up and helped us get into our pajamas. Just when we were giving Dad hugs and kisses good night, we heard knock, knock, knock, again. Dad opened the door and Mr. and Mrs. Green came in. The Greens are old, old and have white, white hair like Grandma.

"I don't want to go to bed. I want to stay up, so I can hear Harry laugh," I told Grandma. But she told me that I had to go to bed. "Besides," she whispered, "Harry laughs loud enough to hear him all over the house anyway."

From our bedroom, I did hear Harry laughing and coughing while he talked, and I heard him say, "You sure have struck a note of bad luck, Johnny." (I think he said 'bad luck' because of that flat tire. Because when we got the flat, I heard Dad say that if it weren't for bad luck, he'd have no luck at all.)

Harry talked about Mama and how nice she was, and then he talked about Mr. Kennedy. "We need a Democrat this time around! He better become the next President of the United States or this country won't be worth a da*mn!*"

"Oh, oh," I said to myself, "Harry said a bad word. If Mama were here, she'd say "Ta Ta, Harry, the children." (I don't think

Harry ever hears Mama ask him not to swear because he keeps saying more bad words.) Harry kept talking and my dad didn't argue with him or say anything to make Harry mad, like Dad always does. Nope. All I heard my dad say was, *nothing*! And after a little while Mrs. Green said, "It's about time you shut that trap about all that President nonsense, Harry, and try to remember why we came here tonight. In fact, I think it's time to let Johnny get to bed!"

While they were going out the door, we heard an old shaky voice coming in our house. "By golly, Johnny, I'd have been here sooner, but I waited for Jerry to get home from town. I knew he'd want to be with Luke."

I knew the shaky voice was Mrs. LaLonde, even if I couldn't see her. She always says, "By golly, Johnny," no matter what else she says. I heard her say that the pies she brought were blackberry. I could hear Jerry talking to Luke across the hall in the boys' bedroom. After a little while, I could hear him crying, just like Luke. (Jerry and Luke always make pies with Mama. Sometimes Mama lets me help, too.)

"I wish Mama would get back home so nobody would cry any more," I thought.

Dad said good night to Mrs. LaLonde and to Grandma, then went to bed. For a long time after, I heard Grandma and Mrs. LaLonde whispering. Sometimes it sounded like they were crying. I thought they were too old to cry, so I had Anna sneak up to see if it was true. Because she's little, she wouldn't get in trouble. But Anna didn't come back to tell us if Grandma was crying. Instead, I heard her asking for a piece of pie. Our grandma said, "No," but Mrs. LaLonde said, "Oh, go ahead and let her have some, Anna." See, Anna's my grandmother's name, too! Catherine and I heard what she said so we got up to have pie, too. Dad heard us, so he got back up.

"It's been a long, long day," he said. "Maybe a couple of you could come and sleep with me to make more room for Aunt Celia and Grandma."

Anna, Catherine and I ran to Dad's bed. "Dad," I said pulling the blankets over us, "When can we go see Mama again?"

"Not tomorrow, but the next day," he said.

"Why can't we go see her tomorrow?"

"Tomorrow," he said, "we're going to pick up Mark at the airport. He's coming home to see your mother one last time."

"Yippee," we said, then we snuggled to each other. "Did you hear Dad?" I whispered to my sisters. "He said the day after tomorrow we can go see Mama." I started to giggle and Anna whispered, "I'm going to show Mama where Puff scratched me."

"I'm going to show her my new haircut," Catherine said.

"I'm going to tell her about all the crying people," I told my sisters, as I looked through Mama's bedroom window. I stared at the stars in the sky until my eyes felt like jumbo marbles.

Chapter Twelve

The next morning, I ran to the kitchen. Sarah was sitting on Dad's lap and Grandma was rocking Monica. Monica was crying, but then she stopped, looked up at Grandma and asked, "Mama gone ta tore?" Grandma couldn't understand what she said, so I told Grandma that Monica wanted to know if Mama was gone to the store. I waited to hear Grandma tell her that Mama was at the hospital and would be coming home soon, but Grandma didn't say anything. So Monica started to cry again.

After breakfast I ran and got dressed. When I got back to the kitchen, Dad was gone. "Where did my dad go?" I asked Grandma. Grandma told me that my dad went to the Funerals' house to pick Mama out a pretty dress to wear home. So I ran to tell Sarah and Luke that they didn't have to cry any more, because Mama was coming home. But when I told Sarah what Grandma said, she cried even harder. Luke blew his nose, like my dad kept doing during the night, and then he screamed as loud as he could, punched the wall, then laid back on the bed and started crying again.

When I got back into the kitchen, I said to Grandma. "I've never been to the *Funerals'* house before, I don't know those people. But I've been to the Guertins' house. They've got lots of chickens. Lots more than us. And I've been to Pscodnas' house. Mama thinks Josephine Pscondna is the fastest potato peeler in the whole wide world." I wanted to tell my grandma about the day Mama took just me to the Cotas' house, but Grandma started talking to my aunts and uncles.

⌒

"Mark's plane will be in at four," Dad said, when he got home from the Funerals' house. "So I'll leave here by two to pick him up. I'll take the bigger girls with me and leave the two little ones here."

"They'll be fine, John," Aunt LuLu said. "I've bought them some new toys to play with."

Inside the big building at the airport, we watched for Mark's plane. Sarah kept crying for Mama, so Dad said, "Wait here!" When he came back he had a bottle of pop for each of us. We all grabbed for the purple bottle, but Dad let Sarah pick first. I got the red pop.

"Why do we get pop, Dad?" I asked.

"To make you feel better," he said.

"Am I sick?" I asked.

"Here comes Marks's plane now," he said, pointing out the window.

"Yippee," I said.

Dad looked like he had tears in his eyes as we watched the plane come to a stop. It took a long, long time before the man with the wagon-like-thing pulled it over to the plane and then opened the plane door. I counted thirteen people come out and walk down the twelve steps, but Mark didn't.

"I hope he's on it!" Dad said. Soon as he said that, Mark walked out of the plane.

"I saw him first," Catherine hollered.

"I did!" I said. "I saw his shiny gold buttons!"

Mark put on his Marine hat and threw his duffel bag over his shoulder. He saw us looking through the big window and waved. We waved back and then ran to wait for him by the door. When Dad opened the glass door, Mark walked through and dropped his duffel bag unto the floor. He threw his arms around Dad and cried on my dad's shoulder, like Mama cried on Mark's shoulder when he left for the Marines. I thought I heard my dad crying, too, but I don't think dads cry.

My sisters and I hugged Mark's legs, except for Sarah. Sarah kept looking out the big window, and crying. Mark let go of Dad, wiped his eyes with the back of his hand, and patted the tops of our hair. "Holy Mary, mother of God," he said as he made the sign-of-the-cross, then hurried to Sarah. He picked her up and she hugged him and lay her head on his shoulder as we walked out to the car.

After we got in the car, Mark turned around to the back seat. "I see that you girls got pop," he said.

"It's to make us feel better," Catherine said. "Because we're sick."

"No, we're not! Mama is!" I said.

"Oh," he said and turned back around. Then I heard him say to Dad, "The whole time on the plane I kept thinking that it must have been the baby that died, but when I saw the girls with pop…"

Mark started to cry—then stopped, waited for awhile, then started talking again. "Then I knew it must be true…that Ma was the one who died."

Mark cried and talked and cried and talked all the way home. And he cried again when he saw all my aunts and uncles and cousins who were waiting for him at our house.

⌒

Dad didn't make us go to school on Monday, or Tuesday, or Wednesday, or Thursday. "If Mama finds out, she's going to be very mad," I said to Dad.

"It's okay," he said, but I still thought Mama would be mad. One time when Aunt Celia came to our house, I begged Mama to let me stay home from school, but she wouldn't let me, unless I was sick.

When we were eating lunch, I asked my aunts why we didn't have to go to school again. "When you're bigger you'll know why," Aunt Gereatha said.

After lunch, Aunt Joanne, Aunt Joyce and Aunt Gereatha washed us up and took the rag curls from our hair that Grandma and Aunt Celia had put in before we went to bed.

"Why are we getting our new dresses on? Are we getting real pretty to go see Mama at the hospital?" I asked. They looked at each other.

"Move right along, girls," Grandma said, walking into the

bedroom. "We want you dressed, so you're ready to leave with your Dad."

"Do we get to wear our new can-cans, too?" Catherine asked.

"Yes," Aunt Joanne said.

Once we were ready, we took turns twirling around in our new dresses. But when Anna got dizzy and feel down, Grandma made us stop. "Mama's going to think were so pretty," I said to everybody, when we were putting our coats on.

In the car, Catherine and I got the back seat to ourselves because Sarah sat up front with Mark and Dad and my other brothers and sisters rode with aunts and uncles. Catherine and I spread out our dresses over the seat. "We're dressed just like Cinderella," I told her. My can-can picked me, right through my tights and so did Catherine's pick her.

"Want to play *Rock, Paper, Scissors*?" she asked.

"Sure," I said. "But you won't be just a rock, will you— like you always are, just a rock?"

"No," she said.

So we played *Rock, Paper, Scissors* until Dad said, "Here we are."

I looked. The hospital was a huge, white house with green around the windows. When Dad was parking the car I asked, "Is this where Mama's at? Is this the hospital?"

"No," Dad said, "this is the Funeral house."

"Who are the Funeral people?" I asked. Dad didn't answer.

A baldheaded man wearing a church suit opened the glass doors for us. He shook my dad and brothers' hands as they went in and rubbed the top of our heads. After everyone got inside, our aunts straightened our dresses and fixed the bows in our hair. Then everything got quiet. Mr. Funeral came and stood in front of my dad and asked him if we were ready. I looked at Dad. He had his hands together behind his back. He looked up at Mr. Funeral and said, "I think so." Mr. Funeral lowered his head, pushed up his glasses and said, "Follow me!"

We followed Mr. Funeral through the pretty white rooms of his house. I counted five pretty white couches. (We only have one ugly green couch.) Lots of shiny lights were hanging from the ceiling, like at our Aunt Geraldine's house. But I didn't see any kids like at our house, or dogs like Aunt Geraldine's Pierre, or any cats like my Puff. Nope. Everything and everyone was very quiet at the Funeral's house. I didn't know why. But then I saw why. Way at the end of the living room, against the wall, Mama was in a hospital bedbox sleeping, just like Monica was sleeping in the big bread-box at home one day.

I looked at Mama. "Mama must have fallen asleep while she was saying her rosary, like she does at home in her bed," I said to myself.

Mama looked just like Sleeping Beauty with her head on the shiny, white pillow. I felt the shiny pillow. It was soooo soft. Her dress was like Cinderella's. It was shiny yellow. I counted seven white buttons on Mama's shiny yellow dress. Pretty flowers were all around her. In front of her bedbox was a kneeler thing, like at church, so I stood on it so I could see her better. I whispered, "Mama, are you sleeping?" But she didn't answer me. Then I said, "Mama, who did you get all these flowers from?" But I don't think she heard me, because she didn't even move, like she always moves when we wake her up. Nope, Mama didn't rub her eyes, Mama didn't scratch her head, Mama didn't roll over onto her side, and she didn't cover the blankets over the head. Nope. She just lay there in the hospital bedbox with her lips closed really, really tight.

"Are you still mad at me, Mama, for drawing pictures on the new wall?" I whispered in her ear. "Are you still at the hospital because I made you sick? I won't write on the wall with my color crayons ever, ever again! I promise," I said.

"Shhhhhh, Mama's doing her rosary," Catherine said. So I went and stood by Mark. Uncle Freddy was talking to him. I pulled on Mark's coat. "Who is Mama saying her rosary for?" I asked.

"Probably for the conversion of the poor souls of Russia, like she always does," he said taking my hand. He looked at Mama and then he put his hands over his eyes.

"When's Mama coming home from the hospital?" I asked. But Mark was talking to Mama, and didn't hear me.

Mama once told me that every time she goes to the hospital to have a baby, she gets flowers from some of her sisters and brothers and from some of her lady friends from church, like Molly. Molly goes to our church. Our church is the church with the pretty windows. The windows have pictures painted on them. I like looking at the pictures. Mama once told me that the pictures tell the story of Jesus. Mama said that long, long, long ago when not very many people could read, painted pictures helped people learn about Jesus. "Like the pictures on the stations-of-the-cross. They tell us about Jesus' death, and when he came to life again," she said.

☞

At the Funeral's house I saw Mr. and Mrs. Thibault kneel down by Mama. They said their prayers, then stood up. I heard Mrs. Thibault say, "Rosie was so beautiful." Then she coughed and coughed. Mr. Thibault started to cry. "Ralph," Mrs. Thibault said, "I better go in the other room." Mr. Thibault didn't go with her. He went and talked to my dad and brothers. Then he lifted Monica up into his arms and hugged her. She was messing up his hair when he carried her into the other room.

Lots of other people looked at Mama and they cried, too. I didn't know why. Then I saw Mrs. Webster kneel by Mama. She said her prayers, too, and when she stood up, she started to cry really, really hard. I ran to tell my dad, because I didn't know teachers could cry.

Once before, when Mama was sleeping Mrs. Webster came to see her, but she didn't cry. She went into Mama's bedroom and quietly called her name and she woke up. Mrs. Webster told Mama that some families from St. John's would be bringing meals to our house.

"No, no, we couldn't have you do that!" Mama said.

"Father Dishaw already had me organize it," Mrs. Webster said. "A different family each night will bring your evening meal until you can get back on your feet again. It's our pleasure."

When Mrs. Webster left that day, Mama cried and said, "Oh, the people from Garden have always been so darn good. And Mrs. Webster is so kind."

☞

I watched when Molly's brother, Dona, knelt by Mama. I saw him pat Mama's hand. When he left, I said to Mama, "Dona was here, Mama. I think he wanted to talk to you." But she didn't wake up. So I told Mama that Dad let us smoke his pipe. But Mama *still* didn't say *anything*.

Lots of my aunts, uncles and cousins, and even some of *my* friends from school came to see Mama at the hospital—I mean the Funerals' house. My sisters and I ran around with them, but then they had to leave. Catherine and I ran into a room where we saw an old woman in a bedbox, like Mama's bedbox, but the old woman's was gray. There were lots of grandpas and grandmas by her, but we squeezed in through them to look at her. I pulled on a lady's dress sleeve and asked the lady with red lips why the grandma had glasses on when she was sleeping. And the lady said, "She always wears them. That grandma is my sister."

"What's her name?" I asked.

"Mrs. White," she said. Then my sister Catherine asked, "Why won't that grandma wake up?" Then a man with a big cigar said, "That grandma is my wife. Now she sleeps with Jesus—just like your mother."

I grabbed Catherine's hand and we hurried back to tell Dad about Grandma White. Dad listened, then asked me to stay by him. "Come and see all the pretty flowers your mother got," he said. But I told Dad that I couldn't stay because Catherine and I were on our way to go look into Mama's bedbox to see if Jesus was sleeping with her.

We looked all around, but Jesus wasn't there, so we ran and told the man with the big cigar that Jesus wasn't sleeping with our mother. The man with the big cigar took Catherine and me into a smoky room. He reached into his brown shiny suit coat pocket and took out matches and lit his big cigar, then smoked on it.

"My dad smokes a pipe," I said.

The man with the big cigar blew white O's into the air. Catherine and I tried to catch them. "Sit down now," he said, pointing his long finger to the couch. I blocked my nose because the smoke stunk. When his cigar was almost gone, he died it out in the ashtray. He looked at Catherine and me and said, "That grandma of mine has died out, like this cigar. There's no more fire in her. She's all used up, like your mother. Know what I'm saying?"

I shook my head up and down. "Yes," I said. "Mama already told us not to play with matches."

"What I'm trying to say, is that your mother died."

"How did she die?" I asked.

"Something must have made her sick," he said.

I threw my hands over my mouth. I turned to Catherine and

whispered in her ear. "Mama said that the flowers I drew on the new wall made her sick! Let's go tell Dad that Mama died."

⤳

I tried to find Dad to tell him what the man with the big cigar said, but lots of the people were talking to him. And lots of the people were crying. I pulled on Aunt Doreen's dress and asked her why she was crying. She looked at me and lifted me up by my arms. "Donna Jean," she said, shaking me. "You're seven years old! You should be crying, too, instead of running all around. Your mother's gone now. Don't you care?"

"No! She's not gone. She's sleeping in the other room. Want to come and see her?" Aunt Doreen put me back down. So I ran to see if Mama was still there.

I thought she'd be awake, because Mama can't ever sleep when it gets real noisy, but when I ran back by her, she was *still* sleeping. I wanted to ask if she had gotten the baby out of her tummy. I wanted to know if it was a boy, like she thought it was going to be. Then I heard Aunt Gereatha talking to a man with a long beard. "Rosie had a little boy. He's doing fine. Roy and Geraldine will care for him." So I ran back to Mama and tiptoed up onto the kneeler. "Mama," I said very loud, "why are you still sleeping? You have company!" But Mama didn't hear me again. She didn't move. She didn't turn over. She didn't say, "Let me sleep!" Or, "Don't be so noisy!" Or, "Can't you kids be quiet?" Nope, she didn't say anything!

"Mama," I said, touching her hand. "Why is your hand so cold? Why are there flowers on top of your legs?" But she still wouldn't talk to me. So I tried to shake her arm to wake her up, but Mama's cold arm wouldn't move. "Get up, get up, Mama, so we can go home!" I said. But Mama still didn't move. That's when I noticed her eyes. Mama's eyes looked like Catherine's doll's eyes. Mama's eyes looked glued shut—like Moe's.

Suddenly, I remembered why Mama was still sleeping. See, when Lily our Guernsey pooped out Daisy, Lily just kept lying on the ground. Luke wondered why she wasn't getting up. My dad said, "Give her some time to rest and she'll get back up." After a while, Lily did get up and go back out to the pasture, just like my dad said she would, so I watched and waited for Mama to get up, too.

125

Chapter Thirteen

When Father Dishaw came to the Funeral's house, we had to sit quietly. He stood by Mama and talked about the good things that she had done. "She has been a means of the living Christ for her family and for many others while here on earth," he said, "but also for *me*. Her example of seeking Christ daily and her divine love of family and generosity for others will never die. God's love has been felt by many, through Rose." Then he talked about Mama going to heaven. That's when I remembered what Mama had told us the night we took her to live with Aunt Geraldine and Uncle Roy.

"See," she said. "When I was seven my mama died, so now she's in heaven with God and the angels."

⌒

Father Dishaw talked for a little bit longer. He told the people about how Mama, Dad and us kids had to sometimes walk to church, but how we were always the first ones there. And he told everybody how Mama read the *Bible* to us every day. Then he said, "I wish her oldest son Matthew could have gotten home from Germany in time to see his mother. The stormy weather has prevented him from getting here, but I'm sure his mother is with him now." I stood up on my tiptoes and looked, but Mama wasn't with my brother Matthew.

126

She was still in her hospital bedbox.

After Father got done talking, we said lots of prayers, then Mr. Funeral said, "This ends things for tonight. We'll see you at St. John's church in the morning."

Father Dishaw came up to my dad. He shook my dad and brothers' hands. Then, one by one, he lifted my sisters and me up and gave us each a hug and a kiss. He talked to my grandma and my aunts and uncles, then he left. Other people started leaving, too. I watched Mama's sisters say good-bye to her. They kept crying and blowing their noses. Mama's brothers cried, too. Uncle Homely almost fell down, but Aunt Alice caught him. "Come on now, Homer," she said. "You know she's in a better place!" So Uncle Homely said good-bye, and when he did, Aunt Alice cried. Uncle Elmer wouldn't come out to see Mama sleeping in her hospital bedbox. He stayed in the smoky room. Even when Mark tried to pull him from the couch, he still wouldn't go see her. "I want to remember her the way she was," he cried.

"It's so hard to believe that I won't see her again," I heard Uncle Roy say to Aunt Geraldine. And Molly said, "I don't know what I'm going to do without my best friend. I don't want to say good-bye!" But Paul, Molly's husband, told her that she had to say good-bye. When they were getting ready to leave, she was crying really, really hard when she was putting on her coat. Josephine was crying, too. She and Molly hugged.

When everyone else was gone, Dad said, "It's time for us to say goodbye, too!" So Mark lifted me up so I could see Mama really good.

"Say good-bye to Mama, Donna Jean," he said.

"Why do you got all these shiny buttons on your Marine coat?" I asked him. I rubbed the shiny gold buttons. They felt slippery. I kissed one of the shinny gold buttons.

"Doesn't Mama look pretty, Donna Jean?" he said. I brushed the top of Mark's buzzed-off hair. "Why is your hair so picky, Mark?"

"I don't know," he said, taking my hand from his hair and then turning my head to look at Mama. Mark lowered me down to Mama's face.

"Give Mama a kiss good bye," he said. So I kissed Mama on the lips. They were freezing.

"Girls don't kiss girls on the lips," Mark said. "Girls kiss girls on the cheek or forehead." So I kissed her again, on the forehead. It was freezing, too!

"When can I come and see Mama again?" I asked. Mark looked at me with puddles in his eyes. "Mama's going to live with God and the angels now."

"Up in heaven?" I asked. Then I told Mark that Mama said that only dead people go to heaven. Mark started shaking. He put me back down on the floor and gave me a hug and cried so hard that his shoulders started jumping up and down.

"Mark," I asked, "is Mama dead?" He looked at me and tried to quit crying. He moved his head up and down. "Yes," he said. He grabbed me into his arms and hugged me really tight and kissed me on my forehead. He stood up, wiped his eyes with the back of his hands, sniffed his nose and said, "I'm going to have one of the other girls say good-by now. Okay?"

"Okay," I said.

Next, Mark picked up Anna. I heard him telling her to say goodbye, like he told me to say goodbye to Mama. I watched Anna kiss Mama on the lips, just like I did, but Mark didn't say anything. The big bow of my dress came untied. I chewed on the tie while I watched my brothers and sisters say good-bye.

Luke stayed by Mama's bed all night long. He wouldn't even move to go eat. Dad put his hand on Luke's shoulder.

"Luke," he said, "it's time to leave. You have to say goodbye to your mother now." But Luke didn't want to go home without Mama. "She's going to heaven now," Dad told Luke.

"Then I want to go with her!" he said. Luke tried to get into Mama's bed-box with her. He tried to put his arms around Mama. Dad lifted him away from her and with his big hands on Luke's shoulders he brought Luke to a folding chair. I went and sat by Luke. Luke kept rocking back and forth and back and forth on the chair, crying out for Mama. I felt really sad for my brother Luke.

My brother John was standing far away from Mama, way in the back of the room. He wasn't looking at Mama. He was looking at the floor. "Come on, John," Dad said. "Come on," Dad said again, with his hand. "Come and kiss your mother goodbye." Dad held out his arm waiting and waiting for John, but John stayed in the back of the room.

"Ma doesn't want any kiss from me!" he said. "She's mad

at me. I didn't do what she asked before she left!"

John ran fast out of the room. I followed and watched John run down the steps and out the glass doors. He didn't even come back three times, like Sarah did to see Mama. Nope. John didn't even take one peek at Mama. I felt sad for my brother John.

When we were done kissing Mama on her freezing face, we went to the big glass doors and waited there for Dad. John, Monica, Catherine and Anna went home with Uncle Herb and Aunt Gereatha., but Sarah, Bernadette, Luke, Mark and I waited for Dad. When Dad finally came into the room, he walked backwards toward us. When he turned around, he pulled up on the sides of his pants, buttoned the middle button of his new suit coat, and then put on his black hat. "See you in the morning," Mr. Funeral said as he opened the door for us. Dad nodded.

"Your mother sure got a lot of nice flowers, didn't she?" Dad said on the way to the car.

"I like the yellow roses you gave her from us. They're really pretty and smell really good," Bernadette said.

On the way home, I asked Bernadette why nobody told me when we first got to the Funerals' that Mama was dead. "I would have stayed by her all night. Now I won't ever get to see Mama again, because Mark said she's going to live with God and the angels now." Suddenly I noticed the Paul Bunyan man. "The Paul Bunyan man," I hollered. "Hurry Dad, turn around. Don't go home. Go back to the Funerals' house and get Mama!"

But Dad didn't go back, so I started to cry. "Come here, by me," Bernadette said. "It'll be okay." She lifted up her arm. "Get under my wing," she said.

☞

In the morning we followed Mama's bedbox into church. The choir was singing *The Old Rugged Cross*. Dad let us sit right up front. I turned around to look at all the people. I saw the high school girls that came and scrubbed the floors. They were crying. I saw ladies up in the choir crying. I even saw Wendy's dad and Anne's dad crying. I thought that my dad would get mad when I kept turning around, but he didn't. He didn't grab my long hair to turn me around, he didn't make mean faces at me to turn around, or scrape his throat, or even tell me to turn around. Nope. Dad didn't say anything to me.

"Dad," I said, "I see Russell, and he's crying."

"Listen to Father Dishaw," he said.

Father talked and talked again, about Mama. Then he said, "In closing I'd like to say that when Rose goes before the Lord for judgment, St. Peter is going to hand her the keys to the golden gate. 'Walk right in.' he'll say. 'Eternal life is yours.'"

Father sprinkled holy water over Mama's shiny brown box. Then Mr. Funeral came up the aisle and put the cover over the top of Mama's head and pushed her bedbox in front of us. I pulled on Dad's sleeve. "Mama said we should never ever put anything on top of somebody's head or they'll get smothered up. Mama isn't going to be able to breathe."

"Shhhhh," Dad said. "Watch Father."

So I watched Father Dishaw lift the gold cup up. He said more prayers and then people went to communion. I saw my godmother Bernice and her husband Joe, and my big cousins Marlyn Ann, Nancy and Bobby.

When church was over, Mr. Funeral asked my boy cousins to carry Mama's brown box outside and put it in his car. We followed. I watched while my boy cousins lifted Mama into the back of Mr. Funerals' black station wagon. Then Mr. Funeral put a little flag on all the cars that were at the church. After everyone got into a car, Mr. Funeral got into his station wagon and drove away with Mama. We followed. All the cars came down the road behind our car, like a choo-choo train, so I started singing, "Choo-choo, choo choo," but Dad shushed me.

We passed our school. I saw kids standing in front of each of the windows. I even saw the teachers looking out, like Mrs. Webster, Mrs. Boudreau and Mrs. Knuth. I don't know what they were looking at—I think maybe a baldheaded eagle was flying by.

"Dad, why are all the cars following us?" I asked when we turned into the place where all the stones are.

"This is the cemetery where they're going to bury your mother."

"Why are names on the stones?"

"That's so we can tell whose grave it is," he said.

"I didn't know they could dig graves in the wintertime," Mark said.

"It's been a mild January," Dad told him. "So they were

able to. Tony Leckson and Ikey Tatrow dug the grave."

When we got out of the car I asked Dad, "Why is that big, green rug on the ground?" But before Dad answered me, I saw the Funeral man and my boy cousins put Mama's brown shiny box on top of the green rug. Dad put his arm around my sister Sarah and me. He bent down, then said, "This is called a grave. They're burying your mother here."

"Are they going to cover Mama up with dirt?"

"Not yet. Those men will do that after we leave," he said pointing toward the men who were far away from us, standing by a big pile of dirt.

Everyone stood around the hole that Mama was on top of. Some of the people shivered. Father Dishaw said *more* prayers for Mama, while he sprinkled holy water. People *cried again*. This time, even my dad cried, so I hugged his leg. My brother Luke put his arm around Dad's shoulder and he cried, too.

When Father said, "May she rest in peace," everyone said, "Amen." Then people started coming up to us and saying good-bye. I kept asking Dad and my brothers for a drink of water, because my spit wouldn't go down, but nobody would answer me, so I went to ask the men that dug the hole. They were looking at each other and talking. "Dad says that it's not nice to bother adults for foolishness," I said to myself. So I stood behind a big tree wondering if asking for a drink was foolishness. That's when I heard one man say to the other man, "No, we're not going to cover her up today. She's going back to the Funeral house. The oldest boy isn't home yet. He'll want to see his mother, too."

"Sweetheart," Uncle Herb said coming up to me, "you have to stay with the others."

I ran and jumped into the car with my sisters. We left Mama's grave and went to St. John's hall. People were standing around waiting for us, like we waited one time for a bride and groom to get to the hall. After Lois and Richard ate, we watched them dance. Then we watched them smash cake into each other's face.

Mrs. Winters took my dad's hand in hers. "The food is ready," she said. "We women will help your children."

We lined up at the table. The ladies helped us girls dish up our plates. When we were eating, I heard a lady that walks with a cane say, "Rosie sure has done a fine job with her children. Too bad she can't be around to watch them grow up."

⁂

Dad and Mark thanked everyone for all the things they had helped us with and then we finally got to go home. Lots of people came home after us. Molly and Josephine came and they started washing clothes. Sarah rocked Monica, because Monica wouldn't go to anyone else. My other sisters and I ran outside and made a mama snowman. We were just finishing it when Mrs. Borga came and brought us the leftover food from the hall. While we were helping her carry the food in, she said she liked our mama snowman. Our hands were freezing, so we stayed in the house. We were in the living room when we heard a knock, knock, knock and then Russell's "HELL-O!" Russell had candy for us kids and a brown jug of beer for Dad. "It's the beer that makes Dad dance with Mama," I said to Catherine.

Dad took the beer and thanked Russell. Russell's face was red. He rubbed his hands together while he held them over the kitchen stove. "Burr, very cold, very cold" he said. Then he told my dad to take a big swig of the beer: "You be bedder din." But Dad told Russell he'd have some of the beer later.

Russell came and sat by my sisters and me in the living room. He said he didn't want to sit in the kitchen. "Too many big people," he kept saying. So he sat by us on the couch and told us lots of stories.

"Once, me saw big, big wolf come up ta house and me was scared of it." Then he said, "When the snow melts, me gonna see lots of bears come up ta house, like every year."

"Are you fraid of bears?" Anna asked. Russell moved his head up and down. So Anna ran and sat on Bernadette's lap. Bernadette put a blanket around Anna and Russell told us about his chicken that got out of the pen and ran all around his yard baulking. Russell thinks it was scared of the thunder. And Bernadette said that maybe it was like Henny Penny hollering that the sky was falling.

Then Russell told us about a giant snake he saw. "Me went in barn last summer and me saw big giant snake curled up on hay, so me run and get hoe ta kill giant snake! Giant snake look mad at me and make me fraid, and it spit out tongue to try to eat me up. So

I take hoe and hit giant snake on head. Giant snake jump right at me and grab me pants so I hit giant snake hard, hard, hard wif all my might and me kill giant snake, but me breakit da hoe. Now me hafta fix it."

"Where'd you put the giant snake?" I asked.

"I trew giant snake really far, far, far but it got stuck on fence post!"

Russell kept spitting when he talked and some of his spit fell out of the corners of his mouth, like my little sister Monica's spit did when she was getting her baby teeth.

When Russell got up to go home, he looked at us. He had giant tears falling out of his eyes, like the giant raindrops that I tried to catch one time. He kept shaking his head and saying, "No more Mama. Just like me. No Mama."

Monica started to cry when Russell said that he was leaving. She wanted him to stay. Grandma came then, took her from Sarah and rocked her.

Russell waved his hand high to Grandma. "So long," he said. Russell looked at us, waved his hand up high. "So long," he said. He went and looked into the kitchen. He told all the big people good-bye as he waved his hand high and then he left.

We ran to the window and watched Russell go down the driveway. We saw him stop and pick up Mama Snowman's carrot nose and put it back on her face. He talked to Mama Snowman for a little while, then he walked backwards down our driveway. When he got to the end of the driveway, he came back and talked to Mama.Snowman again. He looked really mad. After talking to Mama Snowman, he went down the driveway just like before. And once again he turned around. He took giant steps until he got by Mama Snowman. We heard him yelling at Mama Snowman. He yelled really loud and smoke from the cold kept pouring out of his mouth. Then with his big hand that was in his big glove, Russell hit Mama Snowman's head, and it fell to the ground. Her hat blew away so Russell ran and caught it and put it under Mama Snowman's head. He hollered again so loud that it sounded like thunder. His smoky words came right in through the cracked window. "Bad Mama! Bad, bad, Mama!" he said, and he crushed Mama Snowman's head with his feet into the ground.

We watched and watched. Monica wouldn't go to sleep for

Grandma, and she wouldn't let Grandma rock her any more, so Grandma stood with us at the window. All of a sudden, Russell saw us watching and ran quickly down the driveway, bumping into all the cars. He didn't even come back to put Mama back together.

"Wussell!" Monica hollered. "Tome back, Wussell! Mama No-man not posta be like dat!" Then Monica kicked to get down, so Grandma put her on the floor. Monica walked away carrying her raggedy blanket and calling for Mama.

⌒

The next day my dad and brothers went to the train station to pick up Matthew. We waited and waited with Grandma for Matthew to get home. Monica and Sarah were crying for Mama. "Is Mama coming home with Matthew?" Anna asked. I listened to hear if Grandma would say, "Yes, your mother's coming home, too." But Grandma said, "No, only Matthew."

"Why not?" Anna asked.

Grandma looked at us and shook her head. Then she put her hand over her chin and looked down to the floor. "I've got things to do," she said, as she got up from the rocking chair.

"Mama's dead, but our baby brother isn't dead!" Sarah said. "I don't know why Dad wouldn't let us take Jude home with us when we went to see him last night."

"But Dad said that he'll take us every Sunday to see him," Bernadette said to Sarah.

"That's not fair! He's our baby," Sarah said.

"Your dad is going to be busy enough around here with all of you. Your Aunt Geraldine and Uncle Roy are going to take care of him just until he gets a bit bigger," Grandma said.

"Grandma" I said, pulling on her dress, "my dad cried when we went to see Jude."

"He did?" she asked. I moved my head up and down. Then we all started telling her about it. About how tiny Jude was and how funny he looked when he stretched his little arms and legs and didn't even wake up, and how Monica pulled his nose and slapped his face but he *still* stayed sleeping.

"I can't listen to all of you at once," Grandma said.

"I want to tell Grandma. I was first to tell her," I hollered.

So Grandma let me be the one to tell her about my dad crying.

When we were done looking at Jude, Auntie carried our baby brother to Dad. He was standing in the hallway. She put Jude in his arms. Dad stared down at him for just an itty-bit, then hurried him back into Auntie's arms. Then he ran out the back door. I ran to look out the long skinny window that was by the door. I saw Dad fall onto his tummy in the snow. He started doing silly things like Monica does whe she doesn't want to share her toys. He keep hitting the ground with his hands, kicking the ground with his feet, and hollering really, really loud. My sisters and brothers came to the window too, but when Luke saw what Dad was doing he made us all go to the living room by Auntie. But even in there, I could hear Dad crying and crying. But I don't know why he was crying.

"Oh dear, that's too bad," Grandma said. "Run along now or I won't get dinner made."

My sisters and I took turns watching for car lights, but all we could see were zillions of snowflakes coming down. All of a sudden, the back door opened. "Matthew," we screamed, and went running to him. He took turns lifting us up to give us hugs. When he lifted me, I asked him why there was red in his eyes. "I don't know," he said. "Where's Ma?... I mean...where's Monica?"

"Grandma's rocking her," I said.

That night, Dad let us stay up to eleven o'clock! Catherine, Anna, and I took turns wearing Matthew's Army hat and Mark's Marine hat around the kitchen table. We played soldier until Dad made us go to bed.

In bed, Sarah wouldn't play tickle backs with me, like we usually do, so I couldn't go to sleep. My sisters were all sleeping, so I just lay there listening to my dad and brothers talking. I heard my brother Matthew say to Dad, "I sure wish I could have made it home on time for Ma's funeral. Will I still get to see her?"

I thought Dad was going to say, "Sorry, you can't see your mother—she's in heaven!" But instead he said, "Yes, I made all the arrangements for you to see her. We'll go 'up there' first thing in the morning!"

"I'm going to go to heaven, too," I said to myself, and I tried to hurry to sleep, so I could wake up early. "I'll hurry and get dressed in the morning, and I'll do like Catherine did. I'll duck down in the back seat of the car until I hear Dad say to Matthew and

Mark, "We're almost to heaven." Then I'll pop up, out of the back seat, like Catherine popped up out of the back seat when Dad and Luke went to Escanaba to buy the new door. Dad will see me and say, "You've come this far, it's too late for me to turn around and bring you back now!" So then I'll get to go all the way to heaven with Dad, just like Catherine went to Escanaba!"

During the night, I got up three times to see if it was morning yet. When I heard the rooster crowing, I hurried up. My sisters were all sleeping, so I quietly got dressed. I could hear Dad, Matthew and Mark talking in the kitchen.

"Let's go to the barn first and tell Luke and John that we'll be back by eleven. Dress warm; the temperature reads twenty below zero," Dad said.

When they went outside I combed my hair, then ran to get my boots and coat on. I looked out the utility window. "Dad and the boys must still be at the barn," I said to myself. I hurried outside so I could get ducked down in the back seat before they saw me. But when I got to the driveway, I saw the car driving away. "Wait, Dad!" I yelled. I ran down the driveway. "Wait, Matthew! Wait, Mark!" I screamed. "I want to go see Mama, too!"

☞

I threw myself to the mattress and began to cry. Soon my crying turned to wailing. After several minutes I stopped and Elisabeth handed me a pillow.

"No," I screamed, throwing the pillow. I want my MOTHER! NOT A PILLOW!

"That's right, let it out. Let it all out. Let it finally be finished," she said.

I kicked my feet and punched my fist against the mattress while shouting out words of anger. Finally exhausted, I lay still listening to the rapid rhythm of my heart. I closed my eyes and breathed slowly, until I was nearly asleep. Elisabeth sat down beside me and took my hand.

"That's enough work for today. You can share more of the memories again tomorrow if you'd like." Then she stood and softly spoke. "The evening meal will be served soon. We'll convene again in the morning at eight."

Chapter Fourteen

fter a restless night sleep and waking late, I dressed quickly, bypassed breakfast, and hurried to the conference room. As I slipped in between the rows of people to take my place among them, I could see a man around my own age on the mattress. It was Paul, a soft-spoken man that I had talked to briefly during a break. In a gentle voice he had told me that I reminded him of his sister. But now on the mattress, he was anything but gentle. Violently, he was hitting the old directories with the rubber hose while loudly shouting obscenities. As I continued to listen, I realized that he had served a tour in Vietnam and was angry at the country for turning its back on him and the other soldiers.

Suddenly, his disposition changed. He put down the hose and quietly spoke to the group, as tears flowed down his face. "We were first class soldiers. We took our orders as we were taught and tried to carry them out to the best of our ability. Yet, some Americans considered *us* the enemy. Hell, they hated us more than the war itself." He became still and quiet, as if waiting for the enemy's approach. Then, as if he had a Jeckyl and Hyde personality, his disposition changed again. In a rage he began beating the mattress. He stopped again, then shouted, "Do you know what it's like going to bed at night...what am I saying...going to *bed?* It's finding a spot in the *muck,* stepping slowly, wondering if you're about to set off a land mine or if some gook is about to blow your head off! Your few hours for sleeping are spent reliving the day—the people you killed—the people they killed and wishing the gooks had gotten you instead of the other guy. Like Reginald, my buddy. He stepped on a land mine. Shrapnel got him. As he lay there dying, I felt helpless. He called out for his mother. I told him she was on her way as he died in my arms. Earlier that day he had bragged about becoming the daddy of twin girls."

Paul raised his head to us. His eyes looked vacant. Then cursing loudly he vented more of his anger. It was toward the people who had met the soldiers at the airport. His voice was so loud, I placed my hands over my ears and wondered if only opera voices could break windows.

Following a medley of obscenities and fist striking, he collapsed to the mattress, paused briefly, and then continued. My heart ached for him. Secretively, I wished for the courage to stand before him to ask forgiveness on behalf of our country. Instead I reached into my purse, grabbed a wad of kleenex, wiped my eyes, and again, listened intently.

"I remember how happy I was when my tour in Nam was finally over. There were about twenty of us on the plane that day when we flew into L.A. It wasn't only me thinking, 'I'M ALIVE!' We all knew we belonged to the elite group, known as the 'lucky ones' who made it through the war without so much as a scratch. We were throwing punches at each other out of pure joy as we made the trip back to the states. We had heard about the opposition to the war back home, but we didn't know the full extent of it. So we still felt proud to have served our country and honored to wear the uniform. When the plane landed, we could see from the window about a hundred or so people lined up against the fence waiting, for what I thought was a welcome home. But when we walked down the steps of the plane, the people came charging and spit on us!"

Paul hit the mattress again and again and again. It was obvious the mattress for him had become the protestors. His face grew increasingly red. While yelling a finale of obscenities, he tore several of the old phone books to shreds. Finally exhausted, he collapsed once again to the mattress.

Elisabeth put her hand over her eyes, shook her head from side to side as if disgusted, then stood up. She looked around the room at everyone, then pointed her hand toward Paul and said, "It's a shame this young man has had to endure such pain. What were we thinking?" Elisabeth paused for a few seconds, then said, "Go to lunch."

In the cafeteria whispers were being passed from table to table about the Vietnam veteran.

"He needs a hero's welcome," Flossy said.

"Definitely," an elderly woman responded. "But he needs to forgive his country, so the healing can begin."

"You're both right," Steve said. "I was a medic in Nam. I know what he's going through. And I have an idea of what we can do to help him." He stood up and, after getting everyone's attention, told the group what he had in mind.

Paul didn't eat lunch as many of us expected he wouldn't, especially those of us who had already expressed grief. We knew too well how physically and emotionally draining the experience was. Most of us expected that Paul would be gone to his room to lie down, but to our surprise he was still on the mattress talking to Elisabeth when we returned from lunch. A mountain of kleenex lay by his side. He looked up as we trickled into the room. He was preparing to leave the mattress, when Steve gave the signal. Several of the guys walked to the front of the room and lifted Paul up high. The rest of the group gathered around and everyone sang, "*God Bless America.*" Everyone swayed to the music. Tears flowed from Paul's eyes, like water from a sieve. By the time it was over, we were all in tears.

"Thank you so much," he said, after they lowered him to the floor. Then, one-by-one, we embraced him.

"I needed that," he said, as he dried his eyes. "And I'm letting go." Everyone clapped, then we took our seats.

"Do you feel like sharing some more?" Elisabeth asked me.

"I don't know if I have anything left to share," I answered. But with a little coaxing from another counselor, Dennis, I soon was back on the mattress.

"Start where you left off yesterday," he encouraged. "You told us about your mother's death and funeral. What I'm wondering is, did your grandmother continue to live with your family? And

139

what about your brothers that were in the military? Did they have to return to their bases?"

"Yes, my brothers went back. It still seems like yesterday to me. It was the last day of January. It was Grandma's birthday when we took Matthew and Mark to the plane."

⌒

"Don't go away, like Mama did!" Catherine cried. Monica cried too, because she still wanted to play with Matthew's and Mark's Marine and Army hats. Anna and Catherine kept holding onto their legs so they couldn't move.

"Stay home and play *Hide and Seek* with us," Anna begged. "Grandma won't play with us. She won't even give us horseyback rides."

"I'm seventy years old," Grandma said. "Grandma's tires are worn out!"

"You don't have tires, Grandma," Anna giggled.

"No, and I don't have strong legs either!" she said. But when we got back home from taking our brothers to the plane, Grandma gave Anna and Monica each a horseyback ride. When she was galloping Anna around the table, she kept coughing and coughing. And that night in bed, Grandma coughed and coughed again. I had to block my ears.

In the morning, she was really sick. She couldn't even get out of bed. So Dad had Sarah bring her some tea and a piece of bread. Later that day, as soon as Dad got home from work, he went and checked on her. He felt Grandma's forehead. "Ma," he said. "You're burning up. I'm taking you to the hospital." He walked Grandma to the kitchen. "Help me get her arms into her coat," he said.

John helped Dad get Grandma to the car. Then Dad left for the hospital. My sisters and I cried because we thought that Grandma was going to die. John and Luke said that if we'd quit crying, they'd play catch with us. They played *Catch Anna, Catch Monica, and Catch Catherine,* but Sarah, Bernadette and I wouldn't let them throw us to each other.

We were waiting and waiting for Dad to come home with Grandma. When he finally got back, Grandma wasn't with him. "Is

Grandma dead?" Sarah cried out when Dad came in the house alone.

"Grandma has to stay in the hospital for a couple days," he said. "She has pneumonia."

"Is she going to have a baby like Mama and die?" Anna asked.

"No, no," Dad said, lifting her up. "The doctor said that Grandma's going to be okay. But when she can leave the hospital, Aunt Gereatha and Uncle Herb are going to take her home to live with them." We cried, because we wanted Grandma to come home. And we wanted to go see her, but Dad said kids weren't allowed in hospital. So we didn't get to see Grandma again until Sarah's birthday.

It was the first day of spring. Robin birds were sitting on the snow-covered trees and chirping, as we watched for the bus.

"Tomorrow is March twenty-sixth—my birthday!" Sarah shouted.

"See all that snow?" Dad said coming out of the house. "When it's melted, we'll go to your mother's grave."

"When will it be melted?" I asked.

"Pretty soon," he said.

"Dad," Bernadette asked, "why don't you ever shave your whiskers or comb your hair nice anymore?"

"The bus," Catherine hollered.

On the way to school, Bernadette and I were excited about getting to go to Mama's grave someday. And on the bus trip home, we decided that everyday after school we would check to see how much snow was left on the ground. One day when we checked, it was gone. So I asked Dad if we could go see Mama's grave. He said he was too busy. "We'll go tomorrow," he said. But it was thirteen tomorrows before Dad finally said he'd take us to her grave.

Before we left, Sarah and I ran around the yard from dandelion to dandelion until we had a pretty bouquet. Then we ran to the house to show Dad. "We're putting them on Mama's grave," Sarah said, as we watched Dad shave then put Brylcream in his hair.

"Are you combing your hair pretty for Mama?" I asked.

"Get out to the car," he said. "I'm almost ready."

⌒

On the way to Mama's grave I asked Dad if sleeping people in hospital bedboxes turn into dead people when they get covered up with dirt. See, once I put a plastic bag over Monica's head and Mama said, "Get that off her head this very minute or you'll smother her! There aren't any cracks or holes in that bag. Monica won't be able to breathe!" So I thought that Mama got smothered up, too. I asked Dad, again, but he just said, "Look at the trees, they're starting to bud. Enjoy the sunshine. Forget all that other nonsense."

Dad stopped the car in the field of stones—next to the big tree—right by Mama's grave. "Mama must be really mad that we let people put all that dirt on her," I said to myself as I walked around her grave making sure that not even a toe touched it. Because I was afraid her hand would come out of the grave and grab my foot. She might pull me down with her into the ground where bugs and the devil lived.

"I bet Mama misses us a lot, doesn't she Dad?" Bernadette asked.

"She sure does," he said, looking at the cold, gray stone. "Rose Jacques, January 9, 1960," he read.

My sisters and I ran through the cemetery reading other dead peoples' names from the shining stones. "Stay off the graves," Dad hollered. So we did. Except once I stepped on Dr. Bernier's wife and twice on Billy LaMotte, but never ever on Mama, or the little Tatrow baby—the grave with the little lamb. We skipped past the Peterson's tall cross and looked through Bouchard's little white fence. Then I ran and sat under the Christmas tree that Dad says shades Mama's grave. I heard a bird singing and thought of Mama's bluebird song. I gathered needles from under the tree and then took the longest one to give myself a booster shot with it, like the nurse that comes to our school does. I pushed the needle way down into my arm, as I stared out into nowhere, wondering if Mama's hair was still black, if her skin was still white, if her dress was still yellow and especially if her hands were still cold and stiff.

One time my hands were cold and stiff like Mama's because my gloves got stuck in the snow when my sisters and I were making a snow house. Mama heard me crying and had Luke come and get me and carry me into the house. She took my cold hands and put them on her rising bread-dough tummy, where the baby was. Soon my hands were soft and warm. "I should have warmed Mama, too," I thought, as I watched Monica try to climb onto Mama's stone. She chewed on a plastic, yellow rose watching Dad pull long grass from around the stone. When he was down, his mighty arms lifted skinny Monica from the stone and he took the flower from her mouth. "No, no," he said. "Yucky." He held Monica, knelt by Mama's grave, made the sign-of-the-cross and said a prayer. I saw giant tears fall from his blue eyes and land on his smooth cheeks. I ran to him. "What's the matter, Dad?" I asked. Dad turned his head. "Tell everyone to get into the car," he said. "It's time to go."

⌒

Dad's pipe smoke blew into the back seat on the way home from the field of stones. It stunk, so Catherine and I tried to shoo it out through the open windows. We were glad when the car stopped in our bumpy driveway. We hurried out and into the house to see what we could eat for lunch. "Let me take a five," Dad said. "Then I'll get up and make some pancakes."

We sang *all* of *Ninety-nine Bottles of Beer on the Wall* before Dad got up. First he made burnt sugar syrup, then the pancakes. When he got tired of cooking them, he said, "That's enough, I've got washing to do. Someone else can take over."

Catherine and I had to help sort the clothes. "I can smell Mama," I said to Catherine when I put Mama's yellow blanket into the blanket pile. Catherine grabbed the blanket and sniffed. "Me too," she said.

After the clothes were washed, Dad washed blankets. But when he came to put them through the wringer, the wringer popped up. "Damn!" he said. "The last thing I need is for this to break!" He tried to fix it, but couldn't, so he twirled the blankets around and around in his hands to get the water out. While he twirled them, he yelled at my sisters to quit fighting.

Bernadette and Sarah were fighting over whose turn it was to wash the dishes. Bernadette said it was Sarah's turn and Sarah said it was Bernadette's.

"If you two want to go to the gravel pit for a ride with the boys, you better get them done," Dad said as he left to go hang the blankets. So they hurried to do them. Catherine and I took Anna and Monica outside. We ran with them around the house trying to catch a butterfly. It went up into a tree, so instead we tried to catch the blankets on the clothesline as they slapped back and forth. Then they'd fall still to the ground. Catherine and I were pushing the clothes prop up for Dad when the boys said that they were ready to leave for the pit.

I ran to the house to sneak one of the metal spoons from the silverware drawer. I wanted it for a shovel, so that I could help the boys fill the trailer with gravel. I put the spoon into my bloomers so Dad wouldn't see me with it.

When I got outside I heard Dad say, "Luke, have John and Calvin help you fill the trailer with gravel, so we can get the holes in this driveway filled."

John and Calvin bug us girls all the time. Once when they climbed Mama's crab apple tree, then made whistling chirping noises until we came looking—for a hurt bird. When we got under the tree, they plugged apples at us, and that hurt.

"I'm telling Mama!" I said.

"Go ahead," he said. I started running to the house, but then remembered that Mama wasn't alive any more. I started to cry. "If Mama wasn't dead," I thought, "she'd probably be making pies and she'd take one look at my red and white stinging legs and go running out of the house with her rolling pin, yelling, 'Look out boys, if I should catch you!'" She'd be mad, because Mama doesn't like it when the boys do mean things to us. When they put burrs from the sumac bushes into our long hair, she made them kneel in a corner until she picked the burrs out.

☞

Anyway, the boys were mad because they didn't want to take us with them to the pit. "Those brats!" Luke said. His face looked like a bullfrog's when he loaded us up onto the trailer. "Monica," he hollered. "Don't be strolling this way—taking your good old time—get over here!"

"I just need them out of my way for a few hours, so I can get some things done around here," Dad said as Luke climbed onto the tractor seat. John and Calvin stood on the bar of the trailer—the bar that connected us to them—and they held onto the tractor seat.

"You're in charge, son," Dad said to Luke before we left. "See to it that nothing happens to your little sisters, and remember, I don't want them shoveling." Dad looked at us. "If you girls behave for Luke, I'll take you to Aunt Geraldine and Uncle Roy's to see your baby brother someday soon," he said.

"Why does our baby live with them, Dad? I can take care of him. I know how. I changed Monica's diapers, and I know how to hold a baby's bottle," Sarah yelled as the trailer bounced down the driveway, "I can even burp a baby!"

My sisters and I giggled at the farting sounds the tractor made, as it pulled us to the gravel pit on Dad's other land, way down the road, next to where our cows are. Luke was going lickety-split, so we squeezed the sides of the trailer to keep from falling over. We watched our fingers turn from tan to reddish purple, as we be-bopped along. I counted the spider webs in the trailer. "One, two, three and four, a spider web is in each corner," I said, just as Anna stood up. She knew she shouldn't. She almost fell down when she ran to my side of the trailer. A super, long-legged Daddy-Long-Legs scared her, because it was strolling her way.

Luke slowed the tractor. "Jack Rabbit, sit down back there!" he yelled. My brother always calls her that, because she's always hopping around. She never sits still. I'm not afraid of little old spiders, so I stretched out my leg to squish it. Then Anna wouldn't be afraid. But Luke, with his hawk-like eyes, saw me and probably thought I was going to run around in the trailer too, so he hit the brakes. I went sliding across the gravel that was still in the trailer from the day before.

"Ouchies!" I screamed.

"Look at your knees! They're bleeding!" Bernadette said.

I screamed, but Luke wouldn't stop. He kept right on going. Blood dripped down my legs, like the icing on an angel food cake that I once saw in Grandma Jacques' McCall's magazine. (It's the magazine with the paper dolls that have the three sets of paper doll clothes that you can cut out and put on the dolls. Grandma said that next month it's my turn to get the paper cutouts.)

Bernadette grabbed my ponytail to pull me back by her. "You were going to kill that spider, weren't you? Do you want it to rain, you dumb dodo?"

"I don't want it to rain," I said.

I looked down. Tears fell unto my legs and stung my boo-boos. "Ouchies!" I wish Mama were here," I said. "She'd come running lickety-split. She'd reach into her weighs-a-ton purse for the boo-boo medicine and put it on me. Then she'd kiss my boo-boo and make it all better. Then loud like thunder, she'd holler to Luke, 'Stop this tractor, NOW!' Fast like a cat, she'd climb from the trailer and grab Luke by his Dennis the Menace hair. And right through her teeth, she'd say, 'Don't you ever hit the brakes like that again!'"

Luke drove the tractor and trailer down into the gravel pit. I climbed out of the trailer after my sisters, squishing all the spiders with the bottoms of my flip-flops. I even smashed their snarled hair houses where they kept icky, blackish-gray, creepy-feelie things that looked and felt like the moles on my Aunt Lu Lu's face. Luke once told me that those creepy-feelie things are spider eggs and that they'll turn into baby spiders someday. Luke thinks that because he's fifteen he knows everything and he tries to be the Big Charge all the time, but Dad says he can't *always* be the Big Charge. Dad says there are too many chiefs and not enough Indians at our house. I don't exactly know what that means about chiefs and Indians, but whenever Dad says it, Luke is lots of fun again—for a little while. But he's not fun today, because today Dad is letting him be the Big Charge until we get back home from the pit.

My sisters and I walked all around on the inside of the pit. The walls were big like mountains. I was scared. I was afraid that the walls were going to fall down on top of me and bury me up, like Mama. I ran to my sisters and stood with them on the dirt floor where big trucks had made caterpillar-like roads. Then Catherine said, "Does anyone want to play a game?"

"I do, I do," I said raising my hand, like in school.

"Let's try skipping out of the pit," she said. First one to the top wins. But you have to stay on the tire tracks, or you lose."

I tried really hard to get all the way to the top and so did my sisters, but only Sarah made it all the way up. She didn't even have to stop once. She stood at the top edge and started showing off—talking like Mama's cow-milking friend, Josephine.

"Oh, children, I told you Mother could do it! Ha, ha, ha, *I* beat," she said.

I felt like pinching her, because she was making me mad.

Sarah thinks that because she's the oldest, she can be our mother and that makes Bernadette and me mad. But she was way up at the top, so instead of pinching her I rolled on the ground with Anna and Catherine. We rolled and rolled while the boys put shovels of gravel into the trailer.

"Ouch," I said. "Something hurts!" I reached into my bloomers to see what was bugging me, and there was the spoon! "I'm going to help the boys fill the trailer with this," I said to my sisters.

"Where did you get that spoon?" Bernadette asked.

"Home," I said.

"You're going to be in big trouble," she said.

See, my dad got mad at us the other day for taking spoons outside. We use them in our pretend playhouse by the sumac bushes, back of the old barn. My dad doesn't know how much fun we have filling the empty lard cans with batter. First we put in dirt, then salt, and then we fill it to the top with water and stir it all up. We tried stirring with sticks, but the sticks kept breaking, so we started sneaking spoons from the house so everything gets mixed good. Then we dump the batter onto the flat stones. Anna, Catherine and Monica make cakes and pies and cookies. They don't know how to make bread, like me. When we're done, we leave every thing in the hot sun to bake. Once my bread didn't turn out. I think it was because I forgot to make the sign-of-the-cross on it.

One day I asked Mama why she made the sign-of-the-cross on top of the bread dough. "It's like a prayer, so the bread will turn out just right," she said.

"Is that why you make the sign-of-the-cross on us every day, too?" Sarah asked.

Before Mama answered, I started to giggle, but Mama said, "That's right, Sarah. That's the reason. It's so my little girls and my big boys will turn out just right—the way God wants them to."

"Is that why you bless your tummy? So the baby inside of it will turn out, too?" Anna asked.

Mama smiled. "That's right, Anna!"

☞

Anyway, my dad got mad the other day. It was because he

147

couldn't find a big spoon. "How can I make Catherine a birthday cake if you're all going to be taking the things I need?" he said.

"It's Anna and Monica's fault," I told him. "They forget to bring the spoons back to the house."

"They don't belong outside. I blame you bigger girls! Since your mother went away, I can't find a *damn* thing! Nothing has been the same around here!" he said, looking as mean as a bulldog. Then he threw the little spoon back into the drawer, took giant steps to the creaky, old door and slammed it on his way out. He marched down the path, toward the woods. I watched from the utility window. I thought he was going to go look for the lost spoons, but he kept on going. He passed the big flat stones and Anna's muffins baking, he passed the rooster and the clucking chickens, he passed the barn and the boys smoking behind it, and he went far, far, far into the woods. I watched until he looked like a little boy.

"Hurry," Sarah said. "We better clean the house before Dad gets back." But we could have cleaned ten houses, because he didn't come right back.

"Maybe a wolf ate him," I said.

"Maybe a bear!" Catherine shouted.

"Here he comes!" Bernadette yelled.

"Run!" I said.

We thought Dad would be really mad, so we ran and hid behind the wood stove when we saw his marching work boots coming up the path. But when Dad came in, he just looked around and said, "Where oh where are all my little girlicans?" (That's what Dad calls us when he's not too tired and plays dog pile with us on the living room floor.)

First Monica ran out of hiding, then Anna. I watched from behind the stove. Dad lifted them both up, at the same time, and kissed their balloon cheeks. So I ran to him, too. He brushed the top of my head with his hand. Then he gave us all whisker-rubs and horsey rides. Soon we were running around and laughing, like before Mama went away.

⌐

Oh, that's right, at the pit I was about to dump the seventh spoon shovel into the trailer when Luke yelled at me. His yell made my hands shake and the gravel spilled out of the spoon. "Just what do you think you're doing, little girl?" he shouted. "I can't fill this trailer and watch you kids, too!" Slowly I put my spoon behind my back. "Now get the hell out of here and watch your little sisters!" he yelled.

I threw my hands over my mouth. "Mama would soap his mouth!" I said to myself, as I ran to stand by my sisters. I could see my brothers and Calvin jumping on the tops of their shovels to get them deep into the gravel. Suddenly, Luke yelled again. This time it wasn't at me. My heart started jumping up and down. "No, Sarah, no!" he screamed. "Quick! Get away from there!"

I looked up. I saw Sarah still standing on the top edge, right above where the boys were shoveling. I covered my eyes with my hands. "Mama!" I screamed. "I wish you were here. You'd run fast like Walter, our bull, and with your spider-like arms you'd grab Sarah. Wouldn't you?" I said to myself.

There came a big gushing noise. It sounded like when Dad throws out the water from the washbasin onto the ground, but it was a zillion times louder. Slowly I uncovered my eyes and watched the sand and the gravel, and the gravel and the sand pour down the pit, covering up Luke, John and Calvin, like cake batter going onto the bottom of a pan. I screamed again. Dust was everywhere. "Oh, no!" I cried. "They're buried, like Mama!" I ran with my spoon to them and started digging through the dirt.

Only parts of John and Calvin were covered so, soon, they were out of the gravel. John spit dirt out of his mouth and said to me, "Don't go so hard. You'll hurt him!"

I threw my spoon and started digging with my hands. I could feel tiny rocks climbing under my crayon polished nails. Everyone kept digging. Suddenly, I could see Luke's nose lying on top of the dirt. Slowly I swept the dirt from his face. Luke coughed and coughed. He lifted his arms, like Frankenstein did when he first came alive on the doctor's table.

"Everyone, hurry!" John hollered. "Let's each carry a part of Luke!"

John carried Luke's head and arms, Calvin carried Luke's tummy and Bernadette and I each carried a leg. We lifted him to the top of the trailer load of gravel. It looked like Luke was going to cry when we climbed up around him.

149

"I'm driving the John Deer!" John said, as he climbed onto the tractor seat. Calvin sat behind him so that John could reach the pedals. Slowly, John drove us up and out of the pit.

My dad was on the front porch shaking out the living room rugs. He threw them on the ground when he saw us coming, like a turtle down the road. He tripped over a chicken and almost fell, as he ran to meet us. When he got to the trailer, everyone started telling him exactly what happened. "If you all keep talking at once, I'll never know," he said. So he turned to John and asked him what happen. When John told him, Sarah started to cry and jumped off the trailer and ran to the house. "It's not my fault!" she yelled.

Dad carried Luke into the house and laid him on his bed. Dad kept saying, "I'm sorry, Luke. I'm sorry this happened to you."

I don't know why he was sorry. He didn't do anything. He wasn't even there.

Dad moved Luke's legs up and down and up and down, then said, "Well, I don't think you have any broken bones, but you'll probably hurt for a few days. You're a lucky young man." (I thought just dads were called man, but I know my dad said man.)

That night when I went to bed, the thunder kept scaring me. I blocked my ears as I watched the lightning crack open the black sky. I wondered where God lived. Like by our house, or Josephine's or maybe far away in Alaska where my cousin Marilyn lives. Then it began to rain, like the day Mama went away. (Mama once told me that Jesus cries when he's sad and that's why it rains.)

The rain started hitting the window. "I bet God is sad that Luke almost died today," I said to myself. Then lightning lit up the sky like a big splash of fire. I looked at the window. I could see a super long-legged Daddy-Long-Legs running fast up the middle of it. Halfway up, it stopped. Its tummy was Jello fat and its bulging eyes were staring—staring at me! Suddenly I remembered what my sister Bernadette said in the trailer on the way to the pit. "Don't kill that spider! If you kill it, it'll rain, you dumb dodo!"

Quickly, I pulled the blankets over my head. I hollered for Mama. I waited under the smothering blankets to hear her say that she'd be right with me. But under the dark, smothering blankets, the only thing I could hear was my heart pounding and pounding, and Luke, whining and moaning for Mama like the day she went away.

I felt weak and exhausted upon the mattress, so I excused myself and went to my room to be alone for awhile. I lay on the bed wondering how much more pain I could endure. I was missing my mother right then, like I had missed her as a little girl. So much so, I thought my heart would break. Suddenly my roommate came dashing into the room.

"I think I finally have the courage to share with the group, but I need you for support," she said.

Flossy had been there for me during my darkest hours, and now I was going to be able to return the favor. Quickly I got up, and she and I hurried back to the conference room before she had a chance to lose her nerve.

Chapter Fifteen

It was snowing in the valley of the Catskills when Flossy talked about her son's death. Although she had told me bits and pieces surrounding it, she had not explained that the death of her eight-year-old had been due to a drowning. I assumed the *accident* she had talked about was a car accident. She had never mentioned that it had happened at the beach. Almost lifeless, she sat upon the mattress and told the story of that dreadful day.

"The sky was blue, not a cloud in sight. We raced from the car to the beach. I'm so glad I let him win," she said, as she swept strands of her hair to the back of her ears.

Flossy and her son had spent over an hour in the water playing Frisbee when Flossy decided she'd had enough and went to shore and dried off. While she applied lotion, she watched her son dive in and out of the water for the floating Frisbee. She hollered for him to come in closer and he did as she had asked. "He rarely disobeyed me," she said. The sun grew hotter. "I'll be right back," she yelled. "I'm going to the car for the cooler. Stay right where you are."

It had only taken her a couple minutes to run to the car and back. Returning, she looked to the water, but only the Frisbee was in sight. She set the cooler down and put her hand above her eyes to block the blinding sun, as she searched the water. She told herself that he was probably up by a nearby tree going to the bathroom, so she skimmed the area as she called out to him. When no reply came, she frantically sprinted through the water screaming his name. "Get help," she yelled to a teenage girl, the only other person on the beach. She swam to the floating Frisbee and dived in and out of the water in search of her son. Only minutes before she had thought the water to be warm and comforting. But now, as she groped through the darkness, her body felt like it was passing through quicksand, as she treaded along.

"His little hand," she whimpered. "It was his little hand I touched first."

Although of slender frame, Flossy had somehow managed to lift his lifeless body to her own, then run with him to shore. Exhausted, she began CPR and continued until the young girl returned and took over.

"That poor young girl. She was only about fourteen. She worked in a frenzy on Patrick until the paramedics arrived."

Flossy was too depressed to even cry. In fact, the best she could do was to occasionally whimper or moan.

"Depression is often times anger turned inward," Elisabeth said. Then she asked Flossy if she felt responsible for her son's death. Flossy nodded. So with a few more probing questions from one of the counselors, Flossy was soon in touch with her anger. She began hollering and telling herself that she was not fit to walk the face of the earth. She pulled at her hair until it looked as though she'd yank it right out. And she punched at her legs and arms. Elisabeth knelt by her and spoke gently. "Our emotions are neither good nor bad, it's what we do with them that matters. Even anger can be a positive emotion when constructively expressed." Then she encouraged Flossy to use the rubber hose on the mattress instead of continuing with the self-abuse. Flossy heeded the advice and expressed her pent-up anger until she broke down into tears.

After several minutes of crying, Flossy began a lingo of 'if only's.' "If only I would have gotten the oil changed in the car that day like my husband had asked, I would have arrived later at the beach. By then there probably would have been others to see that Patrick was in trouble. If only I'd have hung the sheets on the line and did the dishes, I would have probably drunk a glass of ice tea before I left and then I wouldn't have been thirsty."

"Why didn't you hang the sheets," Elisabeth asked.

"Patrick didn't want to wait. He was so excited about going

to the beach, he wanted to leave right away."

"So out of love for your son, you left earlier than you had planned, right?" Elisabeth asked. Flossy thought for a few seconds and nodded, as she chewed her fingernails. Once again she went to the pile of 'if only's.' "If only I wouldn't have gone for the cooler. If only I'd had gone to work that day like I was supposed to."

"Why did you stay home?" Brandi asked.

"To take Patrick to the beach," she answered. "It was so hard to see him sitting on the porch everyday when I left for work. He'd beg me to take him to the beach, so I promised I would the next day."

"So you're punishing yourself for loving your son enough to be with him," a participant commented.

~

Flossy closed her eyes and sat silent as she recalled Elisabeth's words to a previous participant who couldn't seem to let go of his anger. "Take the shit and turn it into fertilizer," she had told him. Recalling the incident, a light was turned on. And for the first time since her son's death, she said she was able to see the trip to the beach as a measure of her love, rather than through the eyes of guilt. At the suggestion of Brandi, Flossy visualized herself transferring the piles of guilt and anger into a hot air balloon. Then she released the balloon into outer space until she no longer could see it.

"Guilt and anger are very powerful emotions," Elisabeth said. "Most of us will experience them after the death of a loved one. But they are much more intense if you feel responsible for the death. Then these emotions can cripple the way one thinks and feels about oneself, and can destroy a healthy self-image."

Elisabeth handed Flossy a pillow. She took it into her arms and cradled it. "Most often, the hardest thing about losing a significant other is that we didn't get a chance to say good-bye. We didn't get to tell that person how much we loved them, or to take care of other matters of concern. This is what I've termed, *unfinished business*." Turning to Flossy, she said, "What would you like to say to Patrick?"

Flossy put her head on the pillow and began to cry softly. "I'd like to tell him how sorry I am for not protecting him. I'd like to tell him how much I miss and love him." She gripped the pillow tighter. "I'd like…to tell him… how proud I am …that he did so well in karate and how proud I am to be his mother. Patrick, you were the greatest son ever!" she said. Then she looked at Elisabeth. "I am still his mother, right?"

"For always," Elisabeth responded.

Flossy's soft cries became louder and louder. "Oh, my gosh," I said to Steve, the doctor who was sitting next to me. "I thought losing a mother was bad. I don't think I could ever bear losing a child." In a panic I rushed out of the room and down the hall to the pay phone. My fingers trembled as I dialed the numbers. "Once I know everyone's okay, I'll calm down," I told myself. I felt relieved when Bryan answered. I pretended to be on a break and calling just to say hi. One-by-one I briefly talked to each of my boys. The littlest ones talked about the snowman that their daddy had helped them make while the older two talked with excitement about a Wild Game Feed that Bryan was taking them to that evening.

"I better get going," I said when Bryan came back on the line.

"Wait! Don't hang-up yet," he said. "I miss you, Sweetheart! Are you okay? I've been so worried about you. I should have gone with you."

"Don't worry, Bry, I'm fine! I'm going to have a lot to share with you when I get home. But I have to get back to the conference now."

We said our good-byes, and as I hung up it dawned on me that I had been comforting Bryan. "What a change of pace," I openly exclaimed as I rushed back to the room. I felt relieved and even joyful. I knew the kids were safe and having fun with Bryan and his mother. Once again I relaxed, and by the time Flossy returned to her seat I was able to comfort her. "You're doing good. The healing is coming," I said, as I patted her hand.

❧

It was near the end of the day before I felt brave enough to talk about my First Communion Day to the group. It had been the first 'big' occasion in the family after my mother's death. As a little girl I had, somewhat, taken the day in stride. But now, thrashing through my Pandora's box, I found the memories upsetting, rather than joyful.

"Where should I begin?" I asked, looking at Elisabeth and the counselors.

"Just start talking. The memories will come," Larry said.

"Okay," I said, nodding to the counselor, and began.

One day, a knock came on the door when my sisters and I were home alone. "Mama!" Catherine hollered, as she ran to open it. We looked. There was Moonshine Bill, an old man from down the road. "Our Dad's at work!" Catherine told him and slammed the door.

"Catherine!" Bernadette said opening the door again.

"I'll come back another time," he said.

"Why won't Mama come back home?" Catherine asked, dropping her Thumbelina to the floor.

"I told you, Mama's dead!" Bernadette said. "She's up in heaven with God and the angels!"

Catherine started to cry. "I want Moe," she screamed.

I ran and got her Thumbelina from the floor. "No, I want my doll Moe!" she said, and stomped her feet on the floor.

We looked and looked for Moe, but we couldn't find him. Catherine kept crying and crying. She cried so hard, we couldn't even understand what she said when she talked. I told her that if she'd quit crying, I'd jump rope with her and even let her win. But she still kept crying. Finally, when Sarah reminded her that Dad was taking us to see Jude and afterwards to Allen's store to get a baby chicken, she quit crying.

We played four different games of jump rope, but I didn't let Catherine win, because she cheated. She never even crossed the rope for the *O'Leary's*. And when we did *Johnny Over the Ocean,* she jumped on two feet, instead of just one.

By the time Dad came home from work, my legs were wobbly from jumping rope. "We'll be leaving for Jude's as soon as I'm changed, so get in the car," he said.

Anna kept tooting the horn while we waited for Dad. He was mad at her for tooting when he came out of the house. But when we were passing Mama's grave, Anna asked if he'd 'poot' the horn, and he did, for a long ways, until we couldn't see any of the shiny stones.

When we turned onto the highway, Sarah and Bernadette started reading the signs that were along the road and I counted all the cars we met.

"Uncle Roy's green car is number twenty-eight," I said, when we got to Jude's. We hurried out of the car and into the house. Aunt Geraldine was peeling potatoes and she let me help. Bernadette got to cut up pickles and Sarah got to set the table. My other sisters played piano and Dad and my brothers took turns holding Jude.

At lunchtime, Monica and I got to sit on the piano bench that Uncle Roy pulled up to the table.

"Jude's spitting out his peas!" Sarah hollered. My sisters and I giggled. But when Monica started spitting out her peas, Dad told us to stop laughing and Aunt Geraldine said that if we cleaned up our plates, she'd play piano for us. And, then, even before the dishes were done, she played it, and her accordion too. My sisters and I sang to the songs as we took turns holding Jude. Even Monica got to hold him. But when she poked her fingers in his eyes, on purpose, Dad took Jude away from her and gave him back to Uncle Roy.

"I think it's time for us to get going," Dad said. Monica started crying, because she wanted to stay there. She tried to take Jude's teddy bear home, and when Dad made her give it back, she started screaming.

"Monica," I said, taking her hand, "don't cry or Dad won't take us to get a baby chicken."

"A shicken?" she asked.

"Yes," I said, on the way to the car, "a chicken!"

⌒

Dad and my brothers tipped their hats and Sarah, Bernadette and I made the sign-of-the-cross when we passed St. John's church on our way to Allen's store.

"Why do we do that, Dad?" I asked.

"Out of respect for God," he said as he stopped the car in front of the store. We hurried in, and looked at the yellow baby chickens that were in the big box. We each wanted one, but Dad said, "No, only the 'free' one." We picked the littlest one, the one with the big white spot on its back. Catherine carried it to the car. And on the way home, we let it peck our hands and fingers.

When we got out of the car, Peanut Butter, our rooster, jumped up at us. He tried to get our baby chicken, so I hit him on the head.

"Be careful how you treat that rooster," Dad said, as we went into the house. "You know how mean roosters can be!"

Dad took an empty box and made a bed for our chicken, while we tried to think of a name for it.

"Why don't you girls just call it Chicky?" Luke said. So that's what we called it.

One day Chicky was shivering and he wouldn't go to sleep. "Chicky's cold," I said. Dad and my brothers were at work and we didn't know what to do. We looked for a blanket to put inside of his box, but all the blankets were too big.

"Let's use a kitchen curtain for a blanket," Anna said.

"That's a great idea!" I told her. So Anna and I climbed on the counter and took down one of the curtains and put it into Chicky's box. He went right to sleep. Later, when Catherine and I went to check on him, he wasn't in his box. Monica was sitting in the closet with him and holding him by the neck.

"Monica!" I screamed, "don't carry Chicky like that!" Very carefully I took him from her. "Go sit on the couch. If you're nice, I'll put Chicky into your hands and I'll show you how to pet him," I told her.

We love Chicky. That's why we take him wherever we go. One time Dad let us take him to church, but we had to leave him in the car. Dad even let us take him with us when we went to pick up Mark at the train station. Mark came home to live with us again. The Marine people said he could come home to help my dad, because of Mama being dead. And Mark does help my dad. When we get home from school, he has the dirty clothes washed and folded, but he makes us put them away. And he makes us change into play clothes, because he says he's tired of washing all the time.

At bedtime, Mark makes us wash up by ourselves and go to

bed at eight. Even when company is at our house and we ask *Dad* if we can stay up late, *Mark* says, "Noop, bedtime!"

One night he got mad at us for screaming when he tried to brush the snarls out of our hair. So the next day he walked to town and bought us each a hairbrush.

"Line up," he said that night. "Smallest to the biggest."

"They're not in the Marines!" John said.

"No," he told John, "but they can learn to do things for themselves."

So we lined up, smallest to the biggest. Then Mark gave us each a brush.

"I want you brushing the person's hair in front of you," he said. Then he bent down at the front of the line and gave Monica her doll. "Here," he said, "you can brush your doll's hair. Sarah, you're the oldest so you can brush your own when you're done."

We brushed and screamed and brushed and screamed until Mark said, "Okay, it looks like all the snarls are out! You can quit now and jump into your beds." We jumped and jumped and jumped on the beds until Mark yelled, "Enough!"

"Dad," he hollered, "they're all tucked in."

When Dad came in to tell us stories and say prayers with us, Mark said, "I'm heading for bed. I'm whipped."

Dad sat at the foot of the bed. "Don't tell us wolf stories tonight! Tell us girl stories—like Cinderella or Snow White or Rapunzel, like Mama used to," I said. But Dad said that he didn't like telling girl stories. The only girl story he'd tell us was *Little Red Ridinghood*—about how she thought the mean wolf was her grandmother.

"I hope a mean wolf doesn't come to our house dressed up like Grandma!" I said. "I don't want to get eaten up!"

"Shhhh," Dad said, and he started telling us the *Three Little Pigs.* I got scared, but Dad said, "It's just a story." Then he told us about the wolf that ate the Billy Goat Kids.

"Only one of the seven Billy Goat Kids got away from the wolf. He hid in the tall clock case where the wolf couldn't find him," Dad told us.

"If a wolf ever comes to our house," I asked, "where should we hide?"

"Just don't be foolish like the Billy Goat Kids were. They

opened the door when their mother told them not to. If you don't open the door, you won't have to worry about where you're going to hide," he said, then finished the story.

After prayers, Dad turned out the light. We screamed, but he wouldn't come back. I pulled the blankets over my head and yelled for Mama. So did my sisters. Finally, Dad came back.

"I'm not turning on the light," he said.

From the hallway light, I noticed that Dad was carrying something. "I brought a friend for you," he said.

"Chicky!" we screamed.

"Will it make you happier if I let him sleep in your room tonight?"

"Yes!" we shouted. And after that night, Chicky always slept in our room, right in bed with Sarah, Monica, and me.

☞

One Friday when we came home from school, the only one at our house was Chicky—not Mark or Dad, or Anna or Monica. When Dad finally came home, he told us that he took Mark to live with Grandma Jacques. "Mark got a job in Escanaba," he said. "It would be too far for him to drive everyday to work, so he's going to live with Grandma now. She wanted to move back to her own home, so Mark is going to live with her to watch over her."

"Will we ever get to see him again?" Catherine asked. "Or is he dead like Mama now?"

"No, no," Dad said. "Mark will be coming home on the weekends."

"Do we have to help you wash the clothes again?" Sarah asked.

"Yes," Dad said.

On Saturday, just like Dad said, Mark came home. Then one Saturday he brought his girlfriend Sandy home with him, and lots of donuts, too. We hid behind the wood stove, because we were afraid of Sandy. But then, I peeked out.

"Darn!" Mark said, winking at Sandy. "No one's home. I was planning on taking my little sisters for a ride to the store in my new car to buy them each a popsicle."

Monica ran out from behind the stove. "I wanna sicle," she

160

said.

"So do I!" Anna screamed. And one-by-one we all jumped out from behind the wood stove and said that we wanted one, too. So Mark and Sandy took us to the store. My sisters each got a red popsicle, but I got a purple one. Mark made us eat them before he'd let us get back into his car. Then he took us riding to see if the Mayflowers were out. They were, so we picked handfuls and took them home. Sandy put them into jars of water for us. That night they went back to Escanaba. We watched them leave, then started to cry.

"Come on now," Dad said. "He'll be back before you know it. Instead of crying, go decide what you'll wear to school on Monday."

"In school, we're making Mother's Day pins," I told Dad.

"That's nice," he said. I told him how my class was going to fill a tablespoon with Plaster of Paris and then set a safety pin into it. And how, when it hardened we'd paint a flower on it. "Then it'll be a pretty pin and we get to give it to our mother," I said. Dad put his head down and put his hands over his face. He didn't say if he thought they'd be pretty, and I didn't ask him, because it looked like he was going to cry.

On Wednesday when we made the pins, I asked Mrs. Webster if everybody had to color their rose red. "Not necessarily," she said.

"Good," I said, "because my mama's favorite color is yellow."

"Yellow will be very pretty," she said. "Maybe you can give the pin you make to your grandma."

"But I want to give it to my mama," I said. "Mama will like this pin."

"Maybe you could give it to your brother's girlfriend," she said. "Just be thinking about who you'd like to give it to.

When I went to bed that night, I thought about Friday and when I'd get to take the pin home. And how, on Mother's Day, Mark would be coming with Sandy for my First Holy Communion.

"I want to give the pretty pin to Mama—not Sandy. Sandy will take the pin home with her, " I said to Bernadette when Dad turned out the light.

161

"Don't lose your pin," Mrs. Webster said as she handed them out on Friday. "And don't let me see you with a big, dirty face on Sunday when you wear the dress I bought you. Since your mother passed-on, you often come to school with a dirty face."

"What's *passed-on*? Mrs.Webster."

"Never mind that. Just be sure you wash until you're clean," she said.

On the bus, I showed my sisters the Plaster of Paris pin. They felt the painted rose, covered with the glitter.

"I wish I could give it to Mama," I said to Sarah.

"You can give it to Sandy, she'll like it," she said, smiling.

"I know, but I want to give it to Mama—it has a *rose* on it! Rose is Mama's name!"

Sarah, Bernadette, and Catherine showed me the Mother's Day presents they had made for Mama, too. Bernadette and Sarah each wrote poems, but only Bernadette would read hers to me.

To Mama

> *Roses are red*
> *Violets are blue*
> *The world is big*
> *And so are you.*

Love Bernadette

"Mama will like that poem," I said to Bernadette as I reached for Catherine's Mother's Day card.

"That's just a stick person," I said to Catherine when I looked at the picture she had drawn.

"No it's not! That's me handing Mama flowers."

"You colored out of the lines," I said.

"It's pretty," Bernadette said to Catherine when we were getting off the bus.

"Hey, look, Russell's coming down the road," Sarah shouted.

"Yippee," I yelled, and we ran to meet him.

We like it when Russell walks by our house, because he still brings us candy on his way home from the store. Nobody else comes to our house anymore, like when Mama first went away—except for Russell, and Wes, too. Wes is the grater driver. Whenever he goes by our house driving the grater, he throws out packs of gum through the open door. They land on the ground, so my sisters and I run to get the Teaberry and the Blackjack.

⁀

When Russell stopped on his way back from town, I asked him if he was coming to my First Holy Communion. Russell put his hand over his mouth and started laughing. "Oh, oh!" he said. "Now ya hafta tell priest bad things!"

"That's called Confession," Sarah said.

"Sister Janet Marie told me that confession is telling the priest your sins," I said. "Sister said that when we tell a priest our sins it helps us not to do bad things. On Sunday—Mother's Day—I get to make my First Holy Communion, but first I have to make my First Confession, so my soul will be clean. But I'm afraid to go in that little room to tell Father Dishaw my sins."

John laughed, "It's not like there's going to be a big, old wolf behind the curtain."

"A wolf!" I shivered.

⁀

I was shaking when I went into the confessional room on Saturday morning. I knelt on the kneeler in the little dark room. A tiny bit of light came out from behind the little curtain. "In the name of the Father, and of the son, and of the Holy Ghost," I said as I made the sign-of-the-cross.

"Go ahead," Father's 'voice' said, "continue."

"Bless me Father for I have sinned, this is my first confession and these are my sins." Then I told Father that I had three venial sins. He asked me what they were.

"I pulled Bernadette's hair twice, but she started the fight!" I said. "Once I sassed my dad and I told Anna there was a spider on her back, but there wasn't one there."

"So you lied. Are these all your sins, child?"

"No," I said. "I have a mortal sin, too."

"A *mortal* sin? Are you sure it's a mortal sin?"

"Yes," I said. "Sister told us that killing is a mortal sin, and I killed my mother! I made her sick and she died and won't come back home now."

"Why do you think *you* made her sick?"

"I wrote with color crayon on the new wall. I drew flowers for Mama and the flowers made her sick, she said."

"Oh dear," Father said. "You must never think this anymore. Your mother would feel very, very sad if she knew you thought like this. Your mother's work on earth was finished, so God called her home to heaven. You didn't kill her!" Then he told me that I was forgiven for all my sins and told me the penance that I had to do when I left the confessional. Then he blessed me.

In the pew, I knelt and said the three Hail Mary's and the two Our Father's that were my penance. "Dear God," I said. "Father said that I *didn't* kill Mama. Somebody else did. So will you let her come home tomorrow for my First Communion?"

꿈

At bedtime, I went to the closet to look at my pretty white dress that Mrs. Webster bought for me. "Cinderella has a dress just like this," I told Catherine.

"I know," she said, "You're going to be pretty like her. We jumped into bed. "Yippee," I said, "tomorrow I get to make my First Holy Communion!" I lifted my pillow and put Mama's Mother's Day pin under it. Then I asked my Fairy Godmother to come and get the pin and bring it to Mama in heaven.

꿈

During the night the thunder kept waking me. But when morning came, the sun was shining. I lifted my pillow. Mama's pin was still under it. "Darn, my Fairy Godmother didn't come to take my Mother's Day pin to Mama. Now I'll have to give it to Sandy," I said to myself. I hurried to Dad's bedroom. "Dad," I whispered, "is it time to get up?"

Dad looked at the clock. "We all better shake-a-leg!"

I knew what that meant—get ready really fast! So I hurried

to the new bathroom and climbed up onto the sink. I washed my face, but I couldn't get the gum off that was stuck on my chin, so I took Dad's Lava soap and scrubbed really hard. The gum came off, but then dots of blood popped onto my skin. I jumped down from the sink and ran to my bedroom. Sarah took my dress from the hanger. "I don't want you to help me get dressed! I want Mama to."

"Do you want to do it alone?" she asked.

"No," I said. So Sarah took the rag curls out of my hair, that she had put in the night before, then helped me into my dress. "Now where's your veil?" she asked.

"On the bed," I said. But when Sarah and I looked, my pretty white veil was gone. I went running to tell Dad that it was gone, but on the way to his bedroom I saw my veil in the kitchen on top of Monica's head.

"Give that here, Monica," I said. But she thought it was hers and when I jerked it from her the picky stuff ripped.

"Look what you made me do," I cried. Dad came running to see what was the matter. I showed him my ripped veil. Dad hurried and got the needle and thread. Sarah had to hold Monica, because she kept trying to grab my veil while Dad was sewing it. I ran and got my socks and saddle shoes on.

☙

Mrs. Webster was waiting on the church steps to see me. "What on earth has happened to your face?" she asked. So I told her about the big bubble and how it wouldn't come off. She smiled. "You still look like a pretty little angel to me."

I smiled back. "Mrs. Webster," I said, looking at her, "I'm as tall as your lips now." I put my hand up on top of my head and went right to Mrs. Webster's lips with it.

"Oh heavens," she said, moving my hand away, "Look at those dirty shoes!" She grabbed her hanky out of her sweater sleeve and spit on it. She bent down and wiped dirt off the white of my shoes.

"It'll have to do! I'll talk to you after Mass," she said, then went into church.

All of us who were making our First Communion waited outside with Sister Janet Marie and Father Dishaw. After the church bells rang, we walked down the aisle carrying a pretty white candle that had holy things drawn on it. I saw Grandma, Great Uncle Willy, Great Aunt Hazel, Great Uncle Johnny and Great Aunt Eva. They were all sitting in pews by my dad and my brothers and sisters.

The boys from my class sat in the front pew on one side and the girls sat on the other side. I sat between Sister and Celeste.

"Sit still, sweetheart," Sister said. But I kept moving around. "Why are you so antsy?" she asked. I lifted my shoulders. I kept looking around to see if I could see Mama, because Mama once told me, when she was real sick, that she'd come to my First Holy Communion, *even* if she were *dead*. So I stood and turned around to see if she was up in the choir. Celeste pulled me back down.

"You're going to get in trouble," she whispered.

Celeste, Janet and Eileen are my Catholic friends. That's what church we go to—the Catholic church. My friends Krystal and Debbie are my Protestant friends. They can't come to our church and we can't go to their church, and I don't know why.

"I wish Debbie and Krystal could come and see me in my pretty white dress," I thought. "I wish Mama could come and see me in my pretty white dress. Mama would say, 'Hello, Cinderella!' Dad didn't say anything."

Father Dishaw sang, "Kyri e e le i son," then the people sang "Kyri e e le i son." Then he sang, "Chri ste e le i son," and the people sang that too. Father said a lot of other prayers and Sister turned the pages of my little white prayer book for me.

The girls in my class got a white prayer book with a white rosary and the boys got a black prayer book with a black rosary. But everybody got the same color scapular. I'm never taking off my scapular because, at practice, Sister said that if we die and we're wearing our scapulars, we'd go straight to heaven. I'll get to see Mama!

☞

Father lifted the gold cup. My brother John and his friend Danny Tatrow—the altar boys—rang the little gold bells. That's when I remembered what Father Dishaw told us at practice.

"When the altar boys ring the bells, it's a very, very important part of the Mass, so pay attention! Soon the bread and wine will turn into the body and blood of Jesus Christ!"

When the choir sang, "Padre Ome Po tem tem, fa tor im chali at tear rae," we got up and went to the altar and knelt at the communion rail and Father Dishaw came to give us communion. John came with him. John was carrying the little gold plate. He put the little gold plate under my neck, like he had put it under everybody else's neck in case Father dropped the host—that's Jesus! I tipped my head back. And just when I was about to close my eyes and open my mouth, like Sister showed us to do at practice, John made an ugly frog-face at me. But I didn't make an ugly face back. I just closed my eyes and opened my mouth and let Father put Jesus onto my tongue. Then I closed my mouth, made the sign-of-the-cross, stood up, folded my hands and slowly walked back to the pew and knelt down to swallow Jesus and to thank him for coming into my heart.

"Sister," I said, pulling on her long black dress, "Jesus is stuck on the roof of my mouth." I started to put my finger into my mouth to get Him off.

"You mustn't touch with your hands. Use your tongue," she said, and she took my hand from my mouth.

After communion Celeste got up and put a crown on the Blessed Virgin Mary, then the choir started to sing another song. This time I could understand the song. It was in words I knew—it was English—O*n This Day Oh Beautiful Mother*. So I started singing too—to Mama. That's when my tummy started feeling funny. It felt like a zillion grasshoppers were hopping around on the inside of it.

"Sister Janet Marie," I said, tugging on her long black veil. "Sister Janet Marie, I think I'm going to puke." Sister lifted me onto her lap. "It's almost over," she whispered. Then she patted my back until we stood up to walk out of church.

When we got outside, Sister asked me how I was doing. "You miss your Mama, don't you?"

"Yes," I said. "I want Mama to come and see me today in my pretty white dress. I want her to see my little white prayer book and my white rosary, but she's way up in heaven."

"That may be true," Sister said, "But you could write her a letter tonight, to tell her all about today. You don't have to mail it." Then Sister gave me a big hug and kiss. "We better get back to the others," she said.

My friends were getting their pictures taken, so I hurried to have Dad and Grandma take my picture, too. But Grandma and my aunts and uncles all forgot to take a camera and Dad said that he couldn't find Mama's. "I think Monica took it to our playhouse to take pictures of her mud pies," I said.

Uncle Willy and Aunt Hazel brought their grandson Billy with them, too, and he didn't want to be at church anymore, so we all went home. When we got there, Billy ran away. My brothers had to help find him. He was in the woods by our house. Right after my brothers found him, Aunt Hazel said they better get going. Uncle Willy and Uncle Johnny each gave me two dollars.

After they left, Dad told me that someday he'd take me to the Five and Dime store in Manistique, so that I could spend my money. "I'm going to buy Monica a new doll, because she scribbled ink all over her doll from Santa and we can't get it off," I told Dad.

That night, Dad let Monica wear my pretty veil all around the house, because she kept crying for it. Then Anna and Catherine took turns wearing it. When Bernadette got a turn, Sarah sang, "Here comes the bride." My sisters and I giggled.

"Make them stop, Dad!" Bernadette cried. So Dad made us get into bed.

"Today's been a real long day," he said.

"Can we play in our beds?" I asked.

"Go ahead, but don't be calling me for anything. I'm tired," he said.

We played *Press on the Starter*. It's the game that we lie on the bed to play. Someone has to put their feet out and someone else has to put their feet onto that person's feet. Then you have to try to keep their feet pushed down by them, and they have to try to keep your feet pushed way down by you, and everyone sings:

> *Press on the starter*
> *Grind old Lizzy*
> *Come on team*
> *Let's get busy.*

We played the game until our legs wouldn't move anymore. Then I saw the Man-in-the-Moon looking at us through the window. I screamed and hollered for Dad to come by us.

"I'm not going back there!" he said. "Get to sleep!"

⌒

"Your Dad sure had a heavy cross to carry. Just knowing that he kept all of his children together makes me want to call him a saint," an elderly woman said.

I was exhausted but managed to say that I agreed with her. As I was walking back to my seat a man stood and embraced me. "I give your dad a lot of credit. I've been an only parent for one year now, to just one child, and it's been very tough, he said, and began to tremble and cry. Elisabeth motioned him to the front.

Chapter Sixteen

We participants grew closer with each day that passed and many were already feeling they had a new grip on life. Although I had shared more than most, something was still keeping me from moving out of the depression completely. So again, later that afternoon, I decided to talk, but this time privately with a counselor in one of the adjacent rooms. As I took a seat in a recliner, I wondered if there would ever be an end to the painful memories—to the tears. I felt frustrated with my feelings and wanted them to disappear, once and for all.

"Why am I taking so long to get over this?" I asked Brandi. "Other people have only shared once and they're doing fine," I said, hitting the arm of the chair.

"Maybe their pain isn't as old," she responded. "You've spent nearly your entire lifetime carrying this pain. The longer a person has a problem, the longer it's going to take to heal. Think of it as a cut on your leg. If you seek medical attention promptly, the cut will heal quickly. If you ignore the cut, it will fester and infection will set in and it'll take much longer to heal. You experienced a death as a child and were unable to rationalize or understand the consequences that followed losing your mother. So now you're doing it here. The concept of understanding death is thought to be at age eight; you were only seven. You tried in your way to understand it, and maybe with a little help you could have. And you say that some of the other participants seemed to be feeling better. Well, they were adults when they lost that significant other. In no way am I implying that it's *easy* as an adult to deal with a death, just *easier.*"

Brandi handed me a glass of water. "What are you in such deep thought about?" she asked.

"Oh, I was just thinking how scared I felt all the time after my mother died. I became afraid of everything it seemed—animals, noises, people, and even that I might cry and make my dad sad. But I was especially scared that my dad would die."

"Well, we're going to try to help you get over those feelings. So, tell me more about those feelings."

"But all this talking just doesn't seem to be working for me," I said with frustration.

"Keep in mind the old saying 'the darkest hours are just before the dawn.' You're close, you really are. Just hang in there and trust what I'm saying," she said.

"Wow, the darkest hours are just before the dawn," I said to myself. Once again I felt a small ray of hope. Then without much hesitation, I continued down the bumpy, icy, narrow road of the past.

⤚

"Time to get up girls. We've got work to do," my dad yelled. "It's another Saturday and we can't be wasting it away. Your brothers have already been working for hours."

"Here Chicky, Chicky, Chicky," I heard Monica saying. She patted my arm with her cold hand and said, "Donna Jean, I not know where Chicky is."

"I don't know where he is either. Just keep calling him, he'll come," I told her. But Monica, and Anna too, called and called, but they still couldn't find him. So Catherine and I hurried up to help them look. "Maybe Chicky decided to sleep in, like my little girls did," Dad said. Anna thought Chicky was hiding in Wilhelmina's basket, because Chicky liked to sleep with our bunny, but he wasn't there. We looked in the utility room by the chimney, too, but he wasn't in the cubbyhole either. I called outside for him, but he didn't come running. All of a sudden, Catherine started screaming. We all ran to her. "Chicky's hanging on the bedsprings and I can't get him off!" John was just coming in from milking the cows and he heard Catherine screaming and ran to her.

"Watch out!" he said. John took Chicky from the bedsprings and held him in his hand. "He's dead!" he said. Anna, Catherine and I started crying.

"Settle down!" Dad said to me, "or you'll lose your breath like you've done before."

"Can I hold Chicky?" I asked, but Dad turned his head toward the door and motioned for John to go by him. We heard him whispering to John, "Just go toss that chicken out in the field some place where the girls won't find him." We started screaming.

"You can't do that!" John shouted. "The girls like this chicken!"

"But it's just a chicken!" Dad said. "And it's dead! Get it out of here, so they can get over it."

John wrapped Chicky in a washcloth. "Come on girls, let's go bury him," he said.

We followed John to Mama's crabapple tree. He dug an itty-bitty hole in the ground and put Chicky in it. Then he had us say good-bye.

"Bye, bye little Chicky," I said petting him. "Why won't you come back to live with us? Why won't you come back home?" I cried. Catherine was lying on the ground and kicking her feet and hitting her arms against the ground. John lifted her onto his lap. Then we covered Chicky with dirt.

"Chicky's not going to be able to breathe," I told him.

"It won't matter. He's already dead!" he said.

"Like Mama's dead?" Catherine cried.

"Like Mama," John said.

So we covered Chicky with the dirt. "Let's say a prayer now," he said. So we said the *Angel of God*. Then John stood up and told us to follow him. He took us to the orchard and told us to pick some flowers to put on Chicky's grave. Raindrops were getting us wet, but we didn't even care. We just kept picking the Lazy Susans, the Indian Paintbrushes, and the Dandelions. Then we ran and put them on the grave.

"There," John said. "He's going to heaven, now."

"Mama's up in heaven," Anna said.

"That's right," John said. "Now let's get in the house. I think it's going to storm soon."

⤙

It thundered and lightning and rained all day long on Thursday. On Friday night it was raining when we got home from school, so we didn't get to go outside to play.

"I hope it doesn't rain for the school picnic this year," Bernadette said.

"I don't care about the picnic. I'm just glad there's only two more weeks until school's out," Luke said, as he made pip-a-de-pop (that's popcorn).

"Get up to the table if you want some," he said when it was done popping. So we hurried to the table. Luke poured us each a pile. Anna thought that some of her popcorn looked like horses and pigs. Bernadette found a ballerina and a lady's shoe in hers. Sarah found a frog and Catherine found an elephant popcorn. I found a baldheaded man that looked like Mr. Funeral and Monica found an angel popcorn. We all wanted to find an angel popcorn, so I asked Luke if he'd make us more pip-a-de-pop, but he made us go to bed. He and Dad take turns tucking us in now. I heard Dad say to Luke one night that Luke had to start helping him out more. "It's too long of a day when I have to do it all by myself," he told Luke. So Luke tucked us in on Friday night after popcorn time and Saturday night after cinnamon toast and cocoa.

⤙

Wilhelmina's fuzzy powder-puff was tickling my face when I woke up one morning. I laughed and pushed her big butt away. "Wilhelmina, get down!" I said. I pushed her to the floor and she hopped out of our bedroom.

"Wake up, everybody," I shouted. "It's Saturday! Let's play games outside today after we get our chores done."

"Want to do jump rope doubles?" Bernadette asked.

"Let's play *Eenie-I-Over* the house with John's baseball," Catherine said.

"Okay," we said. So everybody got out of bed and got

dressed. Sarah helped Monica, because Monica always puts her shoes on the wrong feet and her clothes on backwards. So does Anna, but she won't let anybody help her. One time she had her slacks on *backward* and her shirt on *inside out*, right at *church.* The pockets of her pants were in the front and the tag of her shirt was sticking out at us. We got the giggles. Dad kept making mean faces for us to stop the giggles, but we still kept giggling and giggling and bubbles kept popping out of my nose. I asked Sarah if she had Mama's hanky, the one with the lilacs on?

"No," she whispered.

"Do you have her other hanky, the one with the R.J. in the corner of it?"

"No," she whispered again. "Donna Jean, we're in church! Be quiet!"

The bubbles kept popping out, so I sniffed my nose. Then John's elbow hit into my side. "Quit sniffing!" he said. But I had to sniff, because stuff kept leaking out of my nose and I didn't want my nose to look like this girl's nose that's in my class. Her nose is always icky. I would tell you her name, but Mama says it's not nice to talk about other people. Mama says if you can't say anything good about a person, don't say anything at all.

Dad was mad at us for laughing in church that day, so now when Anna wears her slacks on backwards or inside out or her shoes are on the wrong feet, I try not to laugh in church. I just say to myself, "Mama's dead." Saying that always makes me sad.

My sisters and I ran outside to play right after our beds were made, the dishes done, and the dirty clothes put in piles. Lots of pretty clouds were up in the sky, so we tried to find the prettiest one, like we always do when there are clouds in the sky. I saw a cloud that looked like a teddybear and pointed to it. "I found the prettiest cloud!" I hollered, but nobody liked the teddybear cloud. Then Anna thought she had found the prettiest cloud, but nobody liked the giant flower, either. "There's the prettiest cloud—that's the Mama cloud!" Catherine yelled. And when we looked to the cloud that she was pointing to, the one that looked like an angel, we all said, "Yup, that's the Mama cloud!" The prettiest cloud is always Mama cloud.

Bernadette ran to get a piece of clothesline from the shelf in the utility room. "Come on!" she said. "Hurry so we can jump rope."

So we hurried to the driveway to jump rope on the gravel. We saw Luke getting into the car. "Where're you going?" I asked.

"To Corky's," he said, and he drove away in our noisy car to his friend's house.

See, lots of times, Dad lets Luke take the car all by himself. But one time when we got to go with Luke to the store, he turned into the driveway really fast and Monica fell out. Luke stopped fast, jumped out of the car, then ran and picked her up. My dad heard Monica screaming and came running. He took her from Luke and said, "You're not going to be taking the car anymore if that's the way you're going to drive."

"The girls should know better than to open the door before I stop!" Luke said on the way into the house.

Dad put a cold, wet wash cloth onto the big bump on Monica's forehead, but she kept crying. But when he called the big bump 'a big egg,' Monica started to laugh. "Chicken not poop egg der," she said. Everybody laughed.

⌒

"I'm first," I hollered when we were getting ready to jump rope.
"Second," Anna shouted.

I watched the rope go around and around as Anna and Bernadette turned it. I waited, then jumped in, and sang with every jump:

Johnny over the ocean; Johnny over the sea,
Johnny broke a sugar bowl and blamed it on to me.
I told my Ma. My Ma told my Pa,
Johnny got a licken, so ha, ha, ha.
How many lickens did Johnny get, 1, 2, 3, 4, 5, 6...

"Ha, ha, ha, you missed, Bernadette said."
"My turn," Anna yelled, dropping the rope.
"That's not fair," I said, pushing Anna. "Anna, you don't know how to turn the rope right! It's Anna fault! She doesn't turn

it high enough. I get to have another turn!"

Anna started crying, because when I pushed her, she fell to the ground.

"Big baby!" Sarah said to me.

We started fighting, so Dad made us quit. "Break it up!" he said. "Don't you think that I ever get tired of that fighting? Get over here and help me finish planting the garden."

Catherine and Bernadette liked to help Dad plant the garden, but Sarah and I hated to, so he said we could make the supper instead.

I liked cooking and wanted to help peel potatoes. "You're too little. You could cut yourself," Sarah said.

"I'm big enough," I shouted. Then I told Sarah how Aunt Geraldine let Bernadette and me peel potatoes at her house."

"Did she show you how to cut the eyes out?"

"Sarah," I said, "*potatoes don't have eyes!*"

"*Oh, yes, they do!*" she said. And she showed me some potato eyes after we brought the potatoes up from the cellar. Then she let me peel six of them.

"Good job!" Sarah said to me as we watched for the potatoes to start bubbling. After they did, she took the bread dough from the refrigerator that Dad had made that morning. She broke off pieces of it and we stretched the pieces out until they looked like little pancakes. Then she fried it. Later, when Dad ate the fried bread dough and the boiled potatoes, he told us that supper tasted great.

☙

The big, red sun was falling down into the ground by the time we played *Eenie-I-Over.* After six games, we were thirsty. Sarah ran to the house to get us a glass so we could pump water into it. When she didn't come back, Anna and I ran to see where she was. When I opened the door, I heard Sarah crying. I ran to her and asked, "What's wrong, Sarah?"

"Dad went to the watering hole," she said.

"He did?" I said. Sarah shook her head, "Yes."

"How do you know?"

"John told me. He said that Dad went out the backdoor so we couldn't see him leave."

I started crying, too, and so did Anna. We didn't want Dad

to be at the watering hole.

"Donna Jeannnn, Annnna, Sarrrrah, are you coming back out to play?" Bernadette yelled, through the open window. When we didn't answer, Bernadette, Catherine and Monica came into the house looking for us.

"Why are you crying?" Bernadette asked.

"Dad went down to the watering hole," Sarah said.

"The watering hole!" Bernadette said, frowning like a sad clown. "Why did he go there?"

"We don't know," we cried. Then Bernadette started crying and so did Catherine and Monica.

See, we don't want Dad to go to the watering hole, because Mama didn't like it when Dad went there.

"What the heck is all the crying about in here?" John asked, coming into the room.

"You said, Dad's gone to the watering hole!" we cried.

"He'll be back tonight. It's not like he's going to get all drunk-up or something." Then he said, "I'm not sitting around here listening to a bunch of crybabies. You can baby-sit each other. I'm going to Calvin's!"

We begged John to stay, but he left anyway. We're afraid to stay alone at night, because of the big bad wolf! Sarah ran and got a butter knife to lock the door. She put the knife under the wood that goes around the door.

"That's not going to keep the big bad wolf away," I told her. "John says that wolves can eat *right through wood*! And our door is wood!"

"Yikes," Catherine said, and we all ran for Mama's closet to hide there.

"Don't you wish we had a tall clock case," I said, "so we could hide in it, in case the big bad wolf comes?"

"The big bad wolf isn't for real Donna Jean!" Bernadette said.

"Shush!" Sarah said. "I hear something!"

"It's probably the big bad wolf!" I whispered. "Or one of the other wolves Dad reads to us about! Like the wolf that tried to eat *Little Red Ridinghood*!"

"Or the wolf that tried to eat the *Three Little Pigs*," Anna said.

177

"I don't hear anything," Bernadette said. "Come on, let's play house. We'll stay right here in Mama's bedroom."

I wanted to be the mother, but Dad gave all of Mama's clothes, shoes, and lipstick, to my cousin Della, so I had to put on Dad's big shirt for a mother's dress.

"Shhhhh," Catherine whispered. "Now I hear something!"

"Ahhhhh!" I screamed. I grabbed Monica and Anna's hands and ran with them and hid in the closet again. "I won't let a wolf get you," I said.

"Donna Jean, be quiet! I think I heard Dad crying, or something," Bernadette said.

We listened. Somebody was crying and crying and crying.

"Maybe it's a wolf trying to eat Dad!" I said.

"It's coming from the back door," Bernadette whispered. "Dad probably fell and is bleeding and will die, like Mama died, if we don't hurry to help him!"

"Don't open the door!" I screamed. "It could be a wolf!"

My sisters couldn't find a flashlight, so Bernadette, Sarah, and Catherine got the big lamp from off the end table and took the shade off of it. Then they put extension cords onto the lamp's plug until the plug reached to the back door.

"Don't open the door," I hollered from Mama's bedroom. "Dad said we should never be foolish like the seven Billy goat kids were. So don't open it!" I yelled. But my sisters just told me to be quiet. They weren't afraid.

When they got the lamp working, I heard Bernadette say to Sarah, "Get over here by Catherine and me. We're holding the lamp, so you open the door."

"Do you think we'll see Dad dying?" Catherine asked.

"I don't know," Bernadette said.

My heart pounded. I held tight to my little sister's hands. See, they're really scared of the big bad wolf, because they're just little—they're not big like me. I didn't even let go of their hands to scratch the itch on my nose.

"Ouch," Anna said, "Don't squeeze my fingers, Donna Jean."

"Ouchies," Monica cried. "Dat hurts. Let go!"

I started to pray. I asked God to kill the wolf. Then I heard Bernadette tell Sarah and Catherine what she wanted them to do.

"When I say, 'go,' Sarah, open the door, fast!" Then she

said, "Get on your mark… get set… go!"

When Sarah opened the door, my sisters screamed. They screamed louder than ever before in their whole wide life. I listened. I could hear my heart pounding and the wolf coming into our house to eat us all up. "I wish Mama were here," I said to myself. I started shaking and the room started spinning, then it turned black.

⤺

"Donna Jean, Donna Jean, Donna Jeeean. Wake up Donna Jeeean."

"Is Donna Jean dead?" I heard Anna saying. I opened my eyes a little. I could see my sisters all around me. "Are we in the wolf's tummy?" I asked. Then I felt a cold wet washcloth land on my forehead, like Mama once put on my forehead when I had a fever. I opened my eyes wider. My sisters were all looking down at me.

"Donna Jean, we're not in the wolf's tummy, you fainted!" Sarah said.

"Is the wolf gone? Did you kill him?"

"Donna Jean!" Bernadette laughed as she looked into my eyes. "It wasn't a wolf! It was just our big old TOM CATS crying and fighting by the back door!"

Chapter Seventeen

The November sun was setting in the valley of the Catskills. The room in which Brandi and I sat grew dark. Laughter echoed in the hallway, where earlier in the week mostly crying was heard. Brandi suggested I take a brief break with the group, then return to deal with more of my troubled childhood. "The traumatic experiences are more than likely responsible for the fears you now live with. Now is the time for letting go. What I'm trying to say is, if you talk about as many of the unpleasant memories as possible, your fears will gradually disappear. The unpleasant experiences will lose their power over you," she said.

Brandi shared why she had so much faith in the workshop experience. It had always amazed her whenever Elisabeth would share letters from former participants who had found new ways to cope with old problems. For her it was proof that the more baggage one dumped the better chance they had of letting go of the past. She had come to a firm belief that talking about one's grief was *truly* the medicine for the soul. It enlightened her to know that in just verbalizing an unpleasant experience, the experience lost its power over that person. She understood that a person had to be ready and willing to let go. The only part she could play in the healing process was to give direction to the grieving person and encourage them along the way.

As I entered the room, after the break, Brandi was in deep

thought. I was about to ask her what was on her mind when she asked, "Donna, have you noticed how much you worry about death? I don't just mean your mother's death. It seems you have spent much of your energy worrying about your children, your husband, your dad and your siblings dying. And for that matter, even your own death."

"I worry about that a lot, I know, but I didn't realize it until a few years ago. I'm always thinking about death! Heck, I've already called home several times since leaving for New York to make sure everyone at home is okay. Sometimes my behavior makes me feel like such a loser, like such a failure. I'm afraid that someday my husband is going to finally get fed up with it all and leave. He desperately wants me to get better, but I don't think he knows how hard I've tried. I feel only God knows that. I bet I've read more books on self-help than anyone has. And I've tried more therapies than most, like Visualization, NLP techniques, meditation, journalizing and different forms of exercises, from aerobics to yoga. I also tried different diets that claimed to help depression, like a diet free of flour and sugar. But nothing seemed to help. That's until I put God first in my life. Then things started to happen. I believe He made it possible for me to be here right now. But yet, I still feel very much afraid that I'm going to go home empty handed. I'm worried how Bryan will react if I return still depressed. Oh, if only I had more faith. "

"That's why I'm encouraging you to talk about those significant events," Brandi said. "Eventually you'll be able to sort them out on your own."

"But how do I know what experiences are bothering me?"

"If a memory keeps lingering and is causing you concern— talk about it. Otherwise it'll continue to fester."

I thought for a minute, then said, "This probably isn't that important, but I've mulled it over and over in my mind since I was little."

Brandi laughed. "Then it probably needs attention," she said, "so, start there."

"Okay," I said, and began.

The morning bell rang and everyone hurried to sit down. Teacher hit the big paddle against the desk. "Settle down," she said as she got out her book to take roll call. "Today might be the last full day of school, but it doesn't mean you're not going to be doing your regular classes. It's report card day, so if you want me to pass them out at the end of the day, you better all be good or your parents will have to come and get them instead." No one said a word. Everyone was quiet as mice for the rest of the morning.

At lunchtime, Teacher told everyone to go single file to the lunchroom and that she'd be there shortly. She handed the lunch boxes to the kids who brought their lunch from home as they went out the door and punched the other kids hot lunch tickets. "Donna Jean," she said as I passed through the line, "please wait for me at the front of the room."

When the last person left, she walked to her desk. "I have a good notion not to pass you this year," she said, pushing up her glasses. "Your grades are all A's and B's, but you have not paid your hot lunch charges!" She put her hand around the back of my neck and lowered my head to the tablet on her desk. "See that?" she snapped.

"Yes, Mrs. Webster."

The light green page of the tablet had lots of little squares on it. Some of the squares had check marks in them, but lots of the little squares had Pd's. "Find *your* name!" she crabbed. So I looked into the tablet for my name.

"You can't find any 'paids' by *your* name, can you?" she asked. "Those check marks are all your hot lunch charges. Did you even bother to ask your Dad for the money to get them paid up?"

I was going to tell Teacher that I did ask my dad and that he said he still didn't have money for the charges, but she jerked my head up and said, "Or were you just too busy playing last night?"

"No, Teacher," I said. "I had to help Sarah do the ironing. I didn't get to play."

Teacher walked me by my ponytail to the door. "Get into the hot lunch line," she shouted.

My friends were almost done eating when I peeked to see

what was for hot lunch. "Oh goodie!" I thought. "Macaroni and cheese or macaroni and tomato, my favorites, and chocolate milk, because today is the last day for hot lunch."

Mrs. McPhee smiled when she handed me my plate of food. I put it on my tray. Then I took my chocolate milk and was on my way to go to sit by Krystal and Debbie when Mrs. Webster grabbed my arm. Some of my macaroni and tomatoes spilled out of my plate and onto the tray and some of the wormy macaronis went sliding onto the floor. Mrs. Webster grabbed my chocolate milk and put a bottle of white milk onto my tray instead. "Here!" she said. "You won't be drinking chocolate milk! Now go set your tray on a table and get a napkin to clean *your* mess off the floor!"

"Teacher's a witch!" Krystal said, when I set my tray on the table, then ran for a napkin.

"Krystal," Teacher said, "you know the rules! If you're done eating, leave the lunchroom!"

My other friends had to leave too, so I sat at the table alone. My stomach rolled around on the inside, like the inside of Mama's washing machine, as I tried to eat. I wasn't hungry anymore. I thought I was going to throw-up like Luke did the night Mama died. But I kept eating the macaronis because I didn't want to get in any more trouble. Teacher told me that everything had to be gone from my plate.

Just as I ate the last macaroni, the bell rang. Krystal, Eileen, Debbie, and Janet were waiting for me in the hallway. As we were walking fast to our classroom, Debbie said, "We thought of lots of fun things to do during summer vacation."

"We'll tell her at recess," Janet said as we took our seats.

When the bell rang to go out for the last recess of the day, my friends and I hurried down the hall. Suddenly I stopped. I spotted some money on the floor. I picked up the half-dollar. I was showing my friends it when a high school boy came by and plucked it out of my hand faster than my dad plucks feathers off of scalded chickens.

"Give that back to her, Billy," Krystal screamed. "She found it! Not you!" Billy went running with the money for a little ways, then turned around and threw it back. I looked at the silver money. "I better go give this to Mrs. Webster, so she can find out whose it is," I said.

"Isn't it 'finders keepers, losers-weepers?'" Eileen asked.

"No," I told her. "Mama said it's a sin to keep something that doesn't belong to you." So I went back to my room and gave the half-dollar to Mrs. Webster. She took it and said that she'd put up a sign that would say, MONEY FOUND.

"Mama can see me from heaven!" I said to Mrs. Webster. "She knows I found that money."

"Are you paying attention, little girl?" she asked as she took the half-dollar from my hand. "As I was saying, if no one comes to claim the money, you can have it. Since we only have one more day of school this year, you probably won't find out until next year if it's yours or not," she said.

"If I get to keep it Teacher, I'll pay *all* my hot lunch charges with it, okay?"

"Oh, dear me," she said as she sat on her chair. She lowered her head, put her hand over her eyes, then moved her head from side to side. "What should I do?"

"What?" I asked.

"You're excused," she said.

I started to run out of the room to hurry outside. "Walk— don't run!" she hollered.

I hurried down the hall to go outside. But just when I opened the big, steel door, the bell started ringing and lots of big boys came running in and the door slammed on my finger. I screamed. Mrs. Boudreau heard me and came running. Quickly, she opened the door. "My Lord!" she said when she saw all the blood.

Everyone was coming in the school and they looked at me. Mrs. Boudreau put my hand into her hand and walked me to the principal's office. She showed Mr. Johnson and Mrs. Richards my finger. Mrs. Richards ran for the First Aid Kit.

"I have to go back to class now," Mrs Boudreau said. "Take care." I started to cry again. "It'll be all right," she said as she wiped the tears from my face. Then she patted the top of my head and left.

Mr. Johnson bandaged my finger, then asked if I wanted to go home. "No!" I said. So he took me back to my classroom. When Mrs. Webster saw my bloody bandage she shook her head, marched over to me and said, "Were you running?"

I started to cry. Teacher took my hand and asked me what

had happened. After I told her she asked me if I was going to be okay. I wiped my eyes, then said, "Yes."

Everyone got out of their seats to look at my finger. "Back to your seats!" Teacher screamed. "Your assigned seats!"

I hurried to mine, too. When I sat down I could feel my tummy spinning around on the inside again, and when I moved macaronis crawled up into my mouth, but I swallowed them again, because Teacher gets very mad if you ask to go to the bathroom after the bell rings. "You should have used the restroom at recess!" she says. So we have to wait until the next recess time.

⌒

When everyone got back to their seats, Mrs. Webster started passing out report cards. As I waited for my name to be called to go to the front of the room to get it, I wondered if I was going to flunk because of my hot lunch charges. Puke popped into my mouth again, so I put my hand over my mouth. Teacher called the A's through H's. Then I waited for the J's to be called, because teacher always says that the only I 's in our room are those in our heads and those in the dictionary.

When she finally called my name, I didn't even look at her when she handed me my report card. And I didn't look at anyone else either on my way back to my seat. I just stared at my dirty saddle shoes. Everyone else sounded happy, like on Valentine's Day. They hollered to each other, "Did you pass?" But I put the top of my desk up and held it there with my head. Janet turned around and asked if I was going into third grade too, but I made believe that I didn't hear her. I pretended to be cleaning out my desk, but I was opening my report card. Arithmetic B, Spelling A, Reading A, Penmanship B. My heart pounded loud like my dad's old tractor and my cut finger pounded, too. I opened my report card. I saw a zillion S's. S's mean satisfactory. (Mama says satisfactory means okay.) My hands began to shake really, really fast and my report card almost flew out of my hands when I tried to turn it to the back where it would say either PASSED into third, or FLUNKED—held back into second.

I turned it over. The first thing I saw was Mama's name, where she had signed it. I stared at her name. "Don't cry!" I said to myself. For a little while, I forgot all about passing. But when Krystal hollered, "Donna Jean, did you pass?" I looked to the bottom of my report card. All I could see was PASSED. I pulled my head out from under the top of my desk. I jumped out of my seat and ran to Krystal. "I passed, too," I said, hugging and jumping up and down with her.

On the bus on our way home, lots of kids were singing, "School's out, school's out, the teacher's let the monkeys out."

"You dingbats," Bobby hollered. "School's not out until tomorrow, so quit singing that dumb song!"

I didn't sing because my finger was hurting. But Debbie was singing, and she stood up and yelled back at Bobby. "We can sing if we want to. It's none of your business!" she shouted.

Bon saw Debbie in his mirror and yelled for her to sit down. His eyes kept watching her. So I told her that she better sit down.

"Let's not sing," Krystal said. "Let's tell Donna Jean about the things we're going to do on summer vacation." So Krystal and Debbie whispered to me all the things we were going to do.

"First, we're going to go to the old white school," Debbie said. "We'll play school there. I'll be Mrs. Webster and you can be my pupils."

"Don't say pupils," I said. "I hate when Teacher calls us pupils."

"Me, too," Krystal said. "We're not eyeballs!"

"Maybe we can ask Edwin and Dennis to come to the old white school. We'll have them climb up into the tower to ring the big bell," Debbie said.

"Going into the old white school scares me," I said. "Once when Mrs. LaLonde was at our house, Luke and Jerry told her they had heard a spooky noise when they were walking around in the old white school. Mrs. LaLonde said that a ghost lives there!"

"A ghost!" Krystal shouted,

"Yes," I said, then told them all the things I heard Mrs. LaLonde tell Luke and Jerry.

꒱

"Who is Mr. Pore?" Luke asked Mrs. LaLonde.

"Mr. Pore? He was a teacher at the old white school," Mrs. LaLonde's shaky voice said. "A real short, pudgy fellow who, frankly, could have used a good shave and haircut. He hung himself one night at the school, down in the wood room. They were going to get rid of him for talking to high school kids about the things that go on between a man and a woman—they called it—sex education. So the old fart hung himself with a chain on one of the beams. The next year, thank God, the new school was built. No one ever wanted to go back in the old one. Kids were saying they could hear a man screaming and the bell in the tower ringing."

꒱

"That's spooky," Krystal said. "Are we still going to go to the old white school?"

"I am," Debbie said, "because there's no such thing as ghosts. At least that's what my dad says. So I'm going. And I'm going to be the Mrs. Webster when we play school there."

"That's not fair," Krystal said. "Why do you get to be the teacher? Why can't Donna Jean or I be the teacher?"

" I don't want to be the teacher," I said. "I want to be Mrs. McPhee, the hot lunch cook. She's nice, like my mama. I'll make bread at home and bring it to the old white school for hot lunch— like Mrs. McPhee makes bread at our school."

"Do you know how to make bread!" Krystal asked.

"No, but my dad does. I watch him make bread all the time."

"I'll bring Kool-aid," Krystal said.

"What else are we going to do during summer vacation?" I asked. So they told me how we'd go walking down the White Barn Road to look for the big eagle's nest, the one we saw on our school field trip.

The bus took us on the field trip. We had to be really quiet on the bus or the eagles would fly away, Teacher said. So we *were* quiet. We all took turns looking out the windows on the one side of the bus. We all quietly walked, looked and whispered. I saw the top

187

of the bald eagle's head sticking out of its nest. But the eagle's head wasn't really bald. It had white hair on its head.

After everybody got to see the eagle, the bus took us back to school. Teacher said that we had been very, very good, even on the ride back to school, so she gave us all a Dixie-cup of ice cream—even me!

I looked at the blood on the bandage wrapped around my finger. Mr. Johnson told me it might keep bleeding. "Don't let the blood scare you," he said. I couldn't wait to show Dad my finger, so when the bus stopped at our house, I hurried out of my seat.

"Ask your dad tonight, and tomorrow let us know if you can come with us to the old white school this summer," Krystal said.

"Wear shorts tomorrow to the picnic" Debbie hollered out the window as the bus was driving away.

"I don't have any," I yelled back, but she couldn't hear what I was saying. "I hope it's freezing tomorrow, then *everyone* will have to wear slacks like me," I said to my sisters as I ran to the house to show Dad my cut finger and report card. I could hardly wait to ask him if I could go play with my friends during the summer.

"I passed into third!" I hollered as I went into the house. Dad was just starting to make bread. He saw my cut finger. "What the heck happened?" he asked. "We're going to have to take a look at that later. It looks like we'll have to change the bandage. I sure hope there's gauze here."

My finger hurt a lot, but I watched Dad as he put the flour and other stuff into the big green bowl.

"Get Monica off the table someone. And give her a drink to rinse the yeast out her mouth," he said.

When Dad got the dough looking like a big white ball, he made the sign-of-the-cross on it, then put the bowl of dough up high.

"Mama doesn't put it there. She puts it on the little white table" I said.

"It's good enough," Dad said. "It's warmer there. It'll rise faster.

When the dough was doubled, Dad let my sisters help him make it into bread and buns. Then he made cinnamon rolls and I got to put them into the pan with my hand that wasn't bloody. Monica made buns that looked like turtles, but Dad said they were good enough to bake. When he put them into the oven, I ran to the bedroom with one of Mama's recipe cards and asked Sarah if she'd write down all the things that go into the big green bowl when making bread. So Sarah wrote:

Dad's Bread

Put 1 handful of salt and 2 handfuls of sugar and 1 stick of butter in Mama's big green bowl.

Pour 3 cups of hot water over the stuff

Crumble I outfit of yeast into a cup of water. Dump into bowl.

Dump a bunch of flour into the bowl. Mix everything with your hands until your hands aren't sticky.

Put the dough in a clean bowl. Make the sign-of-the-cross on top of it.

When the dough gets big, punch it down. When it pops back up, make it into bread or cinnamon rolls. Bake it in Mama's oven.

Two times I had to sneak into Mama's recipe cards so Sarah would have room to write down all the words. Bernadette saw me sneaking cards and tattled on me.

"Daaaad! Daaaaaaad! Donna Jean's into Mama's sttttuuuuuuffff!"

"You're not my Mother!" I said. But Bernadette kept calling for Dad anyway. I heard him say to her, "Let her be tonight. She has a cut finger."

When Sarah was done writing all that I told her, I put the recipe cards under my pillow then ran back to tell Dad that my finger was still hurting.

"Well," Dad said, "as soon as I get the supper done, I'll take a look at it."

At suppertime I wasn't hungry. My tummy hurt, so Dad said I didn't have to eat. "Go lay down and take a nap," he said.

When I woke up everyone was already in bed. Dad was the only one up. He was reading a *Book of Knowledge* that Matthew sent to us for Christmas.

"My finger hurts, Dad," I cried.

So Dad took water from the reservoir and put it into the wash basin, then added some cold water. "Come here. Let's take a look at that cut finger," he said. He lowered my hand into the water because the bandage was stuck and wouldn't come off. Slowly he took the bandage off. When I started screaming for Mama, Dad's eyes got big, like marbles. I looked. The top of my finger was lying in the water!

"Oh my God!" Dad hollered. "Luke, get up! Get out here quick!"

Luke came running into the kitchen. His eyes were almost shut.

"Her finger is only being held on by a tiny piece of skin! I've got to get her to the hospital. Watch her for a minute," he said.

"No, Dad, no!" I cried. "I don't want to go to the hospital! I don't want to die like Mama. I don't want to go to live in the ground with bugs and the devil." Dad put my swinging hands and my kicking feet onto the couch anyway and went out to start the car; he came running right back in.

"The car won't start," he said. I'll have to run to Steve and Josephine's to see if Steve can take us. I'll be back in about half-an-hour," he said going out the door.

"Mama, Mama. Mama," I cried. But Mama wouldn't come. Luke told me that it'd be okay, but it wasn't. It hurt lots. And Dad didn't come back with Steve for a long, long time. Luke and I waited and waited and waited.

"I hear them," Luke said. "They're coming in Steve's big logging truck. Come on, Donna Jean, don't cry, heck you're lucky. You get to ride all the way to Manistique in Steve's big truck. I wish I could. And you'll get to see the Paul Bunyan man that you like."

☙

On the way to the hospital I got to sit on Dad's lap in Steve's big truck, because Steve's car was in Regnold's garage getting fixed. When I saw the Paul Bunyan man, I started to cry because I knew we were almost to the hospital.

"Come on now," Dad said. "You've been to the hospital before. You don't have to cry. Remember the big bright lights. Dr. Waters will make your finger all better, just like he made your face all better after the rooster pecked it up."

See, one morning Mama gave my sisters and me each some soda crackers. I snuck outside with mine, because I liked feeding the chickens—the chickens that walk and bulk all around our yard. But mean old Cockey Lockey, our rooster, tried to get them away from me. I didn't want him to eat them all. I told Cockey Lockey he'd have to share! But he kept jumping up on me until he knocked me down. Then he started pecking at my hands, then at my face. I screamed for Mama. I could feel something really warm dripping down my face, and I could hear Mama hollering, "I'm coming, Donna Jean!" But before she got to me, the ground started spinning around and around and everything got black. When I woke up, I could see Mama and a huge bright light. Mama was holding my hand and Dad was talking to a man in a white coat.

"That naughty rooster pecked you all up, Donna Jean, but the Doctor sewed all the cuts up again," Mama said. Then she lifted me off the bed and took me to a mirror that was hanging over a sink. Mama started to giggle. She thought the threads coming out of my face looked funny. My dad and the Doctor giggled, too. But I cried.

"Doesn't Donna Jean look silly!" Mama said. When she lifted me up to the mirror again, I laughed, too.

On our way home, Dad stopped at the A&P store and bought Mama and me each a bottle of pop. Mama let me sit on her lap all the way home. After lunch that day, Dad killed the rooster. "No rooster like that deserves to live!" he said. And that night, Mama cooked Cockey Lockey for supper, but I didn't have to eat any of him.

⌒

This time at the hospital, when Doctor Waters came with a big needle, I screamed and kicked and tried to get off the table. So he told my dad and Steve to help the nurse hold me down, so he could give me a shot in my finger.

"Ouchies!" I cried.

"There, there," the doctor said. "Now I'm going to sew your finger back on and you aren't going to feel a thing. I just froze it!"

And I didn't feel a thing! When I sat up the cut off part of my finger was back on. I watched the doctor put metal sticks on both sides of my finger and put a bandage over them.

"You were a good girl," he said as he handed me a Tootsie Pop. That's when I remembered that Mama said we must always be polite. So I thanked him when Dad was lifting me off the bed to take me home. I heard Dr. Waters tell him that he wasn't going to have to pay him or the hospital any money for fixing my finger. "The Garden school is going to pay this bill," he said. "They should have known better than to leave her at school with this kind of injury. She could have lost that finger! Even I'm surprised that I was able to save it. Hopefully, she'll get feeling back into it."

On the way home from the hospital, Dad asked Steve to stop at the A&P. I wouldn't stay in the truck with Steve, so Dad took me in with him. When Dad tried to open the store door, the man inside hollered, "We're closed!" Dad hollered back that all he needed was *one minute*, so the store man opened the door for us. Dad told him what happened to my finger and the store man said, "Listen here, this one's on me." I didn't know what that meant, so Dad told me. "The man is telling you to pick out whatever candy you want." So I picked out a Sugar Daddy. Then Dad asked the store man if he could buy a bag of oranges for our school picnic lunches, for the next day. "Oh, sure," the man said.

Dad thanked the man about ten times, then we got in Steve's big truck to go home. On the way, Dad told me lots of poems, like *Lewis and Clark and the Little Cobbler*. I asked Steve if he'd tell me a poem, but he said he didn't know any. So Dad told me *The Village Blacksmith*. It's my favorite poem, and my dad said that it's his, too. I like the part that says:

He goes on Sunday to the church.
And sits among his boys
He hears the parson pray and preach
He hears his daughter's voice. Singing in the village choir,
It makes his heart rejoice
For it sounds to him, like her Mother's voice singing in paradise.

"Does paradise mean heaven? Is that where Mama's at?" I asked Dad.

"That's right!" he said. Then quickly he started singing *I'm a Yankee Doodle Dandy*.

At home, Dad sat me in a kitchen chair so I could watch him peel the eggs that he had cooked in bubble water. They stunk! Dad's mouth kept yawning and yawning and yawning as he made the eggs into egg salad for the school picnic sandwiches. After one huge yawn he said, "It's one-thirty. Morning comes early. Let's get to bed."

I wanted to sleep with Dad, but it was Monica and Sarah's turn, so Dad carried Sarah out of his bed and into her own. I crawled into the middle. "Be careful, so Monica doesn't fall off," he said.

After I was covered over the head with the blankets, Dad got in. That's what we always have to do before Dad gets into bed—cover over the head, because my dad's a boy—not a girl!

Dad let me cuddle under his wing. After prayers I asked Dad if he'd tell me a bedtime story, but he said he was too tired. "I'll hum to you," he said.

"Dad, Daad, Daaaad!" I said laughing. "That's not humming Dad, that's snoring!"

Chapter Eighteen

On the chalkboard in big letters Elisabeth wrote, Unfinished Business. Then when everyone was seated, she said, "The more you deal with the 'unfinished business' of the past, the more you'll be able to enjoy the present. You can ignore the unfinished business, but it won't ignore you! It'll make its way out in forms of depression, anxiety, anger, alcoholism or some other means. And there's a simple way to take care of it—talk about it." Then she explained how in life we need a support system. She compared a person to a house and how a house has four main supports and if one of the supports were to be removed the house wouldn't be as secure. She continued with the metaphor until the house only had one support. "Now if one of life's storms comes, how long do you suppose the structure will survive? Who are your four supports? If you don't have the necessary support system, I encourage you to seek out one after you return home. One support could be your spouse, one a sibling, another your pastor, and finally, a good friend. Now, let's get the day started," she said, as she motioned me to the front of the room.

I quickly walked to the front and sat upon the mattress. I was beginning to feel free from some of the past and was anxious to let go of more painful memories so that I could finally dry my eyes, once and for all. Without hesitation I began spurting out other childhood experiences I suspected helped me to acquire my present fears and worries.

⌒

It was the day of our school picnic. As the bus pulled into Pioneer Trail Park, Teacher stood up and told us all the rules.

"You're to use the steps when climbing up the slide, no one is to play by the river, no one is to go into the woods and certainly I better not catch anyone near the road," she said. Then she nodded to the bus driver and he opened the door. My friends and I ran to the slide, then to the teeter-totter.

"Hey, everybody," Krystal said as she looked to see where the Teachers were. "Let's go walk the railroad tracks that go over the river, then we can look down at the water."

"No," I said. "Teacher said we can't go by the river."

"I know," Krystal said, "but she didn't say we couldn't go on the railroad tracks that go over the river."

So Eileen, Krystal, Debbie, Janet and I ran to the railroad tracks. It was spooky walking on them. When we got to the middle of the bridge, I screamed because my foot fell through the spaces between the boards. My friends were already on the other side.

"Oh, don't be such a big chicken! Keep going!" Debbie hollered. So I pulled my foot out of the hole and tried walking again, but my legs wouldn't go. I started shaking. "Come back for me," I screamed."

"Hurry!" they hollered. I looked down and saw the water below and started crying. All of a sudden, my friends started screaming.

"Run, Donna Jean, run! There's a train coming around the corner!" I looked. "Mama," I cried, "help me!"

That's when I saw Kenny, a sixth grade boy running toward me. Just before the train came, he pulled me off the tracks and to the side with him. As the train went by, I hung onto Kenny and Kenny hung onto a metal beam. The wind from the train blew my hair across my face and the whistle blew loud into my ear. Then the train squeaked to a stop. A man with a blue striped hat, coat and pants got out of the train and came running, and so did my friends.

"Are you kids okay?" the man asked. When we said we were, he started screaming really loud and shaking his finger at us.

"I got a good notion to call the police," he said. "None of you kids belong on this bridge!" We all told him we would never do it again, so he told us to get off the bridge. When we started walking away, he hollered, "What school are you from?"

"Garden," Kenny said as we hurried off the tracks.

"Are you okay?" Kenny asked when we got off the bridge.

"Yes," I said, looking up at him.

"Your friends are at the slide. You better hurry and catch up with them," he said.

I ran to the slide and hurried up the ladder. "Choo choo. Choo choo!" my friends and I sang as went down together.

After we ate our picnic lunches, we played sack races. Some mothers helped us get into the burlap bags. Afterwards, some mothers played tug-of-war and baseball with us.

"Don't you wish your mother could be here, like mine is? Don't you wish she could have seen you playing games today?" Janet asked on our way back to school.

"She did see me," I said.

"No she didn't, she's dead!"

"I know she is, but she can still see me. She's like God— she can see everything!" I said.

I took the Old Maid cards that Eileen was dealing me. I was glad Janet didn't want to play. And I was glad when she fell asleep on the bus on the way back to the school.

When everyone's desk was cleaned out, Mrs. Webster went around checking to see if we had done a good job. If we did she gave us each two pencils that had our names on them. When the final bell rang, Teacher patted each person's back as they ran out of the room. I wanted to hurry so that I could get a good seat on the bus, but Teacher stopped me at the door. "Make sure you use these pencils over the summer. You're a bright little girl," she said. "And tell your Dad I've paid those hot lunch charges for him."

""I will," I said, and hurried out of the room to the bus.

When Bon drove away, lots of kids started having paper fights or water balloon fights. But my finger was hurting, so I didn't. Instead I told Bernadette about all the things I was going to do during vacation. And I told her about the mad man from the train. "Don't tell Dad," I said when the bus stopped to drop us off.

⁀

"Wow!" Sarah said, as we walked to the house. "Whose fancy white car?"

We gathered around the white car and looked at it. There weren't any holes in the doors or any scratches on it like our car. We wondered whose it could be. "I bet it's that lady from the state. She's trying to take you girls away from us," Luke said. "Dad told John and me the other day that a lady from the State came to talk to him when we were in school.

"What's the State?" I asked.

"The State is who can come and take you away from Dad!" Luke said. "The lady came to our house from Escanaba last week, and I bet she has come to take you girls away. The lady doesn't think that Dad can take care of all of us by himself. She thinks that you girls will be better off in a different home. I bet it's her. But don't worry," he said, "I won't let her take you girls! Neither will Dad, because Dad got really mad at her when she was at our house. He called her an Old Duck! He told her to go quack at somebody else for a while. When she was leaving, the lady told Dad she'd be back, so I bet it's her. I *think* she had a white car."

"I wish Mama were here, don't you Bernadette?"

"Of course, I do!" she said.

When we got in the house my heart was pounding really loud, because I didn't want to live with the *State*. I wanted to live at our house. We all walked slowly into the living room to the lady's voice. Dad saw us peeking around the corner and said, "Girls, you remember your Aunt Joanne and Uncle George, don't you?"

"Are they from the State?" Catherine whispered. I lifted my shoulders.

"Boys, you remember them, don't you?"

"Of course, we do," Luke said.

My little sister Monica was sitting on Aunt Joanne's lap. "Well, can any of you say hello to your aunt and uncle?" Dad asked, frowning.

Aunt Joanne put Monica down. She tried to hug Bernadette

and Sarah, but they ran from her. Uncle George lifted Catherine way up high to the ceiling. She giggled at first, but then screamed to get down. Uncle George put her down, then turned to me. "How did you do in school this year?" I told him how I'd *passed* into third grade, into Mrs. Knuth's room!

"How would you and Catherine like to come to our house for the summer?" he asked.

"I can't," I said. "My friends and I are going to build a fort, climb trees and make a rock garden this summer. And my sisters and I are going to do the bellybutton show for my dad, like we used to do for Mama!"

"The bellybutton show?" Uncle George laughed. "What's on earth is that?"

So I told him how my sisters and I hang from the low limb of the crabapple tree. And how Sarah lifts Monica up so she can wrap her hands around the limb, too. Then Sarah runs and sits on the wool blanket, right where Mama and Monica used to sit. She can see our bellybuttons so she sings the Bellybutton song that Mama made up.

> *The bellybutton show*
> *The bellybutton show*
> *Five big bellybuttons*
> *All in a row,*
> *One, Two, Three, Four, Five*

When Sarah calls our number, we have to jump to the ground. Our feet sting when we jump. Once Monica was crying because her feet stung—bad. Bernadette ran and picked her up and told Monica about the time she'd picked up a bumblebee that she thought was dead. "It stung me right on this finger and thumb," she said, showing Monica. We all laughed.

☙

Dad came up to Catherine and me. "You both want to see a big city, don't you?"

"Do we ever get to come back home again?" I asked.

"Before school starts, you'll be back," he said. So we ran to

198

our bedroom to pack. Sarah helped us put our clothes into a little, brown, cardboard box. She kept throwing a pair of John's underwear into the box and Catherine and I kept running behind her and pulling them out. We all giggled, except Anna. She was crying, because she wanted to go with us to the big city.

"Hurry up," Dad hollered. "Your Aunt and Uncle can't wait all day."

Catherine and I hurried with the little box to the kitchen where our aunt and uncle were waiting. We followed Dad and them outside. Dad opened the back door of the fancy white car. "Dad," I asked, "is Aunt JoAnne the lady from the State that has come to take us away?"

"Did Luke tell you about that?" I moved my head up and down. "Hey," he said lifting up my chin, "don't go worrying about that. I went to see her the other day and I told her she has no business here."

"So she's never coming back?" Catherine asked.

"She might come to bring you kids vitamins, or to see how we're doing, but *never* to take you away from Dad. Better get in the car now," he said.

Catherine and I climbed onto the big white seat. "Be good," Dad said, and he shut the door. Dad and our brothers and sisters waved good-bye to us from the front porch as Uncle George backed down the driveway. Catherine and I cuddled together on the back seat. Aunt Joanne turned around. "Are you two going to be okay?" she asked. I moved my head up and down.

In Escanaba we stopped at Grandma Jacques' house to pick up Aunt Joanne and Uncle George's kids. In the kitchen Aunt Joanne stood behind the tallest girl. She put her hands on the girls' shoulders. "This is our daughter Kathy, she's our oldest," she said. Catherine and I watched as she went to the next girl.

"This is our other daughter Mary, she's just a little bit older than you are Donna Jean." Next she took the hand of the little boy. "Here's our son, Bobby, he's three—they're all your cousins."

When we left Grandma's, Kathy and Mary sat in the back seat of the car with Catherine and me. Bobby sat in the middle of the front. Kathy read stories to us for awhile. When she was tired of reading, Aunt Joanne gave Catherine and me each a brand new tablet of paper to write on. We thanked Aunt Joanne for them. I let

Catherine use one of my pencils that Mrs. Webster gave to me.

"You can use the tablets to write home to your family or draw pictures," Aunt Joanne said.

Later, when we passed by the city that Uncle George said made the beer, Kathy let me read her storybooks. But soon it was dark, so we played guessing games, because it was taking a long, long time to get to the big city. Everyone, except Uncle George, was almost sleeping. Finally, I heard him say, "Well, here we are at 106 Oriole Circle, in Rockford, Illinois." My eyes popped opened. I could see their house even though it was twelve o'clock at night. There were streetlights, like in Escanaba. The driveway had blacktop on it, like on our 'new' road at home. The house was pretty, like my friend Janet's house. When we went inside, I didn't see lots of shoes on the floor, like at our house. And everything in the kitchen was clean and shiny, like our kitchen before Mama went away.

Do you need anything to snack on?" Auntie asked.

"Yes," I said.

Uncle George had carried Catherine to the couch and when she heard us talking, she woke up. She started to cry and scream for Dad. When Auntie told her that our Dad was home, she screamed even louder. So Aunt Joanne had me go to bed with her. I tickled Catherine's back so she'd fall to sleep. Uncle George peeked into the bedroom. "Is she back to sleep?" he asked.

"Yes," I whispered. So he came into the bedroom and took off Catherine's shoes, then covered her up. Auntie handed me my cousin Mary's nightie to put on. "We'll unpack your things tomorrow," she said.

Mary's nightie was pretty and soft. I was feeling the Cinderella girl on it when Uncle George came back in the room to tuck me into bed. Then he kissed me. "Goodnight, sweetie," he said.

"Yuckies," I thought, wiping off his kiss.

"Don't you like kisses?" he asked.

"Only Mama's," I said as he turned on the little light that was plugged into the wall.

"Uncle George," I asked, "is Illinois closer to heaven than Michigan?" But I don't think my uncle heard, because he just shut off the big light and closed the door and left.

At first I couldn't see anything. Then I saw something spooky on the little table by the bed. It looked like it had a mean face. I thought it was going to jump off the table and bite me. I shook Catherine to try and wake her up, but she wouldn't open her eyes. I wanted to scream for Mama, but I didn't think she'd come, so I covered over the head with the blankets. When I was under them, I remembered what Sister Janet Marie told me on my First Communion Day. "If you're ever scared, talk to someone." I wanted to call for Aunt Joanne or Uncle George, but then I remembered that Dad said it wasn't nice to bother big people for foolishness. I wondered if being scared was foolishness. Suddenly I couldn't breathe. I yanked the covers from my head. "I don't want to die," I said to myself.

The room looked lots brighter than before. I could tell that the spooky thing on the little table next to my bed was a clock. Next to it, by the little lamp, I saw my new tablet from Auntie. I turned the round switch and the lamp came on. I took the tablet and pulled my pencil from the wire and wrote to Mama, like Sister Janet Marie said I could do.

dear mama

Today me and Catherine came to Elanoy. It is the first time in my whOle widE life that i gOt to go away from MishagEn. i havent even ben in thE haNd of MishagEn. The furthest i ever got to gO iS to GrAndmas hous in Eskanoba til today. I dOnt no if you kin see as gOOd as gOd can see iN heaven bUt me and Catherine are at ant Joanne and Uncle Georges hous. They said they nO you mama cause they ben down to are hous in Garden and even saw me bfore but i don't member em. Cept when they came when you weNt away. antie bOught us pretty new dreSSes to where to the Funerals hous. Uncle George and antie have a prEtty hous. you wood like it cause it has an iNdoor pOtty and a bath tubb tO! I feel funnie here. There are strang smells. The blankits dOnt smell like aPPle blasums. They smell like ant Joannes PerfumE. i wish everybody cOuld be here. I hOpe anna and monica are o k. I miss em. im glad that catherine is here wiTh me bUt shes sleepin and she wOnt wake uP to talk to mE. im gettin sleepy tO. I wiLl tel you tomarOw bout all thE thinGs were goin to dO this sumer at anties hous. BUt kin you come down from heaven and come to ant Joanne and Uncle Georges cause I want to sEE you agen?

Yer

Donna jean

Chapter Nineteen

The next morning I didn't hear the rooster crowing like at our house. I heard weird voices, so I peeked out of the bedroom to see who was talking. "Wow! They have a television like we saw at Josephine's house the night of Halloween," I said to myself. I giggled, because I remembered how Monica kept trying to poke the people that were inside the television box, and how the people got all fuzzy. I thought Monica had broken the television, but Josephine said, "Look everyone. Watch when I turn these rabbit ears. The picture will come in clear again."

We watched as she turned the two shiny sticks that were on top of the television. They didn't look at all like rabbit ears to me. But when she turned the shiny rabbit ears, it made the people come back into the box.

Anyway, when I peeked out of the bedroom, I could see my little cousin Bobby watching a Mighty Mouse on the television. I ran to the bed and jumped on top of Catherine. "Aren't you going to wake up?" I asked. She kept sleeping, so I shook her. She turned over and wiped her hair from her face.

"Are we at Aunt Joanne's yet?"

"Yes," I said. "Want to come and see a talking mouse? It's inside their television." We peeked and saw the Mighty Mouse going all around the world trying to save everybody's day.

"Good morning, girls," Aunt Joanne said, when she saw us.

202

"I thought you two would be up bright and early. You must have been really tired. Would you like some Corn Flakes or Rice Krispies for breakfast?"

"Yummy," we said, looking at each other and rubbing our tummies.

"Just like at Grandma's house," Catherine said, as we ran to the table and sat on the chairs with the flowered pillows.

"Did you bring your toothbrushes?" Auntie asked as she poured milk over the cereal in our bowls.

"No," I said.

"At Auntie's house you must brush your teeth every time you eat something—to keep those teeth pearl white, okay?"

"Okay," we said.

When we finished our cereal, Auntie helped us brush our teeth with the toothbrushes she gave to us. After we were finished, Mary, Kathy, and Bobby showed us their bedrooms.

"Who sleeps in your bed with you?" Catherine asked Mary.

"No one," she said.

"Then who do you talk to at night when you go to bed?" I asked.

"Nobody," she said.

"Then who do you play tickle backs with?" Catherine asked.

"What's tickle backs?" she asked with a frown on her face.

"At our house when we go to bed we take turns tickling each other's back," I said. "We draw pictures with our finger and the other person has to guess what the picture is."

"Sometimes when my dad's at work, we draw pictures all over each other's legs, arms and tummy with a pen," Catherine said.

"But we hurry and wash it off before Dad gets home," I told Auntie.

"Oh, dear, that doesn't sound too good. How would you girls like to take a bath?" she asked.

"Yes!" we screamed. So Auntie started running the water and poured bubbles into the tub. I told her how Mama once let us take a bath in the new silver tub under the crabapple tree, and how she made our hair into princesses' crowns. Auntie giggled. "Before you two hop in the tub, let's see what you have for clothes." She took our clothes out of the little brown box. "Oh, dear!" she said.

That afternoon Auntie told us she was taking us to buy some

new clothes. "Kathy, you'll be baby-sitting your brother and sister. I want to go shopping alone with your cousins."

Aunt Joanne took us to a store that had just clothes and shoes—not food, coloring books and candy or baby chickens, like at Allen's store. We looked at lots of clothes before Auntie bought us some. When we got back to her house, Catherine and I hurried and put some of our new clothes on. Catherine put on her pink pedal pushers with her white blouse. I wore my yellow Moo Moo with the painted blue daisies on it, and my yellow flip-flop shoes. We ran outside and waited for Uncle George to come home from work to show him how pretty we looked.

Uncle George rolled down the car window as he drove into the driveway. "Who are these two beauty queens?" he asked. "It's me and Donna Jean," Catherine giggled as he was getting out of the car. He lifted Catherine to the sky, then gave me an airplane ride. I flopped my wings as I turned around and around above Uncle George's head. "I'm dizzy," I screamed. "Let me down!" He laughed, put me down, and then took my hand. "Let's go eat supper," he said.

Aunt Joanne showed Catherine and me where she wanted us to sit at the table for meals, then she asked us to help our cousins set the table.

"What's this food," Catherine asked with a frown, as we started to dish up our plates.

"Pigs in the blanket," Auntie said, smiling. "Haven't you ever had pigs in the blanket before?"

"Only once," I said, but it wasn't pig food. "Dad took the little pig into the house and wrapped him in a baby blanket. Dad said he was the runt of the litter. Dad was afraid the runt was going to die, so we took care of the little pig in the blanket until he got bigger."

"What's a *runt of the litter*?" Kathy asked.

"It's the baby pig that doesn't get to eat," Catherine said. "The other pigs steal his food."

"Speaking of eating," Uncle George said, pointing to our plates, "let's get going." So everyone quit talking and ate the pigs in the blanket.

Catherine and I didn't have to do the dishes. We got to watch television. We watched *Lassie, What's My Line* and the show with

Opie and Aunt Bea. When it was over, we had to go to bed. Our cousins didn't want to go to bed, but Catherine and I did, because we had new pajamas.

When Uncle George came to tuck us into bed, I asked if I could leave the little lamp on. "For a while," he said, as he somersaulted me onto the bed. He covered us up, kissed us goodnight then he told us that he'd come back later to turn out the light. As soon as he left I wiped off his kiss then got my tablet from under the bed. Catherine watched me write until she fell asleep.

dear mama
at ant Joannes we hafta brush are teeth alot. Even after kookies and milk. Me and Catherine took a bAth in there big tubb and splashed bUbbles and soaped each Others hare uP high. AntiE tOOk uS shopin and bOught us pretty clothes. New bloomers, too. They have writing on eaCh pair. EitheR Sunday or Monday or Tuesday or Wednesday or Thursday or Friday or Saturday. Ant Joanne gave uS some of Marys clOthes to wear tO. And they fit.

Tomarow im gonna ask antie if I kin have a Stamp So me and Catherine kin mail a letter to Dad. i wish i coUld see Sarah and Anna and Bernadette and monica. i miss em like i miss yoU. i wancha to come back home cause antie dont nO how to pUt rag curls in oUr hair.
Yer
Donna jean

During the night it thundered and lightning. Catherine and I got scared and started crying. We wanted to go home to Dad. Aunt Joanne and Uncle George came and talked to us. Uncle George told us why it thunders—how hot air and cold air bang into each other and how that makes a big loud sound. Then I wasn't scared any more, but Catherine wanted Dad to come and get her. When Auntie told her he couldn't come, she screamed so loud, it woke up Bobby.

"What if I say I'll take you home in the morning?" Uncle George asked Catherine.

"Soon… as I… get up?" she cried.

"Yes," Uncle George said.

So in the morning when I saw the sun peeping in through

the window, I ran and asked Aunt Joanne if we were taking Catherine home.

"No, Uncle George had to go to work. Your sister will be just fine," she said.

I watched as Auntie ironed her dress. I wanted to do a job too, so I asked if I could help.

"Only big people iron," she said.

"I iron at home," I told her.

"Really?" she said as she lifted her eyebrows. "Well, I'm not going to take a chance of you getting burned."

"Monica got burned once," I said. Then I told Auntie how one day Monica ran outside crying to where my sisters and I were playing. "Sometin bite me! Sometin bite me!" she screamed.

Sarah, Bernadette and I hurried to her. "Come and show us what bit you," Sarah said. On our way to the house, I thought maybe a spider had bitten her and Bernadette thought it was a bumblebee. But when we got inside the house, Monica pointed to the iron! Later when Dad came home from work, we showed him Monica's red and bubbled-up fingers. He got really, really mad at us. "You know better than to leave her in the house alone!" he said. "And which one of you left the iron on the stove?"

"So someone had left the iron on the stove?" Auntie asked.

"Yes," I said. "We get our iron hot by putting it on the wood stove. Our iron doesn't have a plug, so the wall can't make it hot."

"The *wall* doesn't make the iron hot! It's the electricity that flows through the plug. Like how electricity makes the lights come on."

"Is that why grabbing onto plugs sometimes stings our fingers?"

"Yes! Don't ever touch a plug, especially if your hands are wet! Oh, by the way, I have a surprise for you and Catherine," Auntie said as she slid the hanger into the neck of the dress. "We're going on a boat ride after supper tonight!"

"A real boat? " Catherine asked.

"Yes, a real boat. You girls will like it. Then on Saturday, we're going to the zoo! And Sunday, we're taking you swimming!"

"What's the zoo?" Catherine asked.

"It's where a lot of animals are!" Kathy said. Her eyes got big. "You'll like it there. You'll be able to see tigers, polar bears, monkeys and lots of other animals, too."

"Will wolves be there," I asked. "Because if wolves are there, I don't want to go!"

"The animals are in cages," Mary said, laughing. "They can't get out."

"Oh?" I said.

Little Bobby started laughing and said, "I know that the animals are in cages at the zoo."

⌒

After the boat ride Uncle George tucked us into bed and kissed us goodnight. "Sweet dreams," he said as he was leaving the room. Quickly I grabbed my paper and pencil.

dear mama

We all weNt on a bOat ride today and we gOt to see lights from the city.   it was dark so we cOuld see city ligHts in the water bUt we didnt see any fish Jump out of the water like at Sac Bay. We gOt to see big Tall buildins like you gOt to see in ShcOggO and when we got back hOme we were all sweatin cause it was really really hOt outside. Uncle George turned on a machine that cOld air caMe out of. It felt good. Me and Catherine wanted to Sleep right by the machiNe but Uncle George took us by the hand to our bed. Then he kised us gOOdnight. catherine kiSed him back—I didn't.

When he left i hurried to get My tablet cause hes cOmin back in in 10 minutes to turn out the light cause he said that were gonna havE a big day tomarow cause were gonna go to the zOO. i wish yOu could cOme there to Mama.
Yer
Donna Jean

"Aunt Joanne," Catherine asked the next morning. "Today we go to the zoo, right?"

"Yes, dear," she said.

So after breakfast we all got ready and went to the zoo. We saw lots of animals. And just like Mary and Bobby said, the animals were in cages. It was hot and we got sweaty. So when a little white truck with a ringing bell went by, Uncle George hollered for it to stop. "What kind of ice cream cones do we all want?" Uncle George asked. We each told the man what kind and he scooped the ice cream with a little silver shovel. When we were walking away I said, "Mama would really, really like this ice cream cone. Strawberry is her favorite."

"Wipe your chin," Auntie said to me. "Kathy wants to take our picture with her new Kodak camera."

All day long, we walked and walked and walked at the zoo. Everyone's feet were hurting a lot. "It's time to get some supper anyway," Auntie said. Uncle George pointed to a big building. We walked to it and went inside.

"Is this a hot lunch room?" I asked.

"A restaurant," Kathy said.

"Why does that nurse have a tiny, black apron on?" I asked when she left our table. Aunt Joanne starting laughing and so did Uncle George and my cousins.

"Oh, dear," Aunt Joanne said putting her hand on top of my hand and patting it. "She's not a nurse, Sweetheart—she's a waitress! She took our orders and now she's going to bring the list of food that we want to the cook in the kitchen. When our meals are ready the waitress will bring them out to us."

I got a root beer float and a hamburger on a bun. Catherine got lasagna and some Pepsi. Catherine and I counted all the people that came into the restaurant while we ate. After, when Uncle George was giving the waitress money for the food we ate, we looked at the pretty things in the big glass box.

"Do you each want one of those Mickey Mouse watches?" Uncle George asked.

"Yes," we shouted, and jumped up and down until Auntie shushed us. Uncle George hooked our watches onto our wrist.

"That's the best 'asagna' I ever had," Catherine said, as we were leaving the restaurant.

"That's the *only* lasagna you ever had," I said shaking my head and rolling my eyes at her. We walked to see more of the animals. I whispered to Catherine. "I hope I don't forget to tell Mama about the restaurant and the waitress and the watches."

By the time we found the polar bears, it was time to go home. Bobby wanted to ride on their back, like he did on the camel's back. When Uncle George told him he couldn't, he started to cry, so we had to go quickly through the bird building, then we left to go home.

At home, we took our bath, then went right to bed. Uncle George tucked us in. Before he left he put the little lamp on, then reached under the bed, and then handed me my tablet. "It's okay to write letters," he said.

When he went to tuck Bobby in, I started writing.

dear mama

Today we gOt to go to the zOO. We saw polar bears jUst like you waNted to gO see in Alaska at cOusin MarilyNs hous. Huge snakes were at the zOO to but i didnt gO see em bUt catherine did. Shes not afraid Of snakes nO more.

Kathy said She thiNks were gonna have Even more fUn at tHe Y. The Ys where were gonna gO swim. We sent Dad pictures that we colored. Oh ya. we saw an elephaNt at the zOO just like the elephant that catherine colored fOr Dad. And we saw A liOn jUst like the liOn i colored fOr Dad. We checked when the mailman came bUt we still didnt get A letter frOm hoMe. i hope we get one tomarow cause i think catherine will cry if we dont.

We gOt to go to a restrant. We ate food there. i got a rOOtbeer float. It was ice cream with pop on the top of it and it tasted really gOOd. A watetrEss brote are fOOd. We didnt say grace.

Uncle George jUst came in and said finish up and then turn the light off. he kiSed me gOOdnight. i axadently kised him back. catherine was sleepin bUt he kised her stil. i want to kis you mama. mama why were your lips so cOld at the Funerals hous? Why wont you come back hOme?
Yer
Donna jean

When I woke up in the morning it was thundering and lightning out again. "Catherine, wake up," I said. "We can't go swimming today. It's raining outside."

So Catherine and I made a tent under the blankets so we could play *Duck, Duck, Goose*, but there was only one duck and one goose, so we couldn't play. Then Aunt Joanne came in to see if we were awake.

"What in heaven are you two up to?" she asked when she saw the messed up blankets. We told her we were trying to play *Duck Duck Goose*, but didn't have enough people. So she called Mary, Kathy, Bobby and Uncle George into the bedroom. We all got under the blanket except Uncle George. He was the Goose!

The room kept getting darker and darker every time it thundered and lightened. Suddenly Uncle George said, "Well, are we going to the Y today or not?"

"We can't go swimming in the rain," I said. They all laughed, and then Kathy said, "The Y's inside of a building! Hurry and get ready, so we can go."

After we each ate a banana, we left for the Y. "We'll go out for breakfast after our swim," Uncle George said.

On our way to the Y, we mailed another letter to Dad, in a funny blue mail can that was on the side of the road, next to the Y. Then Uncle George drove the car into a parking spot in front of the big building. A boy with a Davey Crockett hat on held the doors open for us as we ran in the rain carrying our bags. Inside the Y was bright. It looked like the sun was shining.

"What's that funny smell," Catherine asked.

"Chlorine, it's to keep the pool clean," Aunt Joanne said on our way to the dressing room.

⌒

"Wow!" Catherine and I said when we saw the pool.

"You two don't know how to swim yet, so stay in the shallow end," Uncle George told us.

We ran and jumped in and played games in the water. After a long time, I ran to Aunt Joanne. "My fingers are wrinkled," I said, showing them to her.

"Oh, that's from the chlorine," she said.

"Bleach made Mama's fingers like this every time she washed the pail of diapers," I said.

"That's what chlorine is—bleach," Uncle George said. Then he told us that we had enough swimming for one day, but he'd bring us back again in a few days."

⌒

When we got home from the Y, Catherine and I checked the little mailbox that was hooked onto Auntie's house. Still there wasn't a letter from Dad.

"Maybe Dad's dead, like Mama," I thought that night when we were getting our P.J.'s on. But I didn't tell Catherine that I thought Dad was dead. I told Mama.

dear mama

We stil didnt get a letter frOm Dad. We dont nO why he wont right to us. i didnt tell catherine but i think Dads dead like yOu. Tonight ant Joanne came to tuck us in and i whispered in her ear and asked her if Dad was dead and she said Oh heavens nO! Then she said that if Us girls dont here from him sOOn she will let us call mOlly or Josephine and then they kin ask Dad to call Us back cause Dad stil dont have a phone yet.

Today we went to the Y. The Ys where we went to swim in thE pOOl. A pOOl Mama is an iddy-bitty lake inside a Big Big buildin. All us girls went intO a changin room and the boys went intO another changin room to get our swimsuits on. ant Joanne bOught me and Catherine each a swimsuit when we went shoppin sO that we didnt have to cut off our old pants this sumer. catherines has a mermaid on it and mine is 2 pieces like Bettys. Betty is the lady acrOss the road frOm ant Joannes hous. Bettys skinny. she lays out on a long long chair everyday to try and get her skin all brOwn. i talk to her sometimes. i have a swimsuit almOst like hers. She has a litle bottom piece for her butt and a little top piece that gOes over her titties. Mine has a litle botom for my butt to. BUt my swimsuit top is of 2 fish. Thers one fish to cOver each titty.

The changin room is one big rOOm. i didnt want to get undressed in front of all the other People bUt thats what i had to do. Even ant Joanne and Betty got undressed in front of everybody. And mama i saw ther titties! i didnt mean to see em but when i looked up there they were. I turned my head quik bUt i peaked out from under the towel. ant Joannes are round like yours but when Betty bent down to dry her legs hers looked like the Guersey cOws! And when we were gettin dressed catherine asked ant Joanne why her own titties werent big like Ant Joannes. ant Joanne and Betty laughed . i ran and put mY hand over catherines mOUth.

Kathy and Mary dived Off the planks at the Y. Me and Catherine arent alowed to yet. So Uncle George gave me and bobby and catherine piggyback rides in the wAter and we got to jump Off Uncle Georges shoulders. i cant wait til we get to go to the Y agen. Is ther a Y in heaven?

Here comes Dad. i mean Uncle George. Hes comin to kis and hug us gOOdnight. He kises us all the time and we dont eveN care. We like it when he cOmes to tuck us intO bed. Mama can you ask gOd if he will let you come down frOm heaven for my birthday cause maybe Dad dont no hOw to make miracle whip cake and i waNt one for my birthday.

Yer

Donna jean

"What's that loud noise?" Catherine asked when she woke up one morning.

"Aunt Joanne is vacuuming the big rug that covers the living room floor," I told her from under the bed.

"Why are you under there?" she asked.

"I'm looking for my tablet. I still can't find it," I said.

Catherine, Mary, and Kathy helped me look for my tablet after breakfast and again after lunch. When Uncle George came home from work he asked what we were all looking for.

"My tablet," I said.

"You still haven't found it? That means you haven't been able to write in it. You've been missing it since the first time we took you and Catherine to the Y, right? That's been a couple of weeks ago," he said, scratching the bald part of his head.

"Bobby," he hollered, "have you taken Donna Jean's tablet?"

"No!" he said, "I don't have it under my bed!"

"Oh, oh," Uncle George said. "Let's go look under Bobby's bed."

We looked, and sure enough, we found my tablet. It was all

wrinkled up.

"That's a bad thing you did," Uncle George said to Bobby. "What do you say to Donna Jean?"

"I'm sorry," he said.

"That's a sin, Bobby, because you stole my paper!" I said. I looked at Uncle George, "Is Bobby going to go to hell when he dies for stealing my tablet? Because I don't want him to go to hell."

"Oh, no," Uncle George said, "Bobby said he was sorry, so God forgives him."

"Suppertime," Aunt Joanne hollered. I ran to show her what Bobby did to my tablet. "Well," she said, "I think Bobby ought to go to bed early tonight."

"Can I go to bed early too," I asked."

"Why sure you can," she answered. And when it came time to go to bed I hurried so that I could write a long letter to Mama.

dear mama

my tablet was lOst for a long long time but Uncle George foUnd it today under bobbys bed. Weve ben havin lots Of fun at Ant Joannes and Uncle Georges hous. Today is August 12 and that means its just 25 more days til my birthday. im gonna ask Ant Joanne and Uncle George if i can live with em all the time So i kin get a cake for my birthday. One with candles like Bobby got for his. And when i make my wish im gonna wish for a birthday present with wrappin paper On it with a ribbon and a big red bOw. Then i kin unwrap it to see whats inside.

I dont think Dad liked our pictures we cOlOred. Me and Catherine each cOlOred Dad more pretty pictures and i wrote him 5 letters so far bUt he wOnt answer us. Antie said that maybe our letters keep gettin lost in the mail. catherine dOnt want to go home. She likes it here to cause they have a bike to ride. Uncle George taught us how to ride the bike. catherine learned how to ride bfore me but she ran over Bettys tOes cause she didnt no hOw to stop. Today I went around the block 6 times. Mary and Kathy dont ever want to ride their bikes sO we get to ride em all the time.

Ant Joanne said that we kin take the Barbie dOlls she gave back to Mishagen but she said she will hafta think bout givin us the bike. She said that maybe she will let us keep the

little blue bike.   Did you ask GOd yet if you kin come hOme for
my birthday?
Yer
Donna jean

"George. George. George!" Auntie hollered one night when we were watching television. "The doorbell, George. Please get it! I'm in my nightshirt!"

We were all watching Topo Gigio on the Ed Sullivan show—he's funny. Uncle George put down the newspaper and got up to answer the door.

"Luke, what in heaven's name are you doing here? Donna Jean, Catherine, your brother's here! Joanne, Luke's here!"

I ran to the kitchen to see if it was our Luke. Catherine came with me.

"Luke!" we screamed. And ran to him. He lifted us up and hugged us.

"My Lord," Auntie said, coming around the corner. "Are you all alone?" she asked as she kissed him on the cheek.

"Sure am," he said.

"Are you telling me your Dad let you come all the way from Michigan by yourself?"

"I just told him I was going to get my sisters and take them back home where they belong. Ma would want them home!"

"Why you're not even old enough to drive a car yet," Uncle George said.

"I'm almost sixteen," he said. "I always drive at home. I've been driving the tractor since I was eight. Dad says I'm a good driver."

"Well, you're here now," Auntie said, "Let's make the best of it. I can bet you're hungry. Would you like something cold to drink, like a rootbeer?"

"I'll just have a regular beer, if you don't mind," Luke said, then laughed.

After a little while Auntie looked at the clock. "It's time for bed girls," she said.

"Can we stay up later tonight?" I begged. While she was thinking about it, Uncle George said, "Sure, sweetie." So Catherine and I sat on Luke's knees until he was done drinking his pop. When Luke tucked us into bed, we gave him more hugs and kisses. When he was leaving our bedroom I asked him if Catherine and I were going home with him in the morning.

"You betcha," he said. So I told Mama.

dear mama

Lukes here! He came tO take us hOme. ant Joanne and Uncle George dont like his car. anties afraid that it will break down and we wont have a place to go. But Luke said his car is touff. i'm glad Lukes here. tomarow me and Catherine get to see everybody agen. i'm gonna say to Dad why didnt you right to us? mama kin you right me and Catherine a letter from heaven?

Yer

Donna jean

"You're not taking your sisters with, and that's final!" Auntie was saying to Luke when I woke up.

"But Ma would want them at home, I told you!"

"That's probably true," Uncle George said, "but I don't think your mother would ever want you to be driving on busy highways with your little sisters in the car. Remember, you don't even have a driver's license!"

"Luke," Auntie said, "your sisters will be back home in just a couple more weeks. We said we'd have them home before school starts."

"Ya, I know what you're up to. Just like Jude. He never came to live with us after Ma died. He was our baby and he didn't even get to come home. We hardly ever get to see him."

"Luke," Auntie said in a very low voice, "We're not trying to take away your sisters. We're just trying to give your dad a break for a while. He's a busy man. Do you really think your dad could have taken care of Jude, too? I think he has enough with all of you."

"I know," Luke said, and he started to cry.

Luke kept crying and crying and crying, and then he started calling out for Mama. But Mama still wouldn't come.

"Oh Luke," Auntie said, "I wish I could make it all better." She hugged and hugged and hugged Luke. Uncle George patted Luke's back and brushed the top of Luke's hair, but he still kept crying. Then Uncle George whispered for Catherine and me to go over by Luke. I rubbed Luke's arm. Afterwards, Catherine took off his shoes. We took him by the hands and walked him into the living room. Luke lay on the sofa. (That's what they call it—a sofa—not a couch.) Catherine and I knelt down by the sofa. We talked to Luke and we showed him all our Barbie doll clothes that Aunt Joanne and Kathy had made for them.

Finally, Luke stopped crying. He asked if we'd scratch his back. Afterwards he played dog-pile with us on the floor. Even Kathy, Mary and Bobby played. First Luke got on the floor, then Kathy got on top of his back and we kept piling up on him.

"My nose," Luke shouted, "it's digging into the carpet. Get off, you're squishing me!"

Luke stayed at Auntie's house all day long and even slept there that night. In the morning, he left for home. That night when I went to bed I cried for Luke, and so did Catherine. We counted the days until we could to see him again. "Only thirteen more days before we go home," I told Catherine when I reached for my tablet.

"Will you ask Mama how far heaven is and if I can go there to see her?" she asked.

"Okay," I said.

Dear mama

We didnt go home cause Luke started cryin for you. So me and Catherine showed him our barbie clothes. Uncle George bought us each a candy bar from the supermarket today. The super market is a place to buy things to eat. Uncle George and Luke and bobby went to get some meat to put on the outside stove thats called a grill. But braty bobby took our candy bars into the bathroom when they got back home and he ate em all. ant Joanne spanked him and told him that hes lucky his teeth didnt fall out. She made him brush his teeth and sent him to his room. He had to stay there til Uncle George had the meat cooked for supper. Uncle George said that the next time he buys us a Payday he wont let Bobby carry em.

Uncle George let me and Catherine help him mow the grass today. We took turns helping him push the mower. Then he let us help him rake. it was lots of fun. We like Uncle George. We stil didnt get a letter from dad. i think catherine is gonna cry tomarow if we dOnt get one. Catherine wants to no if she kin go to heaven to see you.
Yer
Donna jean

Every morning Catherine cried because she wanted Luke to come back to Auntie's house. She wouldn't even come on the swing set with me. She just kept waiting for the mailman, because Luke said he'd mail us a letter when he got back. One day I heard her holler, "The mailman is coming! He's carrying a present!"

"A present?" I said, as I ran from the swing to the door. I grabbed the present from Catherine. She screamed and tried to get it back from me.

"I got it first!" she said.

"You don't even know if it's ours, stupid."

"Hey, hey, hey," Auntie said. "That's no way to talk to your sister." Auntie took the present from me and looked at the writing. "It's both of yours," she said.

"Yippee," we screamed.

"I suggest you let Catherine open it. She's the one who has always waited for the mailman."

She handed the package to Catherine and everyone watched as she opened it. It took her a long time until she lifted the cover off.

"My baby Thunbelina!" she screamed.

"My marbles!" I said. We dug into the box to see if there was anything else. We found five red-hot burning gums and we started fighting for them.

"Now, now," Auntie said. "Let's read the letter and see what it says," and she handed the letter to me.

Girls,
Got all your pictures. They're very nice. Luke got back home safe and sound. He was suppose to bring this package with him when he went that way, but he left it on the

table. I mailed it out before Luke went to see you, but I had the wrong address on it, so it came back. Hope you get this before you come home. Sorry it's so late.

Monica has had earaches all summer and stays up half the night. I've been busy in the garden. Also busy canning. Anna has been waiting for you both to get home.

They're five gums in the box. You have to share them with your cousins.

See you soon,
Dad

That night after my bubble bath, I hurried to bed and got my tablet and wrote to Mama about the package from Dad.

dear mama

Today catherine played with her baby Thumbelina and i played marbles cause Dad sent them to us. plus gum. Tomarow me and Catherine get to go home. At first we didnt want to but now we do cause we get to see everybody agen. i cant wait to see monica and anna. Just now we had to say good-bye to bobby and mary and kathy. We had to hug em good-bye cause thats what youre supose to do antie said. mary and kathy cried and even Uncle George did. ant Joanne and Uncle George are gonna take us home. kathy and mary and bobby have to stay with their other grandma. We get to bring the blue bike.

if its dark when we get to Our hous im gonna go outside and look up at the stars in heaven. in Rockford there are bright lights and I cant see the stars. Thats why im glad im goin home. im gonna look up to see if a star winks at me cause if it does i no it will be you!

I Love you a skyfull

Yer

Donna jean

PS. ant Joanne gave me 8 candles so i kin put em on my birthday cake if Dad makes me one.

Chapter Twenty

"Well, my two little country mice have made their way home from the city," Dad said when Catherine and I ran inside the house.

"Want to see our new clothes?" I hollered.

"I'll see them later," he said, as he patted the top of my head. Go show your sisters. I'm going to visit with your aunt and uncle now." I ran with my sisters to our bedroom and Catherine and I showed them all the things we got at Aunt Joanne and Uncle George's. We let our sisters play with our Barbies and try on our new clothes. After a little while Dad called us to the kitchen to say good-bye. I didn't want Aunt Joanne and Uncle George to leave. I wanted them to stay at our house for a long, long time, but they said they had to get going.

"When do we get to see you again?" I asked.

"We're not sure when we'll be back," Uncle George said.

I felt sad when they left, and so did Catherine. And during the night I was crying, so I woke up Catherine and asked her if she wanted to run away with me to their house. She said she did so we crept out of our bedroom and through the kitchen and into the utility room. We quietly put on our shoes and coats. But when I opened the door, we screamed and covered our heads because a bat flew into the house.

Dad came running. "What on earth are you two up to?" he

asked. "Get back to bed. You can't be up all night here," he said.

"A bat!" we hollered, pointing toward it.

"Where the heck did that thing come from?" he asked, as he shooed it from the house with the broom. We didn't tell Dad that I had opened the door. We just ran back to bed.

The next day I looked into the refrigerator to see if we had any pears or oranges and I looked on the counter for bananas, but we didn't have any at our house. So I asked Dad if we could go with him to a supermarket and buy some. "Let's get pizza, too," Catherine shouted.

"You're country mice again," Dad said. "You won't be getting those city things here. But you can go pick some apples in the orchard." So we ran outside to Mama's favorite apple tree. We climbed it, then shook it. Lots of apples fell to the ground. We jumped down, stretched out our shirts and put the apples into them until our tummies looked big and fat, like Mama's tummy before she went away.

"Well," Dad said when he saw how many we picked, "Looks like Donna Jean's going to have apple pie instead of cake for her birthday tomorrow."

"Not Miracle Whip Cake?" I asked.

⌒

The next morning Dad made six apple pies and I got to push the eight candles that Aunt Joanne gave me down into the biggest one. After supper everyone sang happy birthday to me. Before I blew out the candles, I made a wish that Mama would soon come home.

"What did you wish for?" Sarah asked.

"I can't tell you, or it won't come true," I said.

After we ate the pie, Dad stretched out his closed-up hand. "Here's your present," he said.

I pulled Dad's rolled-up fingers back and in his hand was an Indian-head nickel. "Thanks, Dad," I said, jumping up and down. I took the nickel and counted the feathers on the Indian's head.

"Get over here," Dad said, pointing to his lap. "It's birthday licking time!"

"No! No!" I screamed. But Dad grabbed me and gave me

the licking anyway. "One, two, three, four, five, six, seven and eight!"
"Ouchies," I hollered, each time he hit my butt.

"Now, one to be good, one to be bad, and a pinch to grow an inch! There, that should keep you out of trouble for a while," he said.

⌒

The day after my birthday school started. It was lots of fun being with all my friends again, but it was fun coming home at night, seeing Monica and playing with my sisters, too. We'd change our clothes, then hurry to the big maple tree to climb it. One night after school we helped Dad and the boys make apple sauce. Dad said he needed us to pick the apples. While the boys peeled the apples, we washed the jars and rings. Dad stirred the apples as they cooked in the big kettle. He'd tease the boys about girlfriends and us about boyfriends.

"I don't have a boyfriend," I hollered.

"Do you get into other mischief at school?" he asked.

"I don't get in any trouble," I told him. "I like my new teacher. She's really nice. She told us that pretty soon we get to have our Halloween party.

"Oh dear," Dad said. "Don't let Monica hear that."

⌒

See, every day when we go to school Monica cries, because she wants to go with us. When we tell her that she's too little to go, she cries even harder. This year Anna's in kindergarten so Monica has to stay home alone with Dad. Everyday when the bus comes to pick us up, she cries. One Friday Dad had to run down the driveway to catch her. He lifted Monica and her raggedy blanket up as I watched from the bus window. She was kicking to get down when I waved good-bye, screaming and putting her arms out for me to take her. Bon started to leave, so I ran up to the front of the bus.

"Stop, Bon, Monica wants me!" I said. Bon stopped the bus and opened the door. "I'll wait for a little bit," he said.

I ran to Monica, because I didn't want her to cry like she cried for about a zillion days after Mama went away. She kept dragging her blanket all through the house looking and looking and looking and calling out for Mama. I tried to tell her that Mama was far, far away—up in heaven—but all she'd say was, "Din go get er." So I would have to tell her again, that I didn't know the way to heaven. But then one day, when Grandma was visiting us, I heard her talking to Molly. Grandma told Molly that if John Kennedy became the President, he was going to send a man to the moon. So I told Monica that if she wouldn't cry any more, I'd write a letter to Mr. Kennedy to see if he'd let Monica and me go up in the spaceship too, so we could get dropped off at heaven. Monica was happy again, because she liked to go for rides.

"Get back on that bus!" Dad hollered. "Monica will be all right." So I blew her a kiss and ran back on the bus. I sat with Catherine and Anna. I held Anna's hand because she was crying. She wanted to stay home with Monica, too. Anna cried all the way to school, but when she saw her friend Mary on the monkey bars, she ran to play with her.

After the morning bell rang, we had reading, writing then arithmetic. We practiced subtracting on the blackboard until recess time. When the bell rang, everyone hurried to the playground, except me. I stayed in our room. "Why aren't you going outside with the other children?" Mrs. Knuth asked.

I started to cry. "I want to go home," I said. "Monica is crying. She doesn't like it when we leave."

Mrs. Knuth sat in the little chair next to mine and lifted me onto her lap. "I'm sure she doesn't cry all day long. After you get on the bus, Monica probably starts playing with your pet bunny," she said, wiping the tears from my face. Then she asked me if I'd like to help her bring the erasers outside to clean them.

"Okay," I said and ran to the blackboard to get some erasers. Teacher and I each carried a bag of them out the back door of the school. Outside, I kept hitting the erasers together until no more chalk came out of them. Teacher laughed because she didn't think I could clean them so fast.

⌒

"If your Halloween party is on Monday, all of you better decide today what you're wearing. I don't want you crying Monday morning and saying you don't have a costume," Dad said. So we all looked and looked, but we couldn't find anything at our house to wear for Halloween. Suddenly Dad had an idea. He took two flour sacks and made Catherine and Anna each into a ghost.

John ran out to the woodshed and came back with the deer horns that were from the deer Luke killed. He tied a shoelace on each side of the horns and then put them on his head. "There," he said, "all I need now is some red lipstick to smear on my nose, then I'll be Rudolph the Rednose Reindeer."

"Mama's friend Molly isn't dead. Ask her for some lipstick," Catherine said.

I wanted to dress up as a Mother, but the only clothes at our house were for Dad's.

"Be a Dad," Sarah said.

"No, I don't want to be a dad, I want to be a mother."

"Then I'll be a dad," she said. So Sarah put on Dad's old clothes and hat and put his old pipe into her mouth. Everyone laughed.

"I got an idea," Bernadette said to me. "Want to be a sister?"

"We are sisters!" I said.

"No, not us. You can be Sister Janet Marie and I'll be Sister Rosalie."

"Okay," I said, and we ran to the bedroom. We took the white sheets from the bed and wrapped them around us.

"What we going to use for a veil?" I asked.

"I got another idea," she said. "Let's use the big white towels."

Bernadette put some of the towel on my forehead, then folded it to make peaks on each side so it looked like Sister veil. Then she pinned it under my neck and let the rest of the towel fall down my back. After she was done doing mine, I made her a veil, and then we ran to the mirror. "See," she said, "We're sisters now, except the sisters, dresses are black."

"We need rosaries," I told her. We ran to our bedroom and got our rosaries from under our pillows and pinned them to our dresses.

223

"Darn," Bernadette said, "Our rosaries don't show up. They're white like the sheets."

"Let's ask Dad if we can use his black one," I said.

We hurried to the living room. Dad was sleeping in his big chair and wouldn't even open his eyes when we talked to him.

"He won't care," I said, as we tipped-toed into his bedroom. We looked under his pillow and under Mama's pillow, but we couldn't find his rosary.

"Where could it be?" I asked Bernadette.

"Maybe it's on top of Mama's dresser," she said.

Bernadette held her hands together. I put my foot into them, then she pushed me up to the top of the big tall dresser.

"It's up here! I can see it!"

"Throw it down, I'll catch it."

"I can't. Dad's rosary is all broken up! We got to go tell him!" I said.

I lay on my tummy and hung my feet down so that Bernadette could catch them. That's when I saw it! It was behind Mama's dresser, way down on the floor. "Bernadette!" I shouted, "I see Mama's big white rosary! It's behind her dresser!"

"No, it's not! Mama took her rosary to heaven with her. Remember, she was saying it when she died."

"Get the fly swatter, so you can push it out."

When she ran to get it, I wondered how Mama could've put her rosary behind her dresser, when she was up in heaven. "Maybe she's home!" I thought. "Or maybe…"

"Got it!" Bernadette shouted, on her way back into the room. "You scared me!"

Bernadette lay on the floor and pushed the fly swatter under the dresser. "Go to the wall…no the other wall…up further," I told her.

Eleven times Bernadette almost pushed Mama's rosary out from behind the dresser. But then Dad came into the bedroom. "You have no business on top of your mother's dresser! What are you two up to?" Dad asked as he lifted me off the dresser. "Skadaddle," he shouted.

We ran to ask Mark and John if we could use their black rosaries. They let us, so we pinned them on. "Now we're going to have to cut off our hair, because sisters don't have hair under their veils, do they?" I asked.

"I don't think so either," Bernadette said. "But we better cut just a little bit off or Dad will be mad. Help me find the scissors then I'll cut yours and you can cut mine," she said.

Dad was sleeping again on the chair when we snuck into Mama's closet and into her sewing basket for her scissors. "I found them!" I whispered.

On our way into the new bathroom we took a kitchen chair with us. I sat on it so Bernadette could cut my hair. She lifted the scissors. When she was lifting some of my long, brown curls, Dad yelled. "Can't you girls ever watch your little sister? I'm trying to nap!"

"Bernadette dropped the scissors and we ran to the kitchen. We each grabbed an arm and carried Monica into the bathroom. I sat back down, and just when Bernadette was finally going to cut my hair, Dad hollered again.

"Get in here, you girls!"

Bernadette and I hurried to the kitchen, again. "Look at this mess! I told you to keep a eye on your little sisters," Dad shouted.

Pepper and salt was all over the kitchen table. "Don't just stand there, one of you get the broom!"

Sarah came skipping with the broom. Dad brushed all the salt and pepper from the table onto the floor. He looked at Sarah. "Get busy," he said, "get sweeping!" He turned to Bernadette and me, "Well, where're your little sisters now?"

"Monica's in the new bathroom, but I don't know where Anna is." I said.

"Anna's outside pumping water," Catherine said.

Dad ran to the door. "Anna, get in here where you belong!" he yelled.

Anna was all wet and her hands were freezing. "I told you, Anna, I don't want you standing on those loose boards. That's a 'no, no'. I don't want you to fall into the well. We might never get you out! Now one of you bigger girls help her into dry clothes."

Just then, Monica came into the kitchen, from the bathroom. "Oh, oh!" I said. "Monica's in big trouble!" Her hair was almost all chopped off, except for three curls hanging down her back.

"It's all your fault," Bernadette said to me, "You found the scissors!"

"But Dad told us both to watch her!" I cried.

Dad was really, really sad. He went into the new bathroom and knelt on the floor. He picked up Monica's hair, and as he held it, he talked to it.

"Your mother loved Monica's goldielocks. Now they're gone! They're dead! Never again to be seen." It looked like Dad was going to cry.

"Dad, Monica's curls will grow back," Bernadette said.

"Not like this," he said, and he started to cry. His tears splashed onto Monica's hair. Then Dad stopped crying. He grabbed the scissors from the floor, then cut Monica's last three curls off and carried them to the kitchen. We followed. He opened the cupboard door and got down an envelope. He put the curls into the envelope and on the outside of it he wrote, Monica's first haircut, October 29, 1960. Then he put the envelope into the black metal box and told Bernadette and me to sweep up the rest of the hair and throw it into the stove. It sizzled, then disappeared into the fire, like snow on wood.

"Monica's head looks like a fuzzy dandelion," Sarah laughed. But Monica thought her hair was pretty.

"Dad," Catherine said, walking into the kitchen. "Look who else's hair Monica cut off." Catherine took Monica's pretty doll from behind her back. "It's an ugly doll, now!" she said.

"Well, I can see that all of you better come with me this afternoon when I go on the back forty to water the cows. If I leave you here, you'll only get into trouble."

☞

See, every morning and every afternoon Dad and John or Dad and Luke have to go lift pails of water from the well that's in the middle of the cow's field. We can never go into the field, because there isn't a fence around the well, and Dad's afraid one of us will fall in. He even yells at Luke and John to be careful. So while they water the cows, we play under the big maple tree—the maple tree where we used to have picnics with Mama.

When we went to water the cows, Dad wouldn't even let us get out of the car. But when they were done, he took us for a ride down the Little Harbor road. As he drove down the dusty, gravel road, he told us about the places we were passing by.

"Right there!" he said, pointing to the river running through the woods, "is a place where none would think, roaring lions come up to drink!"

"Did you ever see a lion there?" Luke asked.

"No, but I heard of a man who did."

Next we passed Corky's house. I already knew that Corky lived there with his Mother and sister, but I didn't know that they had a big brown dog. When we went past Russell's, we saw him getting clothes off the line. We kept going and going until we came to a little creek. Dad stopped the car. We looked out.

"Here's the gold mine," he said.

"Can we look for gold?" Sarah asked.

"There's no gold in there, never was! Years ago some old man said he found gold in that little creek. But no one else ever did," Dad said as we rode away. At the big hill, Dad showed us where a man called Crazy Tony once lived.

"Lots of people called him Crazy Tony because he used to feed the bears. Then one Sunday when Crazy Tony didn't show up at church a few people went to see if he was sick. "I went too," Dad said, "but it wasn't to see if he was sick. No, it was to see if a bear had got him. And sure enough, we found him dead!"

"Dead?" John said. "That's scary."

"There's a lesson to be learned here—stay away from wild animals," Dad said.

At Poodle Petes, the big lake where we once got to go swimming, Dad turned the car around. "This is far enough, we better get back home."

⌒

The next day, Dad had to make Anna's birthday cake and Luke had to change the flat tire on the car, so Dad made us older girls draw straws from the broom to see who had to go with John to water the cows. "I don't want to take a dumb oh girl with me," John said. "What if a wild animal comes? She won't be able to help."

My straw was the shortest, so I rode on the handlebars of the blue bike as John pedaled to the pasture.

"Ouch, don't go so fast," I told him. The gravel road was

really bumpy and my butt was hurting, bad.

"I want to hurry and get back home before dark. I'm going to go lickety-split," he said. "Remember, Dad says there are all kinds of wild animals in these woods."

When we got to the pasture, John let me go into the field with him. "Don't tell Dad I let you go by the well," he said. I watched as John pulled up pails of water from the well. Once I saw him slip, but he didn't fall in. After he got the water to the cows, the cows quit mooing. "Let's get out of here now, before something comes," he said. He lifted me onto the handlebars. "I'm going to hi-tailer, (hi-tailer means to go really, really, really fast), so hold on tight," he said.

After a little ways, John hit the brakes. "Ahhhhh!" we both screamed. It was because a huge, giant black animal jumped across the road right in front of us and we almost hit it!

"Hold on for your life!" John yelled. My butt was hurting again, but I didn't tell John. When we got to the end of the Forty-two Road, John saw a car coming. "Oh, good," he said, "here comes Charlie Chustavich." He braked the bike again and jumped off and ran to the middle of the road. I tumbled with the bike to the ground. John put his arms up really high and waved X's with them so that Charlie would stop. Charlie slowed down and John ran and caught the door handle and opened the door before Charlie even stopped. I ran with the bike to catch up to them.

"Charlie," John said, breathing in and out fast like a bullfrog. "Can my sister ride home with you? I think we just saw a cougar!" Charlie bent his head down toward the seat then tipped it back. "Get er in," he said.

In Charlie's car, I rubbed my hand over the pretty seat. The seat in Charlie's little gray car was really clean and there weren't any holes in it, like in our car. "How come you wear glasses, Charlie? My brother John says your glasses look like Coke bottles. What's this little window for, Charlie?"

I tried to open the little window, then tried to open the glove box.

"Now, now, don't be in dere!"

"What's in here, Charlie?"

"What's that you say?"

So I asked him again really, really loud. "What's in the glove box?"

"A flashlight and some portont papers," he said.

"Charlie," I asked, "what's the name of your car?"

"Ford," he said. "Nutin better din a Ford."

"I know three kinds of cars—Ford, Chevy and Tonka."

"Tonka?" Charlie asked frowning.

"Darn," I said, looking around and seeing John coming fast on the bike. "John's going to pass us up!"

That's because Charlie is really old. He can hardly hear or see anything, so he drives really slow. "Go faster, Charlie. Go really fast, so John can't pass us up!"

But John did pass us up. When he was going by us, I thought, for sure, he'd look at us and do like a ha-ha wave or a toot-da-lou wave, but he didn't even look. John was going so fast, all his hair was going backwards.

"Faster, faster," I said to Charlie, "so we can beat John!" But Charlie still wouldn't go faster. He just puffed on his big cigar and said, "No, dat's how haxadents happen." So we went slow as a caterpillar all the way home.

⌒

That night, before we went to bed, my sisters and I climbed onto the freezer chest in the utility room. See, when Dad has the fire going hot, it's really warm on the freezer—our bedroom is cold. Up there, we can get really warm.

"Tonight," Dad said, "You're each going to tell me a story. But you have to make one up."

So one-by-one we told Dad a made-up story. Anna's story was the funniest.

"Once on a time there was a spider," she said. "The spider liked the pig. The pig liked the spider, so they went to the fair. They got some cotton candy."

"That's not your own story, Anna," Catherine yelled. "That's Charlotte's Web."

"No," I said. Charlotte and Wilburn didn't get cotton candy."

"But we did," Anna said. "Member when we went to the fair?"

We all did remember, especially Dad. See, Dad took us to the fair and he took us through the cow and horse barns and through the sheep and pig barns. When we were going through the chicken

229

coops, Dad had to carry me, because the roosters scared me. When we got back out into the sunshine, Sarah asked Dad to buy us some cotton candy. "No," he said. "We'll walk to the car to eat the peanut butter sandwiches I made for us."

At the car we gobbled the sandwiches down, then Dad took us to the dairy barn and bought us each a glass of ice cold milk. "That cost me five cents a glass, so make sure you drink it all," he said. We did. It was yummy.

Dad made us rest with him in the shade, under a big tree before we could go on any rides. Monica wouldn't lie down on the ground. She was playing by the tree and found a black and orange caterpillar climbing up it. So we all looked for bugs, too. When we all tried to catch a yellow butterfly, Sarah tripped over Dad, so he got up.

"Guess I might as well take you on some rides if I can't get a nap," he said.

My favorite rides at the fair are the little cars, the boats and the merry-go-round. Everybody, even my dad went on the Merry-go-around. The man with the dirty clothes and the funny hat made Dad go on the ride with us, so Dad could hold onto Anna and Monica. Dad went on the Ferris wheel with Sarah and Bernadette, too. I was a big chicken to go, and so were my little sisters. We just watched. When they got done, we asked to play games, but Dad wouldn't let us. "I'm not going to let you waste money," he said.

The sun was going down when we came out of the big, huge building where you could buy things. "Time to go!" Dad said.

"Can't we just go on one more ride?" I asked.

"No," he said, "all I have left is a couple dollars."

"Can't we go look at more cows?" Anna asked.

"No, we've been here since morning. I want to get back before dark. Where the heck is Catherine!" Dad asked looking over and between the people. We all looked, too, but Catherine was gone.

"Quick! Hold onto each others hands!" Dad said.

We looked and looked and looked for Catherine. No one had seen her in the 4-H building or in the grandstand or by the food stands. I don't think she could have made it all the way back to the rides or the barns," Dad said. "I hope no one took her! We better get to the police station."

Sarah started to cry. "Where would they take her?" she asked.

"Shhhh," Dad said. "Listen, I think I heard something over the speakers."

We all listened very quietly and when the voice came again, it said, "A little girl has been found. She says that she's six years old, but she won't tell us her name. If she's your little girl please come and pick her up at the police station located here on the fairgrounds."

We hurried there. "Catherine!" Dad shouted when we saw her. She was just finishing a Carmel apple. A woman with red hair was standing by her. "I found her in the Exhibition building by the Carmel apples and taffy. She was alone and crying, so I figured she was lost. She said that she was trying to find her mother. Is her mother still looking for her? I could page her."

"No," Dad said, "her mother isn't here." I thought Dad was going to say that her mother was up in heaven, but he didn't. He just thanked the women for taking care of Catherine. "Let's get going before I lose another one of you," he said.

"Can we *please* get cotton candy?" Sarah begged.

"Oh, okay," Dad said. We each got a different color—I got blue.

On the way to the car Dad made us play follow-the-leader. "I'll start, then smallest-to-the-biggest," he said.

We licked on the fluffy cotton candy on the way. When we got to the car Dad turned around. "Where are your cotton candies? You couldn't have eaten them already!"

"I threw mine away," I said. "It felt picky, like the insulation you put in the new house."

"Mine did too," Catherine said.

"So did mine," Sarah said. And one by one all my sisters said theirs, too, felt like the insulation we played with when Dad was building the new part of the house.

"That cost money!" Dad yelled.

"We know," Bernadette said, "but we didn't want to get pickies down into our tummies!"

⤳

Dad let us talk and talk about the fair—about the clown on stilts that gave us each a Tootsie-roll, about the spook house we were

231

afraid to go in, about the tilt-a-whirl that made Bernadette and Anna dizzy and the roller coaster that made our tummies tickle.

"That's enough story telling for one night," Dad said. "It's bedtime!"

Chapter Twenty One

Anna woke up screaming for Mama, so Dad came running. He told her exactly what he told Catherine one night when she woke up crying. He said that we'd all get to see Mama again someday in heaven. It was still kind of dark outside, but Dad said it was time to get up for school. I ran to the window to see if it had snowed during the night. I could see the leaves blowing and feel cold air blowing in through the picky insulation that was around the window.

"Donna Jean," Dad shouted. "Get out from behind that shade and get ready for school.

"Dad," I said, "how did the moon get so little? How did it get way up into the sky? At bedtime it was sitting on the ground behind the garden."

"It's because the earth turns. Now get ready for school."

"How can the earth turn without us falling off?"

"Never mind all that," he said, "just get ready!"

"Where's my shoes?" Anna cried.

"The bus will be here soon. Let's help her find them," Dad said. But none of us were ready either, so Dad looked by himself, under clothes, beds and dressers.

"Where did you take them off last night?" Bernadette asked Anna.

"I didn't take them off," she said. "My feet were freezing,

so I wore them to bed."

And sure enough, when I lifted the blankets, there were her shoes.

Anna hurried, but she put her shoes on the wrong feet. "The bus is up by Chucky Lovell's. Now is almost to the forty-two corner!" John yelled, just as Dad hooked the last buckle on Anna's shoes.

On the way to school, lots of kids were pretending to be smoking, because there wasn't any heat on the bus. By the time we got to school my fingers felt like sticks whenever I tried to write my spelling words, especially the finger I got sewed back on.

After lunch we got dressed up in our Halloween costumes and then we paraded through the other classrooms. Then the other classrooms paraded in for us to see them. I saw my brothers and sisters. Everyone laughed at John. They liked his Reindeer costume. John was lucky. He won a candy bar for having the funniest costume. On the way home from school, he wouldn't give anyone a bite of his giant Hershey bar.

That night Dad took us trick-or-treating in down town Garden. We didn't have any thing to put our candy in, so Dad took us to Molly's first, and she gave us each a bag. When we got home, we counted all our candy. Dad begged us to give him a candy bar, so we each did. I gave him an Almond Joy. "That's Mamas favorite kind, right, Dad?" I asked.

"Why don't you keep that one," he said, and he got up and went into his bedroom. He didn't even get back up to say prayers with us or tuck us into bed, so Luke did. And for about a thousand days Luke tucked us into bed at night, because Dad was tired all the time and went to bed right after he hauled in the wood for the night.

⌒

"See you all after Thanksgiving vacation," Bon said, when he opened the door to let us out. When the bus left, I asked Catherine if she wanted to go collect pop bottles from the ditches with me, then walk to Cal's store to get the money for them. "We get two cents for the little pop bottles and a nickel for the big ones," I told her.

"Okay," she said, "but first we have to ask Dad." So we ran to the house.

"It's too cold to walk all the way to the store. You better stay put," he said.

"But there still isn't any snow yet," I told him.

"No, but snow could come any minute now. You have to understand, Donna Jean, that maybe I just might know more than you do. So no, and that's final. Did you already forget about the last time you walked to the store? The day the road got blacktopped?"

"I remember," I said, wrinkling up my nose.

"If you would've listened to me that day, you wouldn't have gotten your feet burned—burned so bad your skin peeled off."

That was the day our road—the Little Harbor Road—got thick black tar rolled onto it. The black thick tar looked like licorice when it got poured onto the road. It made the road nice and smooth, so I walked all the way to the store without my shoes on. I had found a nickel pop bottle in the ditch, and I wanted to buy some red Kool-aid with it. Red Kool-aid taste like Juneberries.

See, in the summertime when it's hot, Dad takes us berry picking on the Garden plains. And when the Juneberries are ripe, he parks the car under a Juneberry tree and we get to stand on the hood, so we can reach the berries. We get to eat as many as we want. Dad and my brothers pick blueberries and then they can them for winter. Dad makes my sisters and me pick blueberries too, but we only have to each fill a lard pail.

Anyway, when I left to go to the store, I skipped bare foot on the new blacktop road. When I got almost to the store, I saw Cal's big dog, Chief, sitting by the tiger lilies. I'm afraid of Chief, because he looks mean. He's a big, white bulldog and growls a lot. Whenever I go to the store with my dad, I hold Dad's hand so that Chief can't get me. Dad always says, "Just keep walking and don't even look at him." So I don't.

I was scared to go by Chief without Dad, so I turned around to go back home. My arms were tired of carrying the pop bottle and my feet were burning, so I stopped at Pete-the-Bear's house. Pete isn't really a bear, we just call him that. His real name is Pete Lambert. Pete is really, really old. He's probably about two hundred years old, I think, because once I heard my dad and Luke arguing about who was older—Pete or Charlie and I heard my dad say, "Oh no way, Pete is way, way, way older than Charlie!" I think Charlie's about one hundred and fifty, so Pete must be about two hundred.

Pete lives all by himself in a tiny pink house next to Dorian's house. Pete only has one room in his house. But he has lots of stuff in it, like a bed, a stool to get up onto his bed, a table with a chair, a dresser, a refrigerator with beer and milk and eggs in it, and a spooky deer's head that's hooked onto the wall. He has candy in his house, too.

I knocked on the door. I could hear, Skippy, Pete's little black dog, barking loud. It scared me, so I ran from Pete's house. Pete opened the door and hollered at me to come back. Skippy ran right by me and growled. I could see his pointed teeth. He was trying to bite my toes. I kept jumping away from him until I got into Pete's house.

Pete told me to sit down when I got inside, so I sat on his chair. He sat on the bed. I told him my feet were hurting. When I lifted up my feet to show him, Skippy tried to bite my toes.

"Look, Pete,' I said. "Both of my feet have blisters on them." I rubbed over the bubbles of skin while Skippy growled and snapped. I screamed. Pete got up, and with a fly swatter shoed Skippy away from me.

"He's just wittle," Pete said. "He won't hurt ya."

"But Chief could hurt me, because he's big," I said. "I don't like Chief!"

"That big oh dog, he knocks me to the ground when I go to the store," Pete said. "Chief too big a dog to have around."

I knew my dad would be really, really mad if he knew that I was bothering Pete for foolishness, but I still tried to get Pete to give me a ride home.

"My dad will probably be really mad at me if I walk all the way home with blistered feet," I said.

"Naaaa," he said. "Your dad, he not ever get mad. He's a good man." So then I thought that maybe if I asked Pete if I could see the inside of his new car, then he'd take me home.

"Pete," I said, "I've never ever got to see the inside of your black car. Can I now?"

"Someday you come back to Pete's when you got clean feet and Pete will show you inside of it," he said.

I got off the chair. "I better go home, so my Dad doesn't worry about me."

Pete went to his dresser. He took something from the top of

it and handed it to me.

"A candy maple leaf!" I said, taking it.

"To eat on your way home," he told me.

"Thanks, Pete!"

As I walked home I ate the maple leaf, but my feet still kept hurting.

☞

After Dad had reminded me about the day I'd walked to the store bare feet, I said to Catherine, "It's okay if Dad won't let us go to the store. We can do something else."

All of sudden Sarah hollered. "Hurry, get in here. A bird just hit the window!"

Bernadette, Catherine and I ran outside with Sarah to see the bird. When she started to pick it up, Dad knocked on the window. "Don't touch it! It could be diseased!"

"But Dad, it's still alive. Can we take it into the house and make it all better?" Sarah asked. So he let us take the hurt bird into the house. We put it into Chicky's old box. Luke tried to give it drops of water, but the bird still died.

"Is someone we know going to die now, Dad?" Sarah asked.

"No," he said. "What made you ask that?"

"Because Mrs. Lalonde told us if a bird hits the window and dies, it means someone from your family will die, too."

"NO, NO, NO!" Dad said. "That's not true!"

"But Mrs. Lalonde said that one morning a bird hit her window and that day a big tree fell on her husband, and he died," Sarah said.

"I don't want anybody to die!" I said.

"Quit believing all that garbage!" Dad said, "And get washed up for supper."

When every potato and every piece of venison was gone from our plates, we flipped them over and Dad gave us each a slice of apple pie. While we ate, Dad and my brothers talked about the fences they had to fix, and we talked about the pretty clothes that were in the Sear's catalog. When we were done eating the pie, Dad said, "You girls get your dishes done. I'm going to water the cows. I'll tell stories again tonight when I get back."

After Dad and Luke left, we hurried and got the dishes done,

237

then we climbed up on the freezer chest. We could hardly wait for
Dad to get back. We like the stories and poems he tells us. Lots of
times Monica won't even go to bed until Dad sings *Twenty Froggies*.
She knows most of the words, so we all sing it.

> *Twenty froggies went to school*
> *Down beside a rushing pool.*
> *Twenty little coats of green*
> *Twenty vests all white and clean.*
> *We must be in time said they*
> *First we study, and then we play.*
> *That is how we keep the rules*
> *When we froggies go to school.*
>
> *Master bull frog brave and stern*
> *Called the classes in their turn.*
> *He taught them how to noble stride*
> *Likewise how to leap and dive*
> *From their seats upon a log*
> *He taught them how to say "Kerchog."*
> *He showed them how to dodge a blow*
> *From the sticks that bad boys throw.*
>
> *Twenty froggies grew up fast,*
> *Bullfrogs they became at last.*
> *Not one dunce was in the lot*
> *Not one lesson they forgot.*
> *They were all polished to a high degree*
> *As each froggie has to be.*
> *Now they sit on other logs*
> *Teaching other little frogs.*

"When Dad gets back from watering the cows tonight, he's
going to teach us *The Village Blacksmith*!" Bernadette said.

"Wonder what the heck is taking him and Luke so long,"
John said. "It's almost six o'clock! It's too dark for them to see
what they're doing now."

"Here comes a car! And it's stopping," Sarah said.

The back door flew open and Luke came running in hollering

for John. "Grab your coat and hat! We need help! Hurry!"

When they were going out the door, I heard Luke say something like, someone fell into the well when they were watering the cows, so I told my sisters. "It must have been Dad," I said. We all started crying.

"Oh no!" Sarah said, " Mrs. Lalonde was right about a bird hitting the window! Dad's going to die just like the bird did!"

"We won't ever get to see Dad again! He'll be up in heaven, like Mama!" Catherine cried.

"Let's quit crying and pray, like Mama said we should do when we're in trouble," Bernadette said.

"Are we in big trouble?" Anna asked.

"No," I said, "but Dad is. He fell into the well when he and Luke went to water the cows! His foot slipped and he fell right in and nobody can get him out! He's going to die, if we don't pray!"

"Let's say the rosary; I'll do the first part of the prayers and you can all do the second part," Bernadette told us. So we ran to get our rosaries. Sarah let Monica use hers, because Monica started crying for it. And I told Anna I'd share mine with her, because she doesn't have one yet, either. Catherine used Luke's.

We made the sign-of-the-cross and then Bernadette said, "Hold the cross, because we have to say the Apostles' Creed."

"Let's say the Child's Apostles'Creed, like Mama taught us," I said.

"Okay," she said. She looked at Monica and Anna and said, "Just move your lips, because you don't know the prayers yet."

We knelt on the floor, in the middle of the room. "Kneel up straight," Bernadette said. Then she started the rosary.

We believe in you God, You are the Father the Almighty, you are the maker of heaven and earth, and all that is seen, or unseen. And we believe in you, Jesus. You are the only Son of God. You were conceived by the power of the Holy Ghost,

"Don't say ghost," I said. "I don't want a ghost to come here."

"Donna Jean," Bernadette whispered, "We're trying to say the rosary. Be quiet! Okay, let's start again right where we left off."

"And born of the Virgin Mary," Sarah said.

"Oh yes.

And born of the Virgin Mary. You suffered under Pontius Pilate

"Dad said a pilot is a man that drives a plane," Catherine said. "Once I thought I saw a white plane up in the sky, but when the plane got to our house, it was a seagull!"

"Like the bird that hit the window?" Anna said.

"That wasn't a seagull!" Sarah said.

"We're trying to say the rosary, remember?" Bernadette shouted.

Then you died and were buried.

"Like Chicky, right, Bernadette? Catherine asked.

"Like Mama, too," I said.

"No," Monica said, "Mama's gone ta tore. She be back!"

"NO," Bernadette said, "Mama's not gone to the store!

BUT, on the third day you rose again. Then you went up into heaven.

"Mama's in heaven, right?" Anna asked

"Let's not say the rosary anymore, Bernadette, let's play records," Sarah said. And Sarah ran to put on Dad's *Wings of a Snow White Dove.*

"Can we play the heaven song next, Sarah?" Anna asked.

"No, don't" I said, "I don't like that *How Far is Heaven* song. It makes me cry." But Sarah played it anyway.

"Dad must be dead!" Bernadette said when the clock coo-cooed nine times.

We all started crying again, but then we heard Monica talking. "Monica," we screamed.

She was talking on the telephone. The telephone that Dad had the man with a funny yellow hat come and put into our house. Dad told us that only he and our brothers could use the phone unless it was for something really important.

We heard Monica say, "My mama gone ta da tore."

I grabbed the phone from Monica. "No, Mama's up in heaven!" I said, then I listened to see if someone was still there. A lady started talking. "Are you one of the little Jacques' girls?" she asked.

"We're *all* Jacques' girls," I said. "Our dad doesn't want us playing on the telephone."

"Well, we better hang up then, don't you think?"

"Yes," I said, and hung up the phone. When I did, Sarah hollered, "I have a idea. Let's dial numbers until we can talk to a policeman. Then we can tell him we're really scared."

So Sarah dialed lots of numbers. Finally, we thought, she was talking to a policeman. But when she got off the phone she said, "It wasn't a policemen, it was John Bartus. He said we don't have to be afraid."

"Did you tell him about Dad falling into the well and how nobody can get him out and how we don't want him to die," I asked.

"No, I forgot to," she said. So we all started crying again, except for Monica.

"Donna Jean," Monica said, taking my hand. "I want to go to bed."

Monica looked like she was going to fall asleep on the floor, so I took her onto Dad's bed and took off her shoes. Then I took off mine. Soon, Monica fell asleep. I tried to keep my eyes open, but they kept shutting, like Monica's. When I woke back up I could hear my sisters. They were still crying. Suddenly I remembered that I'd had a dream. I got up and ran to tell my sisters about it. They were all sitting together in the middle of the floor yet, because when we're scared, we don't ever sit on the couch or on chairs that are by the windows.

"We don't have to be scared anymore," I said. "A pretty lady came and stood by Dad's bed and said, 'Donna Jean, wake up. I want you to go tell your sisters they don't have to cry anymore. Tell them your dad will be coming home soon. He's all right and so are your brothers. I'm Jesus' Mother and I've come to bring you God's PEACE and LOVE."

"What else did she say," Bernadette asked.

"Nothing! The pretty lady disappeared and that's when I woke up."

So my sisters stopped crying and we talked about the lady until we saw car lights coming into the driveway.

"It's Dad," Catherine yelled. We all ran to the door. When

Dad came into the house, he and John and Luke were really dirty. "Where were you?" Sarah asked.

"What a night," Dad said. "The cow slipped butt first into the well. We tried and tried to pull her out, but we couldn't do it. So Luke went downtown and asked Nick Thennes to come with the county bulldozer. We tied rope around her horns, then finally, with Nick's help, we pulled the Guernsey out of the well."

"She sure was weak, hey Dad," Luke said.

"You betcha! But she'll still probably make her way home, like she always does," he said. And sure enough, right after we ate the cinnamon rolls, Dad had made that morning, we heard the Guernsey's bell. We all ran and looked. She was walking by the barn.

"Well, it's just like I said. She's made her way home." Then Dad looked at my sisters and me. "By the way, what the heck are you girls still doing up? It's eleven o'clock! To bed!" he said, "or I'll make you sleep with the Guernsey tonight!"

Chapter Twenty Two

My sisters and I watched from behind the curtain of the utility room window for Dad and John to come home. They went far into the woods to cut down a Christmas tree. I wanted to be the first to see them dragging it home, but when I saw Monica's hand holding her crotch, I hurried and got our coats and ran with her to the outdoor toilet. We were shivering on our way back to the house when Monica said, "Wook, da tree's toming."

"Everybody, they're coming!" I hollered as I opened the door.

"It's only three more days until Christmas," Catherine said, jumping up and down.

"I can't wait," Anna said. "Because when Santa comes down the chimney, he'll bring us presents!"

"And he'll put peanuts, candy, an orange and an apple in our sock," Bernadette said.

"And an onion and the potato, too," Sarah said, laughing.

I always give the onion and the potato to Mama, and so do my sisters, but this year we're going to give it to Dad.

We watched as Dad cut a piece off the bottom of the tree. Then he nailed the tree to a board. He and John took the tree into the house and put it in the corner of the utility room. Catherine and I brushed the snow from it while Dad and John warmed their hands over the stove.

"Can we put the decorations on the tree right now?" Anna

asked.

Bernadette, Sarah and I laughed, because we didn't know that Anna knew that big word—decorations!

"Not tonight," Dad said. "First we have to let the tree dry off."

"Are we gonna put da paper trains dat Sarah made in kool on da tree?" Monica asked.

Sarah laughed and shouted, "Paper *chains*, Monica, not *trains*!"

"I'm going to put my paper lanterns on the tree—the ones I made," Catherine said.

"Me too!" I shouted, "and my spray painted pine cones."

"I'm hanging my Christmas bells over the door," Bernadette told us.

Sarah, Catherine, Bernadette and I ran to get the decorations we made from our bedroom closet where we had hidden them from our little sisters, and Dad got the Christmas box down from the attic. We dug through the box looking at every one of the decorations. We found a picture of Matthew—when he was just a baby. It was glued to a paper angel. There was a card with a picture of Jesus, Mary and Joseph in the manger that Mark had colored at school, with words on it that said, "MERRY CHRISTMAS 1947, TO MOM AND DAD, FROM MARK.

"I figured it out!" John said, holding the card. "Mark must have been in the first grade when he colored this picture."

Sarah found a picture of Santa she had colored for hanging on the tree, but it was all wrinkled up. Luke found a little sleigh that he had made out of popcicle sticks when he was in Mrs. Knuth's room. Bernadette and Sarah looked and looked for the clove apples they had made for Mama last year, but couldn't find them.

"I know where they are," I said, and I ran to Mama's dresser and opened the bottom drawer. There they were, but none of Mama's clothes were in the drawer getting pretty smelling, like last year. I took the clove apples and gave them to Sarah and Bernadette, then dug into the Christmas box some more.

We took out all the Christmas tree balls, and I counted them. There were fourteen of them. Luke and John found the cord with the lights on it. They plugged it into the wall and laid the lights out over the floor. Some of the lights didn't work.

"Let's put everything away now, until tomorrow," Dad said. "Then I'll tell you the story of Little Piccola." But Dad didn't end up telling us the story until bedtime. He told us how Little Piccola and her mother lived alone and how they were very, very poor. On Christmas Eve her mother told her that she didn't think Santa would find their house. Her mother told her that because she was too poor to buy Little Piccola anything for Christmas. But Little Piccola said, "Santa will find us! You'll see, mother."

When morning came, Little Piccola ran to her stocking that was hanging by the fireplace. In it she found a little bird. The little bird had gotten lost in a storm. He was cold, so he sat on their chimney to keep warm. But he went to sleep, and fell down the chimney and landed right into Little Piccola's Christmas stocking.

The bird belonged to a real rich woman. When Little Piccola heard that the woman was looking for her bird, she took her bird to the woman to see if it was hers. The woman was so happy to get her bird back that she gave Little Piccola and her mother lots of money and they were never poor again and lived happily ever after.

"Bedtime now," Dad said.

"Didn't Santa put the bird in Little Piccola's stocking?" Anna asked, on the way to our bedroom.

"Maybe not," Dad answered, "Sometimes God does it for him."

"Oh," she said, as she hopped into bed.

☞

The next morning Dad and Luke put the tree in the living room and John sprayed it with fake snow. Monica tried to lick the fake snow from a branch, but Dad said it would make her sick, so she watched Luke put the lights on the tree. Catherine and I counted them. There were twenty-five lights, but only thirteen lit up. When he was done, my sisters and I put the decorations on. We put on the Christmas balls, the picture of Matthew, and all the things we had made at school. Sarah dug through the box to see what else she could find, but she got some glass in her hand from a broken ball that was down in the bottom of the box. Dad pulled the shiny blue glass out of her hand, and her hand didn't even bleed!

245

"Hey, Dad," Bernadette said, "here's the Christmas card I made for you and Mama last year! Do you want it?"

It had a Christmas bell on it and Bernadette had filled the Christmas bell with glitter. My sisters and I took turns feeling the glitter on the bell.

"Look, Dad," she said. But Dad turned his head. He wouldn't even look at the pretty card she had made for him and Mama.

"I have to go fire the stove," he said, and he left the room.

Bernadette waited to show him, but after he fired the stove he went outside, even though it was pouring down snow, and split wood. After he piled the wood, we saw him walking down the road. When he finally came back in, Bernadette couldn't find the card.

I found the star for the tree in the bottom of the box, but it was broken, so we didn't have anything to put on top of the tree. Sarah asked Dad if he'd buy us another one.

"No, get an angel; the kind with hair," Bernadette said. But Dad said we'd have to wait until next year to get a new top for the tree, when he'd have more money. Last, we put Sarah's paper chains on the tree and the shiny icicles.

After lunch, Bernadette hung the Christmas bells she had made at school on the front door. She had made the bells with the top parts of three small bleach bottles. Dad cut the tops off the bleach bottles, because she was afraid to use the butcher knife. The tops looked just like bells. Bernadette took the bottle tops to school, and so did the other kids in her grade. Her teacher told them to paint them silver. When the paint was dry, they hung a red ribbon down through each bell and made a little shinny silver ball of tinfoil to hang on the ribbon. After they tied the ribbons together, they put a big red bow on the top of them. "That's when the bleach bottle tops turned into Christmas bells," Bernadette said. "The prettiest Christmas bells in the whole wide world!"

That night Dad plugged in the tree lights and turned off the lamps. It looked just like Christmas. The icicles sparkled in the dark. "That's not such a bad looking tree after all," Dad said, looking at Luke and John. Then he said, "Let me hear my little girls sing *Oh Christmas Tree*." So we sang it and lots of other Christmas songs, too.

"Donna Jean," Dad said. "You have to learn how to carry a tune."

"What's a tune?" I asked.

"You have to learn how to sing like your sisters. Listen to them." So while my sisters sang *Jingle Bells*, I looked at our pretty tree. I was glad Dad had cut it down, because I didn't want our tree to be outside freezing. "I wish Mama didn't have to be freezing outside," I thought.

"Hey Dad," John hollered, "the radio just said that it's supposed to snow again tonight!"

I don't think my dad heard John, because he just kept staring at the tree, picking at his fingernails and humming *I'm So Lonesome, I Could Cry*. The icicles kept twinkling and my tummy kept spinning on the inside. "In just two more days Santa will be coming!" I shouted.

"Dad," Catherine asked, "do you think Santa got the letter Sarah wrote to him?" But again, my dad didn't answer. He just kept staring at the tree and humming that song.

"Dad," I said moving his arm, "do you think Santa got our letter?"

See, Mama always asked us what we wanted Santa to bring us, but Dad didn't. So Sarah wrote a letter to Santa, like Mama used to do. But first, Sarah let us look in the catalog at all the toys and clothes. Then after we each picked something out, she wrote the letter.

Bernadette picked out a bride doll and fingernail polish. Catherine wanted a doll and a dollhouse that had lots of rooms with furniture in them. Anna asked for a doll crib and highchair. Monica pointed to a new baby doll and a tricycle. Then she kept pointing to other stuff too, but we told her that Santa only brings two presents—one big present and one small present. She cried, so Sarah asked Santa to bring Monica three presents. Sarah asked for a hula-hoop and a dress. I asked him to bring me play hi-heels, like Mama's real ones and a Ben Casey blouse.

When Sarah was done writing the letter, I ran to the kitchen to see if I could help Dad and Luke. They were making pumpkin pies for Christmas dinner. Dad said I could, so I put on Mama's butterfly apron. When Dad saw me with it on he looked mad, like a bulldog, and he told me to get it off.

"That's your Mother's!" he said. "If you want to help, you better stay out of mischief. Some things in this house aren't for touching. And you know what they are."

I shook my head up and down and said, "I know what they

are. Mama's yellow glass teapot, her watch, and her butterfly apron."

"That's right," he said.

⌒

Dad looked at the pies baking in the oven. "They're done," he said, and took them out. Next he gave the turkey a bath, then put it in the roaster, then back into the refrigerator.

"Everything's ready for tomorrow's dinner. We'll peel the potatoes and rudabeggies in the morning," Dad said.

"Can we make Jell-O to put out for Santa?" Anna asked.

"Go ahead," Dad said. He reminded us that Santa's favorite, is green Jell-O. When we were done making it, we helped Dad sort the dirty clothes. Monica must have put my new blue blouse from my godmother into the white pile, because when Dad took the white clothes out of the wash machine, my blue blouse was part white and part blue.

"Oh, no!" I cried. "My new blue blouse from my godmother is ruined!"

"See what happens when you open your Christmas present before Christmas. You should have waited," Dad said.

Monica kept getting into things, so Dad made us all go outside to play. "I'm tired of you under foot," he said. "I've got things to get done. Go make a snowman."

I helped Monica get her hat on and then put socks over her hands, because she didn't have any mittens. Then we hurried outside.

"The snow's just right," Bernadette hollered. "It's packy!"

My sisters started rolling the snow into balls. John and Luke were outside, too. They were making snowballs and throwing them at each other, then they started throwing some at us. We screamed. Dad looked out the window and hollered to the boys. He made them go play in the back of the house. Sarah had Monica help her roll the snowman's bottom and Bernadette had Anna help her roll the snowman's top. Anna kept saying things that made Bernadette mad.

"Bernadette," Anna said, "we're rolling snow off the world, right?"

"No, Anna! It's not the world, it's the earth!" she told her. They rolled the ball a little bigger.

"Bernadette," Anna said, "can I help lift the snowball off the world and put it on the snowman with you and Sarah?"

"Anna!" Bernadette shouted, "it's not the WORLD! I told you before, it's the EARTH!" Then Sarah, Catherine and I told Anna that it was the e*arth*—not the world, but every time she talked about the snow that was on the ground, she kept calling the ground the world.

"Donna Jean and Catherine," John shouted, coming around the corner of the house, "if that's the snowman's head you better quit rolling it or it'll be bigger than the body." So we quit rolling and ran to the maple tree to see if we could find some sticks for the snowman's arms. The sticks were buried under the snow, so we yelled for John and Luke. They came and broke branches off the tree for us.

"Let's make a Mama Snowman!" I said when Luke and John put the snowman together. All my sisters thought it was a good idea, too. We wondered what we could put on the snowman to make it into a Mama Snowman. We thought about a hat, but my cousin, Della had taken Mama's hat home after Mama died. I was mad at my dad for giving it to Della, because I wanted it. I was going to save it and wear it when I got big. But Dad said that we'd only wreck it, so he let Della have it, for keeps.

"Mama's purse!" I shouted. "Let's use Mama's brown purse and her black kerchief." I ran to the house to ask Dad if we could use them.

"Oh, go ahead," he told me. So I ran back with Mama's purse and black scarf and put them on Mama snowman.

"I'll be right back," Bernadette said. She ran to the house, then came back with Mama's coffee can of sewing buttons. She dug in the can until she found two big brown buttons. She pushed them on the face while Catherine dug for red buttons for the smile. When Sarah gave Mama Snowman a carrot nose, we all laughed. Bernadette ran and knocked on the window.

"See Mama Snowman!" she shouted when Dad came to the window.

"Wow!" he said.

"Come outside, so you can see her face," Sarah hollered.

"In a little bit," he hollered back.

"Can we come in now?" I asked.

"It's nice out, play for a little longer," he said as he folded a towel.

Monica started crying because her hands were cold, so I took the wet socks off of her hands. I lifted my coat and put her hands onto my warm tummy. After her hands were warm, I hurried in the house to find other dry socks for her.

"Want to make snow angels everybody?" Catherine asked when I got back outside.

"Yes!" we all shouted.

"Let's lie down on the snow right in front of Mama Snowman," Bernadette said. Sarah thought we should make two rows of snow angels, so she showed us where to lie down. Catherine, Anna and Monica lay down in the front and Bernadette, Sarah and I lay down behind them. We moved our legs and arms as far out as we could. We yelled for John and Luke to come to watch us, but they were having snow ball fights again, so they wouldn't come.

We giggled when it started snowing. The big flakes kept landing on our eyelashes.

"Father Dishaw's here!" Luke yelled, when a car drove into the driveway.

"No one move," Sarah said. "So we can show Father Dishaw how we make snow angels."

So nobody got up. Even Monica stayed still. I heard Father's car door shut. I watched as he made a snowball and threw it at John, and then John threw one back at Father. When Father started walking past us, we giggled. Father looked down at us, then laughed. "What do we have here?" he asked. "Are the little Jacques girls making snow angels?"

"No," Anna hollered, "We're making Earth Angels!"

"Earth Angels?" Father asked, just as my dad came outside.

"Did you see their Mama Snowman?" Dad asked, as he shook Father's hand.

"I sure did," he said, as he lifted up Monica.

"Supper's almost ready, would you like to stay and eat with us?" Dad asked. But Father said he had to get right back, because of church.

"John and Mark," Father hollered, "I need you to do me a favor. Go to my car and get what's on the back seat and bring it into the house please." We went with Dad and Father into the house and waited by the door to see what Father had brought for us.

"Merry Christmas," he said when John and Luke set the

two big baskets wrapped in shinny see-through yellow paper onto the table. There were apples, oranges and bananas in the baskets with chocolates and candy canes on top of them.

"Can we have some of that candy?" Catherine asked Father. Father started to say yes, but my dad took the baskets and put them on the refrigerator.

"Tomorrow," Dad said, "on Christmas." Monica started screaming for one of the candy canes, so Dad gave her one.

"Give them all one," Father said. But Dad said, "No, they can wait until tomorrow. Heck, they've already gobbled down the Moose-oil fudge their cousin Marilyn sent them from Alaska."

"Midnight Mass tonight!" Father said. "I better be going. I'll see you all at church." When Father was leaving Dad thanked him for the baskets.

At suppertime, John kept bugging everyone. He kept calling the food by different names. "Pass the beater," he said, instead of the butter, "pass the mamaters," instead of the potatoes, and "pass the elk," instead of the milk. We never knew what he wanted. Dad hollered at him and told him to straighten up, so John stood up really straight. "You know what I mean!" Dad said.

"Otay, Tad," he said. We all laughed, and John giggled so hard food started spilling out of his mouth.

"Well," Dad said, "I know how to solve this problem. "Whoever laughs next, does the dishes!" Nobody laughed again.

෴

It was pitch black for a long, long time before we finally got to get ready for midnight mass. My sisters and I helped each other button the backs of our dresses. Monica wore the dress that Anna wore to the funeral house. Anna wore Catherine's funeral dress, Catherine put on mine, I put on Bernadette's and Bernadette wore Sarah's. Sarah got a new one!

"That's not fair," Bernadette told Dad the day he came home with a new dress for Sarah. "Why does she get a new one?" But Dad said that things aren't always fair. Bernadette got mad and Dad got mad back.

"Money doesn't grow on trees, so unless you don't have a dress that fits, you can forget getting a new one!" he said.

At Midnight Mass, Monica fell asleep on Dad's lap, like last year. My eyes kept shutting, too. One time I went right to sleep and my head dropped onto John's arm. For a minute, I thought it was Mama's shoulder. But then John bounced my head off and whispered for me to get my cooties off of him. I tried to tell Dad John was being mean, but Dad lifted his finger to his mouth and shushed me. Anna was being bratty too. She was standing on the pew. She grabbed my scarf and pulled it right off. "It's a sin for girls to be in church without our hair covered," I told her. Quickly I put it back on, but I think God still saw.

I didn't tell Dad about Anna pulling off my scarf because he would've been mad at me for talking and he would've made mean faces at me to be quiet. Like the mean faces Mrs. Webster made when I turned around to see who was singing in the choir. Her spying eye saw me, and her pointer finger made me turn back around. So instead, I looked up front to where Bernadette and Sarah were sitting. They were dressed as angels for the Christmas mass. "Next year, it'll be my turn to be an angel!" I said to myself. "Then Sister Janet Marie will put the round gold halo on my head and the sparkling gold wings over my shoulders."

As I stared at Sarah and Bernadette, I thought of something really funny. I wondered what a Bernadette or Sarah angel would look like on the top of our Christmas tree. I started to giggle. John pulled my hair. "Stand up and pay attention!" he whispered, as the choir started to sing *Silent Night*. I watched as Bernadette's friend Colleen put baby Jesus into the manger. Then Father Dishaw told us the story about baby Jesus. How long ago and far away in the little town of Bethlehem, Mary and Joseph looked for a place to stay. Nobody had room for them, so they found a barn and Mary had baby Jesus right in the manger. "And now," Father said, "Jesus still lives, even though nearly two thousand years have gone by!" I wondered why Mama didn't have Jude in a manger. Then I would get to see her for two thousand years, too.

But then I remembered how Mama hated the smell of the barn. And one time our Guernsey kicked her, so she wouldn't go back in the barn, except to collect the warm eggs from the chickens.

Mama liked Henny Penny and our new rooster, Peanut Butter. (Peanut Butter isn't mean like Cockey Lockey was.) The boys think Peanut Butter is a stupid name for a rooster, but Mama thought it was a nice name. She helped us pick it out. Mama always helped us to name our animals. She hated when Dad killed them. She wouldn't let Dad kill Henny Penny, because we'd scream loud when he or the boys would try to grab her from the coop.

See, every year before it snows, Luke and John help my dad chop the heads off the chickens with the ax. It's really yucky. Mama used to holler at my sisters and me when she saw us watching. But we stayed outside anyway and watched as head after head got chopped off chicken after chicken. Mama heard scream after scream.

"Get in here this minute!" she'd holler. But we would wait and watch the headless chickens dance around the yard until one by one they'd drop to the ground. Then we'd run to the block of wood to look at all the chicken heads on the ground. "Ah!" we'd scream when we'd see their eyes looking up at us. Then we'd hurry to the house to tell Mama all about it.

Afterwards, Dad and the boys would bring the headless chickens into the house and drop them into the water Mama had bubbling on top of the stove. Then Dad would take the chickens out of the bubbling water and set them on the table, on top of the old newspapers from Harry, then everyone would have to pluck the feathers out of them. "Yuckies!" I'd say when I touched their, wrinkled, naked bodies.

One time after Dad scalded chickens, Luke cut a foot off of one of them and he hid behind the utility door with it until Anna came in from going to the toilet. When she saw the chicken's foot, she must have thought it was a monster's hand, because her eyes closed and she fell to the floor.

"Is she dead?" Sarah screamed on her way to Anna.

Dad was very mad at Luke and told him never to scare anyone like that again.

Oh, I almost forgot, at Midnight Mass, John was pushing my head off his arm when I woke up. "Hey, lame brain, church is over," he said, snarling his face at me. And he snarled again when

Dad told him to carry me to the car.

"Look at all the stars up in the sky," I said to John when he set me down by the car. But John said he didn't want to look at any stars. The wind was blowing hard. Jack Frost was scribbled over the car. It was cold in the car, so I rubbed my fuzzy tights to warm my hands and legs. When we got home, we hurried and got into our P.J.s. Then Dad knelt with us by our bed and we said the *Angel of God*. "I think we've said enough prayers for one night," he said. But I asked if we could pray for something.

"Go ahead," he said. When it was my turn, I prayed that Santa would bring Mama home for Christmas.

Bernadette laughed. "That's stupid!" she said. "You know that Mama can't come back home, she's dead!"

"She can too, Bernadette!" I said. "Mama said that the Bible says "God can do anything, right, Dad?" My dad didn't answer. He turned his head. We climbed into bed.

After Dad left, Bernadette said, "That's dumb, Donna Jean. Do you really think God can send Mama back home? How could he do that?"

"God can tell Santa Claus!" I said.

Bernadette laughed, again. "I'm going to sleep!" she said, and covered over the head.

I couldn't go to sleep, because I kept wondering how Santa would get Mama down the chimney. Then I saw a star shining in the sky. "Maybe it's the star of Bethlehem, the one that Father Dishaw told us about," I thought. So I wished upon the star.

> **Star light, star bright**
> **First star I see tonight**
> **I wish I may**
> **I wish I might**
> **Have the wish I wish tonight.**

I closed my eyes and wished for the best Christmas present ever—Mama! I tried to stay awake, so I could be the first to see Mama when she got home, but my eyes kept closing. Suddenly, it was morning! "This must be Christmas day!" I said to myself, as I jumped out of bed. Everyone else was already up. I wondered why no one woke me up. I started to run to the living room, to see under the tree. But when I got to the kitchen, I stopped. I could see Mama's dish towels hanging on the towel racks and they were very, very clean again, like before she went away. By the kitchen table, I saw Monica's old hi-chair. Dad had broken Monica's hi-chair into pieces when Mama died, but now it was all back together again. And my baby brother Jude was sitting in it, eating a chocolate Easter Bunny. I went up to him and asked if I could have a bite of it. Jude squeezed the chocolate bunny through his fingers and threw it at me. It hit me in the face. In a Mama's voice he said, "Whyja kill me?" I tried to tell him I didn't kill him, but my mouth wouldn't move. I was about to clean up his chocolate mess when I noticed Santa Claus sitting at the table eating the Jell-O we had made for him. He was eating it with Dad's big snow shovel and it was spilling all over, none of it was getting in his mouth.

"Santa's here!" I screamed, and ran to the living room to tell everyone. My tummy tickled when I saw the twinkling lights of the tree. "Wow! Dad must have fixed all the burned out lights," I said to myself. I looked to the very top of the tree. I saw the most beautiful angel sitting on the highest limb. She looked like Cinderella's fairy godmother, but was really, really tiny. She smiled, then winked at me. I noticed all my brothers and sisters and my dad. They were watching me. My sisters were jumping up and down. I could tell by the way my brothers were smiling, we all got what we wanted from Santa.

Under the tree I saw Bernadette's bride doll with pink fingernail polish next to it. I saw Catherine's doll and felt its hair and noticed she had got the dollhouse she asked for. Anna's doll crib and highchair were under the tree, too. I saw a tricycle for Monica and a sweater for Sarah. "My Ben Casey blouse and hi-heels!" I said, jumping up and down and hugging them. Lots of other stuff was under the tree, like guns and basketballs for my brothers. I could even see a new coat for my dad.

"My blue blouse," I screamed. "How did this get under the tree?" I picked it up. I looked at it. "It's not bleached any more! It's all blue again!" I said, showing it to everyone.

"Isn't it supposed to be all blue?" Dad asked.

"Remember, Dad, you accidentally bleached it!"

Suddenly, I noticed my brother Matthew. He was home from Germany and sitting on the couch. I jumped up on him. "I didn't know you were coming home for Christmas," I said to him. Everyone just kept smiling, then Matthew said, "Donna Jean, everyone's waiting. Aren't you ever going to see the present under the tree?"

Just then, all I could see was a big white box under the angel-topped tree—there it was! The biggest, longest, deepest present I'd ever seen. It was wrapped with white tissue paper and had a cover to match. Red ribbons were wrapped around it and on the top was a big red bow. I hurried to the box. I read the nametag. TO-EVERYONE—FROM SANTA. Mark took out a ruler from his shirt pocket. "How the heck big is this box?" He measured it. "Five feet, four inches," he said, "I wonder what it can be?"

We pulled hard and played tug-of-war with the ribbons. Dad took his scissor-sharp teeth and broke the knot. My heart started pounding, like Dad's old tractor when we lifted the lid. There was Mama! Her cheeks were pink and her lips were as red as the ribbons and bow. Her hair was still black and her dress still yellow. I looked for her big tummy, but it wasn't fat any more, like when she went away. It was skinny. Mama smiled at us and reached out her hand for me to help her out of the box.

"Mama," I said, "your hands aren't scratchy or bloody any more." Your hands are soft, like Wilhelmina's fur!" I rubbed her soft hands onto my cheeks. "And your hands aren't cold either. I helped her out of the big white box. Mama was smiling, then she started hugging and kissing us. Then everybody was hugging and kissing and kissing and hugging and hugging and laughing.

Mama went into the kitchen. I followed her. She put on her butterfly apron. I watched as butterflies flew right out of her apron. Everybody tried to catch them—even my dad. A yellow butterfly zipped past me and said, "Isn't your mother wonderful?"

"Yes," I said. I laughed because I didn't know butterflies could talk. I watched Mama climb up unto the counter over the sink. She put the red and white curtain back on the window again. Then she stuffed the Christmas turkey with candy canes, apples, and the fudge from Alaska.

"I thought we ate all the fudge from cousin Marilyn," I said to Mama. She just giggled and kept tying the turkey legs together with dandelions. Then she put the turkey into the oven. When she started to close the oven door, the turkey wasn't the turkey any more.

It was the mean old rooster.

"Cockey Lockey!" I screamed, and ran to hold onto Mama. Cockey Lockey saw me. With mad eyes he hollered, "Don't you care about me at all? Why did you kill me?" He started coming out of the oven to get me.

"Mama," I screamed. "Where are you?" I ran looking for Mama, but she wasn't in the kitchen any more. She wasn't in her bedroom, either. Cockey Lockey chased me all around our house, even into the closets and down into the spooky cellar, while I looked for Mama. "Mama, Mama, where are you?" I cried.

That's when Anna jumped on me and in my ear half-spitting she said, "It's Christmas morning, Donna Jean! Hurry! Get up, so we can open presents!"

"The big white present!" I said to Anna, throwing the blankets off of me. I jumped out of bed and quickly I ran to the Christmas tree to open the big white box with the ribbons of red and the big red bow.

⌒

I raised my head and looked to the workshop participants. "I never... did find... the big white... box." I threw myself to the mattress, then cried uncontrollably, for what seemed hours.

"Yes," Elisabeth said. "Let it out. Let it all out. We're not afraid of your tears—no more Band-Aids. Now the wound will begin to heal."

After several more minutes I wiped my eyes and sat up. Elisabeth stood and took a seat and motioned for me to take the seat next to her. She patted my leg, then spoke to the group.

"Now you should have an understanding of what can happen when a child is left to comprehend death on their own. It wasn't only the absence of her mother's physical being that Donna Jean grieved, but also the death of the friendship she had with her mother and the protection she felt from her. Death was also apparent in the absence of hugs and kisses, unattended scrapes and bruises, and even in the simple, yet necessary nurturing, like drying her tears. Many, many small deaths followed throughout these years because of the death of her mother. And she will still, at times, long for her mother. That's normal."

Elisabeth turned to me. "How are you feeling right now?"

"Buzzy," I said. "I feel like my whole body has fallen asleep."

"Actually," she said, "it has just awakened after a long nap of denial! You have worked very hard this week at the workshop and I, for one, am very proud of what you have accomplished."

With that statement, the other participants of the workshop began to applaud and Brandi excused herself from the conference room. "I'll be right back," she said.

When she returned, she gave me a dozen yellow stem roses. I began to weep, but this time the tears were tears of appreciation, for the freedom I felt.

Afterwards, several participants embraced me and congratulated me on my new beginning.

☙

That evening, a closing ceremony was held. Everyone lit a candle to signify what he or she would be leaving behind. No one was at all surprised when I said I was leaving the pain of my childhood. Then I approached Elisabeth.

"I was told this final evening would conclude with a dance," I said. "So I rummaged through the selection of music and found a song I'd like to dedicate to you, for all you have done for me."

While Carly Simon's, *I Haven't the Time for the Pain* played, I smiled with a sense of confidence I had not experienced in years. In fact, some of the participants had already remarked that I didn't even look like the same person who had first arrived at Shanti Nilaya. When the song ended, I thanked everyone for their support, and said, "The only grief I have now is the grief I feel for all of you, knowing we'll be parting in the morning."

Chapter Twenty Three

arly the next morning I boarded the resort shuttle. When it arrived at the Greyhound station in Phoenicia, I bid farewell to Flossy and the others that were with me, then transferred to Greyhound. Again, as in the beginning of my journey, I felt emotionally and physically drained as I stepped onto the bus. But this time it was due to letting go of the sorrowful memories, rather than suppressing them as before. Tired as I was, I felt a sense of exhilaration knowing I had left the depression behind, back in the valley of the Catskills.

Collapsing to a window seat, I grabbed my pillow and propped it to the window. Laying my head against it, I stretched my legs onto the seat next to me. Before long, I fell into a deep sleep. I didn't awaken until Pittsburgh, when an elderly woman nudged me. "Do you mind, child, if I sit here?" she asked.

"Sorry," I said, straightening up and rubbing the sleep from my eyes.

As the bus drove away, the elderly woman settled herself then turning to me she said, "Southern Alabama is a long way off, I may as well make myself useful."

I peeked at the cross-stitch the lady had taken from her bag and noticed the design, when completed, would be the face of Christ.

"I's been gone way too long. My sister was a needing me. But now the good Lord has taken her on home, so I's figured I'd better get on back to my family."

"My condolences," I replied.

"No need to offer sympathy. Francisca has now begun the rest of her life."

"Maybe she's already met up with my mother," I said, enthusiastically.

"Oh, heavens child, your mother already passed on?" she asked rather loudly, with disbelief in her voice.

"Twenty-five years ago," I responded and explained that I was returning home from the workshop and how it had helped me finally deal with my mother's death. I could hardly believe how freely I was conversing with the stranger. To me a miracle had happened over the past few weeks. I had gone from refusing to ever mention anything about my mother, to enjoying talking about her with just about anyone. In fact, I felt like standing up and telling the whole world all about her, both before and after her death. Or, at a minimum, spreading letters from a plane across the sky, reading, "Yes! I, *too,* had a mother."

Since a few years after my mother's death, I felt anything but born. *Hatched,* seemed like a much better analogy of my presence on earth. Desperately I tried to feel in common with my peers, but continued to feel abnormal. My thoughts roller-coastered from my mother having been the most wonderful person, to that of never having laid eyes on the mother of my birth.

☞

"Forgive me, child, I'm Rosa Marie," the woman said, as she crossed another stitch.

"Rosa Marie! What a coincidence! My mother's name was Rose Marie!"

"Was she born in 1901, too?"

"No," I said, with a chuckle, "1921."

"I suppose she had a slew of kids, like me."

"Yes, as a matter of fact, she did. She had eleven. I'm lucky number seven! How many children do you have?"

"Nine, and all boys!"

"Oh, my gosh!" I said. "Nine boys. I can't quite imagine that. I have four boys and I think that's a handful!"

"They're a handful, all right, but they've also been my most wonderful blessing," she said. Then she smiled a smile that put a shiver up my spine.

"You just smiled *exactly* like my mother used to smile. She was always smiling. In fact, over the years I've often wondered how she could've been so cheerful. She certainly didn't have any of the luxuries of life. And with all us kids to care for, I have been both amazed and envious at her ability to still experience the joy of life."

"Remember child, you said you lost your mother while you were very young, that makes a big difference."

"But so did she! She and I were both motherless by the age of seven."

"Then I suspect she never lost her means to the living God. You probably did."

"The living God?" I asked, with a sense of confusion.

"Yes," she answered. "Mother's are *the living God* in action. So if a mother dies, or a father for that matter, someone else must step in to take on that role, or troubles are sure to come. Maybe your own mother had someone there for her—to take her mother's place, at least somewhat."

"Yes," I said, "her sister, my Aunt Celia was like a mother to her, at least that's what I've been told. And I guess you're right about needing someone to stand in for my mother, because I often wished I could've had someone, motherly like, to talk to about certain things. You know, like when I first started my menstrual cycle. I didn't know what the heck was happening. I had two older sisters, but unfortunately my oldest sister started on Monday, Bernadette on Thursday and me on Friday—all the same week! It's almost unbelievable it happened that way, but I think it was God's way of making sure we didn't feel alone in it. Thank goodness for an occasional visit to the school by the county nurse. She had shown filmstrips on the female anatomy to Sarah's class, so at least Sarah had been somewhat informed, or I know we would've thought we were dying. Although, for years, I blamed the whole 'period thing' onto little green apples."

"Little green apples?" Rosa asked, with a puzzled look. Her forehead wrinkled as she pondered how on earth 'little green apples' could be linked to such a *natural* occurrence of the female body.

"Yes," I smirked. "My sisters and I had a contest to see who could eat the most little green apples from the crabapple tree. Sarah ate seventy-seven, Bernadette ate one hundred, and I, of course, had to out-do Bernadette, so I ate one hundred and one. Needless to say, we had more then our periods to deal with! A few months passed, when one day Anna, who was eight at the time, and Monica six, had asked Bernadette what was in the big blue box in the closet. Of course it was the kotex, but rather than her explain it to the girls, she simply said, 'socks.' A couple days later when I went into the bedroom, I could hear the two of then talking in the closet. They were sitting on the floor when I looked in to see what they were up to. Each of them had a kotex at the bottom of a foot. Anna looked up at me, 'How do you get these sock on?' she asked. I laughed and grabbed the pads from them.

'We want new socks, too!' Monica screamed as she tried to get them back."

"Oh dear, I wish I could've been there for ya all. I would've taken on some of those tasks your mother would've done, like making sure you and your sisters knew what to expect in regards to your own body, at least."

"Thank you," I said, patting her arm. "I appreciate your saying that."

As the elderly woman cross-stitched, she shared how she and her mother had a very close relationship. "I don't know what I'd do without her," she exclaimed. "She's always been there for me. She was there to give me courage when I went out on my first date and dried my eyes when I came home early from my first dance. And, of course, with every child born, she came to my rescue. When my husband of forty years died, she was one of my main supports."

"Forgive me for interrupting, but did I hear you right? Your mother's still alive!"

"One hundred and six," she said chuckling. "And still as sharp as a whip."

"I can't even imagine having a mother *that long*. But I must admit, for awhile over the years I did imagine how wonderful it would've been having a mother to talk to about some of the things that were bothering me. Or just to be able to sit by her side would've been nice. But as the years went by, I quit imagining and started packing my problems into the depths of my mind. And my joys, too. I felt that if I couldn't share them with my mother, I didn't want to share them with anyone.

"Such as what joys? What sorrows? Do you mind my asking?"

"Heavens no," I said. "The workshop I just came from tore down the walls of silence. I feel different now. I'm not afraid to talk anymore about my past." And without much thought, I started to tell her about an experience that I had shared one night with Flossy.

"What comes to mind is President Kennedy's assassination. First, I should tell you that Elisabeth Kubler Ross, a grief expert, explained to those of us at the workshop that when we cry it is usually because we have stirred up grief within us. So even though we may think we're crying for another, it's usually for ourselves. Like with me, when President Kennedy died. Day in and day out, I cried for Caroline. I had even written her a letter, and although I never sent it, I reread or rewrote it every night for about a month. I had that letter memorized!"

"Do you still?" Rosa asked, raising her eyebrows.

"Oh, yes," I chuckled, "I just shared it with one of my new friends at the workshop. I don't believe it will ever leave my memory because it was such a devastating time for me."

"Well, child, don't just be sitting there, let's hear it."

"But…"

"But nothing, girl. You got me as curious as a nosy neighbor now."

"Okay," I said.

Dear Caroline,

I was tracing my hand at school, because we were going to make turkey decorations for Thanksgiving, when Mr. Johnson knocked on our door. He asked Teacher to go out into the hallway for a minute. When she came back in, she told us the President was dead. Everybody from the whole school got to go into the kindergarten room, because there was a radio in there. We listened very quietly to a man talk about your dad.

My mother died at a hospital too, but she didn't get shot. Dad took us to Mr. and Mrs. Green's house and we saw on the television the bad man that killed your dad. We saw the white horses pull him and the American flag to the cemetery. My mother got dropped off at a cemetery, too, but she was in a big black station wagon.

I like your coat. I want a coat like yours. I'm glad that the bad man is dead. My dad said, "No way, no how, did just one man do that!"

Last night when I said my prayers, I crissed-crossed my heart, raised my right hand to God and promised him to pray for you and Jon Jon and your mother, too. She's pretty. Dad said your dad and my mother are both up in heaven.

Yours truly,
Donna Jean

P.S. Why don't you ask your mother if the secret men can bring you to our house to play? You could jump rope with my sisters and me. We jump the O'Larry's. It helps us not to cry.

"My goodness gracious," Rosa said, wiping her eyes. "Maybe I shouldn't have been so persistent. Do you have anything joyful in that Pandora's box of yours?"

"A joyful experience? Ah, yes. Actually, I do. I had always wished I could've talked to my mother the night of our Junior-Senior prom. It wasn't just the fact I had been crowned queen and my boyfriend, who is now my husband, crowned king, but I had wished she could've seen my dress. It was beautiful! It was the only formal I had ever gotten new. It cost twenty-one dollars. It was sleeveless, a turquoise chiffon in an empire style. Oh, how I loved that dress. One of my best high-school friends, Cheryl, had gotten a pink one just like it. We were both so excited while we were getting ready. Before we left her mother grabbed her camera, and while the flashes were going off, I visualized it being my own mother taking the pictures.

Heck, I felt like a queen long before they crowned me that night. And when I got home, I ran to the bedroom to tell my dad. He was happy for me, but I still longed for my mother. I wanted to show her the beautiful tiara and the dozen yellow roses I'd received. Yellow was my mother's favorite color, and roses her favorite flower.

When I went to bed, I couldn't sleep. As I lay there reliving the night, something extraordinary happened. A warm sensation came over me. It was as though someone had poured a warm liquid into the top of my head and it flowed, like osmosis, through my entire body. Instantly, a total peace came over me, followed by my mother's presence. I couldn't see her, yet I knew she was with me and was proud of me."

"I do, believe honey, that the dead have their ways of communicating with us," Rosa whispered. And for several minutes we talked about the experience of my prom night.

Rosa looked at her watch. "You have about an hour before I transfer buses, so spill your guts while you can, Honey. Tell me more of the things you wish you could've talked to your mother about."

"Actually, I did sort-of talk to her. I kept a diary for a long time, but then one day I got angry and never journalized again. I was tired of having to talk to a piece of paper, I guess."

I gazed out the window, then turned back to Rosa. "My wedding day, it was a hard day," I said and I began to cry. "I'm sorry, I don't mean to cry. I thought I had shed every tear possible at the workshop." We both began to laugh. "It's just that when I think about how much I tried to include my mother in my wedding day, it actually amazes me. Rosa, do you know any bride who picked *On This Day Oh Beautiful Mother* for her wedding song? My brother Jude, who was born when my mother died, sang it at my wedding. He was only eleven. Even the recessional song astonishes me. It was *Put Your Hand in the Hand of the Man*? The words to that song are so powerful. They correlate to my life. A few of the lyrics went like this:

Put your hand in the hand of the man who stilled the water
Put your hand in the hand of the man who calmed the sea
Take a look at yourself and you can look at others differently,
By putting your hand in the hand of the man from Galilee.

My mother taught me how to pray before I reached the age of seven
She said, "There'll come a time when there'll probably be room
in heaven."

"We'll be in the windy city in twenty minutes," the bus driver announced. "And it's a cold one today, a minus two."

"Rosa," I said, clearing my throat. "I'll probably never see you again, so I'd just like to say how wonderful you've been—listening to my stories, and all. I believe you were a necessary link in my chain for the healing of memories and I want to thank you. I know now that when I get back to my family, I'm no longer going to be consumed by thoughts of my own mother, but instead be able to be a full-fledged mother to my children. You have helped me to achieve that long awaited goal—a goal I have secretively prayed for—to be free of the past."

"Well, child," she said, reaching into her purse for paper and pencil, "I don't feel like it's the end of the road. I feel like our journey has just begun." Then we exchanged addresses.

"Can I ask one final curiosity question before I have to transfer?"

"Of course," I said

"Well, I was wondering, if you could be granted time with your mother, what's the one thing you'd say or do?"

Without the slightest hesitation I answered. "I'd ask my mother to put ringlets in my hair."

"So, what you've missed most was your hair not being fixed?"

"Oh, no, it wasn't that at all. It's been my mother's *touch* I've missed, and still do. See, for a year after her death, I really believed I'd see her again. I spent a big part of my time in wishful thinking. This week I learned that as the seven-year-old child, I didn't understand the concept of death. Most children don't, until the age of eight. So I believed my mother *could* and *would* come home. After all, even at church I heard of Jesus coming back to life, and Lazarus, too, so why would I have thought it unrealistic for my mother to return?"

The bus came to a stop. "People underestimate the complicated thoughts of children," Rosa said, as we made our way off the bus.

I walked behind the wise and witty woman as she slowly ascended the steps and then into the terminal. We were both starving so we picked a place to eat, and there shared a Reuben sandwich, then headed back to catch our appropriate bus. Rosa took my hand. "I wish I had more time, child," she said as we hugged goodbye. She kissed my cheek, then boarded her bus.

Through my tear-drenched eyes, I made my way to my own bus and boarded. As it rolled out of the terminal, I noticed there had been a change of drivers. I shifted my aching body until comfortable and soon, thereafter, fell asleep.

Dreams of reuniting with my family awoke me. I looked out the bus window. "We're only to Green Bay," I said to myself. Gazing at the city lights, an idea came to me. I switched on the overhead light, then reached into my carry-on for pen and paper and began to journal for the first time in years.

Dear Mama,

As you probably know, I've been to the workshop. It was exactly what I needed in order to let go of the past. For some time now I've been thinking of how, so often as a child, I prayed and pleaded to God. I thought that if I were a real good girl, he'd let you come back home.

During Lent, that first year following your death, I walked to the church nearly everyday from school for the Stations of the Cross. Mrs. Webster would ask before lunchtime which of us students would be leaving for church. I was the only one from our class that went. "Be sure to walk with the bigger kids," she'd say.

I went, because I wanted to be a saint, like so many people said you were. So away I'd go to the church. There, the sisters told me how proud they were of me for being so little and yet attending the service. "God is going to find favor with you," Sister Janet Marie said one day. I didn't know what that meant, but I did know how good her comment made me feel. I recall one time when the sisters had to correct one of my superstitions when I arrived at church crying. I thought I'd broken God's back. I believed the saying I'd picked up at school, "Step on cracks, you break God's back." So I always hopped over the sidewalk cracks, but that day I'd failed.

Looking back, I believe I went to the Stations at first to seek holiness, but soon it was for love and affection. On that first day, I told the sisters my feet were cold, so they each grabbed a foot, took off a shoe and rubbed my bare feet until they were warm. They repeated this procedure each day when I arrived so that my feet would be warm before I'd have to go back to the school. To this day, I'm addicted to seeking out love through a foot rub!

Over the years I have often pondered how slowly each day went by when you were gone to Chicago. I thought you'd never return. Yet you did. God brought you safely home, just when I'd given up hope. So after your death, I thought you'd eventually return, too, but you didn't. For a full year I prayed and waited. It wasn't until after that fateful Christmas dream that I realized you'd never return.

From the time of my birth you only had seven years to consecrate this physical heart of mine into a spiritual heart also. What a mother—you achieved it! For, although lately I have been feeling God was no longer with me, I've come to realize it was the sorrow and anger that separated me from Him. Now I believe He was always there.

I feel so fortunate for having wonderful siblings and a dad who kept the family together. Dad could've been easily persuaded, because of the heavy burdens he carried, to allow some of us to be adopted, but he kept the faith.

I realize, also, how tuned into God Father Dishaw was to have come bearing gifts of great joy on Christmas Day, before you died. Especially the gift you received in the Blessed Sacrament of the Holy Eucharist.

I no longer see the church experience with the nuns as just sisters warming my feet, but God working through them, giving them the courage to be liberal in their church behavior at a time when behaviors, as such, were forbidden. Yes, Mama, I believe now that God did not abandon me. It was He who came in the tearful eyes of so many people during the time of your death. He was there in the hearts of every person who gave, from the locals all the way to an Indian Mission in California who had heard about our hardship and sent five hundred dollars. I feel blessed, Mama, knowing that even your 'death' couldn't destroy my love for God.

⌒

"Look to your left," the driver hollered. "Must be a meteorite shower. They usually take place in November."

I quickly closed my journal, turned out the overhead light, and looked into the darkness. I watched as stars fell like fireworks. I chuckled. The display, to me, was a sure sign of my mother acknowledging what I had written. "I love you too, Mama," I said, as the bus pulled into the Escanaba station. I took in a deep breath. It felt wonderful to be alive. Quickly, I gathered my belongings and started for the door.

"I was told this November is the coldest on record," the driver said, sounding a bit hoarse. "I'm glad I'll be moving on. Twenty-two below zero, is way too cold for me!"

"I'm used to that and worse!" I said, as I bounced down the steps. I thanked him, then ran inside the depot.

"Mama," my boys hollered as they ran to meet me. I lowered myself so they could each take a place in the circle of my arms.

"Dad took us to a wild game feed when you were gone," the oldest one said. "We got to taste turtle!"

"TURTLE! Oh, my," I exclaimed as I kissed my little boys. "I guess I should be glad I had to go away!" I smiled and looked up at Bryan. I saw him wipe a tear from his eye. Gently he took my hands and helped me up. With skepticism, he asked, "How was the workshop?"

"It was wonderful!" I said. "Now I can finally admit my mother died. And you know what, Bryan? It's okay!"

Bryan grabbed me into his arms and dropped his head onto my shoulder, then began to cry.

"Why are you crying, Dad? Mama's home!" my five-year-old said.

Bryan lifted his head. He looked at the kids. "I know she is," he said, half-crying, half-laughing. He lifted me from the floor and as he spun me around, he shouted, "Yes! Mama is *finally* home!"

⌒

To a child whose mother is temporarily gone a day passes like a year, but to a child whose mother has died, a day never ends.

Mama

Mathew and Mark

L-R Sarah and Bernadette

L-R Anna, Mark and Monica

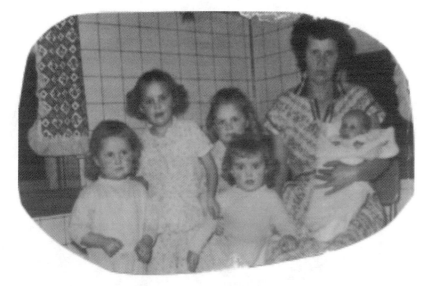

Mama & her Daughters

Dad & the Gang

L-R Sarah, Bernadette,
Dad in Background

Jude age 1

Dad with the Girls